CON
GAME

THE TRUTH ABOUT
CANADA'S PRISONS

MICHAEL
HARRIS

M&S

National Library of Canada Cataloguing in Publication Data

Harris, Michael, 1948–
Con game : the truth about Canada's prisons

Includes index.
ISBN 0-7710-3961-1

1. Prisons–Canada. I. Title.

HV9507.H37 2001   365'.971   C2001-900947-X

We acknowledge the financial support of the Government of
Canada through the Book Publishing Industry Development
Program for our publishing activities. We further acknowledge the
support of the Canada Council for the Arts and the Ontario Arts
Council for our publishing program.

Typeset in Bembo by M&S, Toronto
Printed and bound in Canada

McClelland & Stewart Ltd.
The Canadian Publishers
481 University Avenue
Toronto, Ontario
M5G 2E9
www.mcclelland.com

2   3   4   5   06   05   04   03   02

For Kim Hancox

CONTENTS

Reform MPs Myron Thompson, Art Hanger and Randy White will be visiting us on December 1, 1995. These gentlemen are known to be ardent critics of CSC [Correctional Service of Canada] and are quite vocal in expressing their views. I want to ensure the Edmonton Institution is at its best, giving very little reason for criticism. THEREFORE this institution will be spotless, areas needing paint will be painted, inmates will be visibly at work during their tour (as they should be anyway) and programs will be in full swing. . . . I do not want inmates lying about doing nothing (not that this would happen anyway). I have not seen a lot of activity that involves inmates shovelling snow. The walks should not be cleared with snow blowers. Push shovels are more appropriate. Buy them if we need them. Suggestions are welcome. I want a commitment from all of you though that you will ensure that we are well represented during this visit.

– E-mail from Jack Linklater,
warden of Edmonton Institution, to staff

"They tell us we have to have respect for the inmates. Here in Warkworth, that's pretty hard. How do you respect a sex offender when you see him masturbate in his cell watching *Sesame Street*?"

– correctional officer,
Warkworth Institution,
Campbellford, Ontario

INTRODUCTION

Canada's prison system is in crisis. It neither reforms criminals nor protects the public, and for those reasons it enjoys the enthusiastic support of just 6 per cent of Canadians.

Behind the grey bureaucracy of the Correctional Service of Canada (CSC), which Madam Justice Louise Arbour has called the "least visible branch of the criminal justice system," huge value judgments affecting the safety and security of Canadians are being made with virtually no public input. The CSC has reached the subjective conclusion that prison is the right place for violent, high-risk criminals, albeit for the briefest possible time, but the wrong place for those who it decides are non-violent, low-risk offenders, regardless of their crimes.

Despite ritual public denials, one of the key corporate priorities of CSC is to reduce the length of time convicted criminals spend in jail, as an arbitrary means of reducing the incarceration rate in Canada. The sentences handed out by the courts are not the final word on a criminal's fate in the justice system. It is the National Parole Board, acting on information and recommendations from

CSC, that really determines how much of his sentence a convicted criminal actually serves. For reasons that have nothing to do with crime and punishment, court sentences are reduced to such a degree that crimes which inflict great misery on innocent citizens are routinely trivialized in CSC's zeal to reduce Canada's prison population. With an 80 per cent concurrence rate between CSC's parole recommendations and the NPB's decisions, the one is virtually a rubber stamp of the other.

Canadian criminals currently serve an average of just 32 per cent of their sentences before receiving day parole, and only 39.8 per cent of their time before getting full parole. Other than those serving life or indeterminate sentences, inmates are normally eligible for parole after serving one-third of their sentences or seven years, whichever comes first. In cases that meet the criteria for accelerated parole review (APR), federal inmates may be paroled after serving one-sixth of their sentences. APR is reserved for first-time federal offenders who are considered non-violent.

Bill C-51, which introduced APR in Canada, was enacted on May 1, 1999. The legislation allowed fraud artists, thieves, money launderers, and drug traffickers to be released from prison after serving just one-sixth of their sentences. It was a mockery of justice that left the police community demoralized and angry, while the criminals were delighted. Antonio LaRosa, working with the Caruana Mafia family, was sentenced to four years for conspiring to import 1,500 kilograms of cocaine into Canada from Colombia. The RCMP spent $9 million on Project Omerta to smash the drug ring and arrest criminals like LaRosa and others. LaRosa qualified for APR as a first-time, non-violent offender and was paroled in eight months.

CSC frequently justifies alternative approaches to incarceration by citing the high cost to the public of locking up convicts. In 2000–2001, it cost an average of $66,381 a year to keep a male inmate in a federal prison, but only $14,534 annually to supervise that same inmate on parole. The savings to the system for female

inmates on conditional release is even greater, since the average cost of their incarceration is a staggering $110,473 annually. But here is the irony. After remaining fairly constant for most of the 1990s, Canada's corrections system actually had fewer offenders in it by 1999–2000, yet costs to taxpayers rose by 11.4 per cent over the previous year.

It is the classic example of the public getting less for its money from a bloated federal bureaucracy; 12.5 per cent of CSC's 15,000 employees work at national headquarters in Ottawa. CSC cost taxpayers $1.4 billion in 2000–2001, with the National Parole Board accounting for $30.9 million of that amount. The cost of running Canada's justice and prison system both federally and provincially is $10 billion. That number jumps to $46 billion if the personal costs to victims and lost productivity are taken into account. In fiscal 1999–2000, it cost $2.5 billion to operate the federal and provincial prison systems, a jump of 10 per cent over the previous year. The provinces run a much tighter ship than Ottawa. It costs on average $123 a day to keep an inmate in the provincial corrections system, compared with $185 in a federal institution. Six students could have their university fees paid for what it costs to keep a single male inmate in a federal prison for a year.

The 6,221 men and women who guard Canada's inmate population operate in one of the most dangerous and poorly managed workplaces in the country. Prisoner-friendly reforms have taken away their weapons, made search and seizure procedures perilous or impossible, and weakened security in the country's sixty-nine federal correctional facilities.

On the other side of the bars is Canada's criminal class. As of January 4, 2000, there were 12,379 men and 338 women in federal custody, a decrease of 9.1 per cent from 1996–1997. Another 8,649 male offenders and 508 female offenders were under federal jurisdiction in the community. Parole jumpers, persons on bail, and escapees are excluded from CSC statistics. Security has become such a low priority of CSC that prisoners routinely "walk away" from

minimum-security institutions, which account for about 95 per cent of all escapes from federal custody, clear evidence that they should never have been put there in the first place. In 2000-2001, 81 prisoners escaped from federal institutions.

The inmate profile shows that Canada's federal felons are young and violent, regardless of gender. Nearly 55 per cent are aged twenty to thirty-four. Five per cent of the men are serving sentences for first-degree murder, 13 per cent for second-degree. Eighteen per cent of male federal inmates were sentenced for sexual offences. Fifty-six per cent of female inmates are aged twenty to thirty-four. Seventeen per cent of them are serving sentences for first- or second-degree murder. Fifty per cent of female inmates have committed acts of violence, but only 3 per cent are imprisoned for sexual offences.

Behind the raw numbers, the social histories are dismal. Fully 50 per cent of inmates claim to have had dysfunctional parents, and 75 per cent have unstable job histories and are considered "poor" at problem solving. Approximately 70 per cent abuse alcohol or drugs and are considered to be chronically impulsive and unable to "generate options" other than a life of crime. Seventeen per cent have been hospitalized in mental health facilities. As of December 1999, 3,599 men and 129 women were serving life sentences in Canada, one-third of them in the community on conditional release.

According to a November 1999 report by the National Parole Board, thirty-seven convicted killers paroled during a twenty-four-year period killed another fifty-eight people after their release. But the report didn't include murders committed by parolees who had originally been convicted of crimes other than homicide. Over those twenty-four years, the grim toll of innocent victims of criminals who kill while on parole is actually 367, 130 from 1975 to 1986 and 237 from 1987 to 1999-2000. Criminals on parole or statutory release also committed 194 attempted murders in the twelve years from 1987-1988 to 1999-2000, as well as 2,647

other serious offences, including sexual assaults and armed robbery. If a court system in a jurisdiction with capital punishment ever executed 367 innocent victims in twenty-four years, it would be abolished. Yet CSC and the National Parole Board trivialize this horrific record behind heartless statistical percentages and charges that the media are whipping up zero-tolerance hysteria. Their sin is not imperfection, as CSC executives sarcastically claim, but a deadly arrogance that is blind to the human misery their policies cause.

Telling this story has been the most difficult task of my journalistic career. Federal privacy law forbids publication of the names of inmates, so many are referred to here by pseudonyms. The names of several guards have also been changed, but for a very different reason. It is a violation of their terms of employment with CSC to talk about what goes on inside their workplace. It is for these reasons that CSC is, as Madam Justice Arbour correctly says, such a secretive institution. Fortunately for me, hundreds of courageous guards spoke out for this book, some even granting permission to use their names, putting their jobs and pensions on the line because they knew it was the only way the public would ever find out how Canada's prison system really works.

I wrote this book because I have seen too much pain caused by criminals over a writing career that includes two books about murder and another about the odious sexual abuse at the Mount Cashel orphanage in Newfoundland. When I began, I expected to find a generally well-run prison system managed by politicians and bureaucrats who still had a lot to learn about victims' rights. What I discovered, with a few notable exceptions, was a secretive and blinkered collection of administrators who ran a system where the criminal was king after he was sentenced to prison. Awash with drugs and alcohol, violent, and frighteningly unaccountable, Canada's prison system is a place where criminal behaviour is rarely altered, true recidivism rates are hidden from the public, and the so-called "restorative justice model" is embraced with all the

fanaticism of a cult so sure of its philosophy that it is openly hostile to criticism and reform.

Never has a department of government been more in need of both.

Michael Harris
Lunenburg, Nova Scotia
January 2002

PART ONE

The Slammer

I

MILLHAVEN

Going to the slammer confers a vast boredom that stretches between the fateful day of entry and the distant day of release. No one really knows what will emerge from the steel cocoon when a federal inmate's warrant finally expires. But like most other encounters with big government, serving time is a dreary process that begins and ends in mountains of red tape.

After their day in court, male offenders sentenced to two years or more in Canada are transferred from provincial custody in the jurisdiction where their crime was committed, usually within fifteen days of sentencing. Sentences of less than two years are administered by the provinces and territories, as are juvenile corrections under the Young Offenders Act.

Almost 90 per cent of all federal inmates – there are more than twelve thousand of them – have a criminal history, as either young or provincial offenders. Provincial detention centres are often overcrowded, dirty, and dangerous, relics of a previous era that are now being replaced. Accused murderers, child molesters, and armed robbers sometimes languish in jail for as long as three years awaiting trial. Special segregation units are often filled with suicidal

or mentally ill inmates, instead of the dangerous or unruly offenders they were originally designed for. For most inmates, transfer to federal institutions, which generally have more and better amenities, is a relief, even if it is only to begin the slow crawl toward parole after twenty-five years of a life sentence for first-degree murder.

An "intake assessment" of a new federal offender is completed within seventy days of sentence commencement. It normally takes place at a Regional Reception Centre, although in fact the process is started as soon as a Correctional Service of Canada (CSC) community office is notified by a court or a provincial detention centre that it has a new offender for the federal system. Either a case management officer or a parole officer interviews the offender and begins to collect community information – normally a brief social and criminal history. The inmate's version of the offence is also documented. Information obtained in the community is then sent to the Regional Reception Centre as quickly as possible in order to be available when the new inmate arrives. Health information is considered to be of such importance that it accompanies the offender when he is transferred to the reception centre.

An inmate's first conversation with the people who hold the mortgage on his future is strictly practical. In non-judgmental language, the officer tells the new inmate what to expect during his sentence and discusses his institutional placement decision. The officer notes suicide concerns, medical conditions, or any special family issues that the offender may have. The courts, Crown attorneys, and the provincial corrections service all provide information about the offender's crime. The law requires that this information be shared with offenders. In fact, inmates are given every scrap of information that is used to make decisions about them during their entire prison stay, all of which they can respond to or appeal.

If an offender commits his federal crime in Ontario, Millhaven Institution is his first stop in the system. When you first turn off Highway 33 outside Kingston, you can't see the prison. Even when prison buildings loom up just after the road forks, the sight is

deceptive. The first structures of the low compound actually belong to Bath Institution, once a minimum-security prison, now a medium-security one.

Architecturally, Bath looks like a medium-budget university campus. Security was so lax here in the 1980s that inmates regularly went for drinks at a nearby hotel, or even to the liquor store in Kingston twenty kilometres away. Shrimp and lobster were sometimes served at inmate socials, followed by partying at a local trailer park. On more than one occasion, inmates built a bonfire by the shores of Lake Ontario after a swim. As long as they didn't embarrass the warden and made it back to the institution for the mandatory counts, their extramural pursuits were tolerated. The remarkable levels of liberty sometimes reached comic proportions. On February 13, 1988, a Bath inmate called a taxi for a run to the liquor store. Unfortunately for him, the cab driver turned out to be an off-duty Millhaven guard doing a little moonlighting to make ends meet. The driver recognized the thirsty inmate and instead of driving him to Kingston dropped him off at the prison.

Millhaven, which is not only the reception centre for Ontario but also one of two maximum-security institutions in the province, is a much more daunting sight. Its twenty-foot-high fences are topped with coils of glistening razor wire and studded with eight towers manned by armed guards. The officer in the main tower watches new arrivals through binoculars as they approach the prison. Everyone who enters Millhaven must pass through security in the identification building outside the main gate. It is a dramatic moment. When the inmate walks through the first gate, it closes behind him as the second gate opens. The sound of the lock of the second gate clicking into place removes all doubt of what he has left behind and where he is going.

Millhaven has three administration buildings and three living unit buildings. The maximum-security wing houses approximately 125 inmates, fewer than half its rated capacity of 276 and dramatically fewer than the 600 inmates it held in 1993-1994. Announced

in 1965 by the federal Liberal government, the complex suffered several construction delays. State-of-the-art in its day, Millhaven was supposed to replace Kingston Penitentiary, the other maximum-security institution in Ontario. After a major riot destroyed the interior of KP in 1971, inmates were sent to Millhaven. Even though it was not yet ready to open, authorities felt it was secure. They were wrong. Fourteen inmates embarrassed the brass at CSC's national headquarters when they escaped from the system's flagship maximum-security institution in 1972. Since then, Millhaven itself has been plagued by major riots in 1976, 1988, 1996, and 1997.

When an inmate reaches Admission and Discharge (A&D) in the reception unit at Millhaven, all personal property he brings to the institution is recorded on CSC Form 514: "Inmate Personal Property Record – Cell and Stored Effects." The inmate retains a copy and displays it in a designated area of his cell so it is visible to all staff. The inmate is given essential hygiene items on arrival, and his personal cell contents are delivered within five working days. The inmate records all articles received during his incarceration on a personal list. During the first thirty days of incarceration, the inmate can receive personal effects from the community. After that, additional items can be purchased only through the Social Development Department of the institution. If an inmate wants to go to A&D to store, exchange, or pick up items, he has to submit a request and be placed on a "call-down" list.

Within twenty-four hours of arriving at the intake assessment unit, the inmate is interviewed by staff to supplement and verify the information already gathered about him. The inmate's immediate needs are flagged. He is then put through the orientation process, which includes a medical checkup, clothing distribution, information about how the institution operates, and, most important, an in-depth suicide screening. A new inmate's first weeks in an institution are the most taxing. The initial interview enables the case management team to identify offenders who may be violent or at risk in a federal institution.

Millhaven is one of the most modern and secure of the country's maximum-security institutions. The living units contain ranges on two levels, with twenty-nine cells per range. The steel cell doors, painted vivid shades of green, pink, and purple, run along either side of a walkway. The floor is plain grey cement, since the original flooring was destroyed in a 1997 riot. The windowed cells feature a bed and a desk and are bigger than their counterparts at the older KP. Although there is double-bunking in A Unit at Millhaven, all J Unit prisoners have their own cells.

J Unit is reserved for the most dangerous offenders and houses five ranges: 1K, 2K, 1L, 2L, and 2M. Prisoners in J Unit take their meals in their cells, and guards at J Control have weapons and do not walk the ranges when the inmates are outside their cells. (In fact, there is no national standard for maximum-security institutions. At others, like Kingston Penitentiary, unarmed guards walk among offenders on the ranges, and the guards backing them up at the control stations are also unarmed. J Control at Millhaven, an octagonal command post on J Unit, is manned by two armed officers, who back up three more officers on the floor.) There are roughly 125 inmates in J Unit, including Clinton Gayle, the killer of Toronto police officer Todd Bayliss, and the Colombian drug lord Rivo Conofrio.

Until 1984, Millhaven was one of three maximum-security prisons equipped with a special handling unit, or SHU, the highest level of security in the system. Now only Sainte-Anne-des-Plaines Complex in Quebec retains a SHU, but Millhaven has been designated as the segregation holding unit for the Ontario region.

On arrival at Millhaven, each inmate is given two sheets, a pillow, four towels, and a blanket. Institutional clothing issued is two pairs of jeans, a summer jacket, a winter parka, three golf shirts, a pair of shoes, four T-shirts, four briefs, and four pairs of socks. Institutional clothing must be worn at all times during the normal working day. If unemployed and called off his range, the inmate has to dress

correctly or he will not be allowed to leave the range. During visits, institutional jeans must be worn, but personal shirts – other than muscle shirts – can be substituted for prison garb. Leisure clothing can be worn for recreation, after hours in the living units, and on weekends and holidays. Inmates can purchase personal clothing through the Social Development Department.

The cell rules for Millhaven include: Inmates shall sleep in their cells with their heads away from the cell doors. Cells are to be kept clean and neat. Unless the cell is double-bunked, there is to be only one inmate permitted in each cell at one time. No pets are allowed (though the Prison for Women used to provide pony rides for one inmate who officials believed would benefit from the activity). Hobby crafts, including leatherworking, basket weaving, carving, and painting, are done in the cells. Requests for the necessary materials are directed through the social development officers. Combustibles such as newspapers, books, and craft supplies are not allowed in excessive amounts because of fire regulations. Inmates must go to their cells immediately after returning from other areas of the prison, such as common rooms, the yard, or the hospital. No pictures or photos depicting nudity are to be posted in cells, a rule honoured more in the breach than in the observance. Metal foot-lockers are to be stored under beds.

Inmates at Millhaven are issued a picture ID that must be worn at all times when they leave their living units. Replacement cards cost the inmates $5. No privacy curtains or window coverings are allowed, and each cell is equipped with an emergency call button. Inmates are also financially responsible, at least theoretically, for damage to their cells: it costs $910 to replace a toilet, $150 to paint a damaged cell, and $165 for "joint-issue" bedding and clothing if it is destroyed. (In practice, this regulation is seldom enforced because most inmates are simply unable to pay.) An inmate can keep $1,500 worth of personal items in his cell, such as a TV or a PlayStation, and a computer worth up to $2,500. Today almost every prisoner in the system has cable TV in his cell, at a cost much lower than what citizens pay on the outside.

"Muscling" is frowned upon at Millhaven and other institutions. If caught intimidating others for money or goods, the offending inmate undergoes a counselling session and three weeks of increased observation. In an effort to control muscling, the inmate is allowed to store no more than $90 worth of goods from the canteen in his cell, including a limit of three cartons of cigarettes or two unopened cans of tobacco. Only $300 worth of jewellery is allowed, with no item to exceed $100 in value.

Purchases made in the canteen are delivered once every two weeks. The maximum anyone can have in a canteen account at one time is $90, the amount every inmate is provided with when he begins his sentence. An inmate's canteen money comes from his current account. Inmates are paid an allowance of $2.50 a day while taking programs, which normally run from 8:30 to 11:30 in the morning and 13:15 to 15:45 in the afternoon, a five-and-a-half-hour day. Offenders may also be assigned jobs for either a half-day or a full day. (Level A pay, the highest, is $6.90 per day.) Premium jobs outside the unit, including work in the canteen, in recreation areas, and with the paint gang, are reserved for the best-behaved offenders. Those who refuse to participate in programs or interviews are given a basic allowance of $1 a day and restricted to their cells during normal working hours.

Schedules for unit activities at Millhaven – including showers, telephone calls, visits to the yard, gym, and weight pit, and any other activity requiring inmate movement – are posted on each range. Since inmates hate variations in their routine, staff notify inmate "range representatives" if there are to be any changes. Inmates must have a pass for any movement from their unit to anywhere else in the institution. If an inmate is not on a pass list, he is not permitted through the main control area of Millhaven, called N Control. It looks like a barred-in space ship, its octagonal mass controlling all barriers in the prison. The guards who work here can train weapons out through N Control's gun ports. In order to proceed to any other part of Millhaven, all inmates must pass through N Control. Those on the list of inmates authorized

to move through the institution are not to loiter and must travel directly to their work location, meeting, or classroom.

Telephone calls are permitted from 13:30 to 22:30 and must not exceed thirty minutes. Three-way calling, by which inmates can reach people not on their authorized list, is not permitted, although it is common. Those caught making such calls can lose their telephone privileges. For privileged calls, to lawyers, a written request must be made to unit staff twenty-four hours before the call. Unlike other calls in prison, such calls are not subject to interception. Emergency calls from the unit office are authorized for valid reasons. Depending on the schedule of the chaplains, a call-out for chapel is issued to the Millhaven population after 13:00 on Saturdays or Sundays. Offenders who go to services are not allowed to make phone calls during that time, except in emergencies.

In 1998, there was a rash of fatal drug overdoses in prisons across Canada. In most cases, the drug involved was heroin. Since the majority of drugs come in with visitors, especially during private family visits, it was decided to have thirty days of "closed" visits (behind glass) at institutions like Kingston Pen. Authorities reasoned that the drug supply would dry up if there was no physical contact between inmates and their visitors. But guards say the plan was cancelled because it was going to cause too many problems. Officers claim that CSC will always elect to save money when faced with a choice between security and higher costs.

Officially, inmates are expected to be drug- and alcohol-free during incarceration. On paper, drug-related activities can result in a review of the inmate's Correctional Plan, the restriction of "open" visits (without glass between inmate and guest) or private family visits, a review of his security classification, suspension from a job that requires a degree of trust or affords movement in the institution, or a pay cut. If an inmate commits a serious offence such as assault or muscling, he appears before the Disciplinary Board, chaired by an independent person who is not an employee of the institution. If sentenced by the board, the

inmate can appeal to the warden for a review. The maximum penalty is loss of privileges for thirty days, $500 restitution, or thirty days of segregation, penalties far less severe than for similar offences under the Criminal Code. The reality of what happens to drug users in prison is very different.

Inmates mail out CSC Form 653 – "Visiting Application and Information" – to people they want approved for their visiting lists. All visits are closed until an application for open visits is approved. Inmates and their visitors are expected to dress and behave "in a manner considered reasonable for a public place." They are also responsible for controlling their children in the visiting area. After application and a community assessment, the inmate's parole officer makes a recommendation to the Private Family Visit Board, chaired by the unit manager. Mail is delivered daily by the Visits and Correspondence staff, and outgoing mail is picked up from the ranges each weekday morning.

If an inmate in Millhaven requires medical attention, he completes a medical request form to be placed on "sick parade" and deposits it in a request box in the unit. The nurse who comes to the unit every day to dispense medication collects the forms, and inmates are placed on the sick list as soon as possible, depending on the urgency of their condition. Emergency matters are dealt with by unit staff who call the health care department immediately when circumstances warrant an emergency response.

Once an inmate is "processed," the regimen that will dictate his life at the institution kicks in. At Millhaven, a typical day in J Unit, the wing for inmates who are either new or in some degree of trouble, begins with the 7:30 range walk by correctional officers. At 8:00, the food stewards, who are usually CSC staff, check the breakfast meal with the offender food server, who slides trays through the cell food slots. By 8:30, the trays are picked up and returned to the food carts, and the inmate server is locked up after cleaning the green plastic trays. The food slots are locked and staff

conduct another range walk. Each offender is asked if he is going to participate in his programs and appointments that day, and the staff then pick up yard lists.

At 9:00, there is a staff briefing, then preparation for the movement of offenders to interviews and programs. Next, offenders employed in the unit are let out. Shortly after 9:00, there is another range walk of the units, and the more difficult inmates are released to the unit cloister across from the J Unit office for exercise. At 10:00, staff conduct another range walk to check cells, and the inmates in the exercise yard come back. Since orientation inmates are kept separate from the others, offenders housed in 2K for orientation are released to the yard for recreation five minutes later. At 11:00, staff conduct another range walk. Offenders in E Unit are cleared for recreation, gym, or yard, then returned to their cells and locked in at 11:20. Five minutes later, all inmates on 2K are locked in their cells and counted. Only then are the food slots opened.

After J Unit offenders have returned from work or programs at 11:30, medication is delivered from cell to cell. Once the count of prisoners is verified, lunch is served through the meal slots at noon. Half an hour later, the trays are picked up and returned to the food carts. Staff then complete another range walk. Unlike KP, where a single unarmed officer walks the range with up to thirty-eight cell doors open, Millhaven keeps its inmates secured in their cells while the officers do their "winds." Two officers complete the walk, backed up by a weapon pointing down the range for extra security. Guards at KP tried to change their procedure in 1997 but were told by their bosses, "Well, if they take you hostage, and there is only one of you, they can't kill you, because if they kill you, they don't have anyone else left."

At 13:00, Millhaven inmates go to interviews, programs, and work stations. There is another range walk at 14:00 and one at 15:00. At 15:55, all 2K offenders are locked in their cells, and another count is conducted at 16:00. Once the count is verified, supper is served in the cells at 16:10. By 16:30, the food server is picking up the trays and staff are preparing for evening range activities.

After a range walk at 17:00, staff pick up the list for range activities, which commence at 17:40: showers, cell cleaning, phone calls, laundry, library, and kitchenette. Lock-up is at 19:55, and the count is done at 20:00. At 20:15 the orientation inmates are allowed range activities for an hour and forty-five minutes. By 22:00 all offenders are locked in for the night and there is a range walk. The final count for the day is done at 23:00. The unit is completely locked down from 22:00 to 8:00.

The realities are a little different from the official version of how the assessment unit and the prison run. Asked what a typical shift at Millhaven was like, one correctional officer agreed to take notes during his working day.

At 15:30 the officer reports for duty at the Keeper's Hall (staff room), then reports to J Control. An inmate cleaner from 1K demands to see the officer in charge because he wants to make ice and deliver ice cream on the other ranges. The request is granted.

By 15:45 the inmates are returning from work or various programs, and they visit one another in their cells. When the officer in control announces "count-up" over the loudspeaker, several inmates yell, "Fuck you!" Most inmates ignore the order to go to their cells, and some go to the kitchenettes on the range instead or block their cell doors so that they can't be closed. One inmate from 1K is talking to another in 1L through a barrier; when ordered to return to his range, he responds, "Fuckin' relax, pig."

By 16:05 the inmates are finally locked in their cells for the formal count. Meanwhile, the food carts are locked and secured on the ranges to prevent inmates from using them to pass on weapons or drugs. Then the cells are opened, and the inmates are served their supper at 16:15. One inmate on 1K yells for the control officer to bring the food steward because his vegetables are overcooked. He wants a fresh portion. The steward informs him that there are none left, and the inmate responds, "This is fuckin' bullshit. This has been brought up before and nothing is fuckin' done about it." He pitches his tray of vegetables in the garbage can. An inmate on 2L is also unhappy with the diet. "You give us the same fuckin' shit

all the time. I am supposed to get fish, not just chicken all the time." The food steward tells the inmate to put in a request to see the dietitian. The inmate walks away complaining, "Now I have to wait two more weeks to get this fuckin' bullshit straightened out."

At 16:40, the inmates are given the five-minute warning for lock-up and count. In response, they all step out of their cells and start mingling on the range or proceed to the kitchenette. The cell doors are closed automatically at 16:47, but several inmates are still out on the range or loitering in the kitchenette. Some start yelling out their cell numbers and begin to scream, "Open the fuckin' doors, goof." Floor staff have to help control officers lock up individual inmates. One inmate on 1K is still on the phone. He ignores the control officer who twice orders him to get off the phone and lock up.

After being ignored, the officer switches off the power to the phone, and the inmate slams down the receiver and screams, "What is your fuckin' problem, goofs? I was talking on the phone, you fuckin' punks. Don't ever do that again, you fuckin' pig." The inmate then turns to the floor staff and demands, "Who is that fuckin' punk goof up there? What a fuckin' asshole!" The inmate finally locks up. At 16:58 the unit is secured and the floor officers do their range walk.

At 17:30 some inmates are released for recreation "on" the yard, while the remaining offenders are secured in their cells at 17:50. (Inmates say "on the yard" rather than "in the yard" since "in" connotes being inside and controlled, and "on" implies being outside and free.) Five minutes later, a cell emergency alarm goes off on 2L. The inmate complains, "I have got no fuckin' power and I want it back."

An officer draws a key from J Control and proceeds to open the ducts to reset a fuse. At 18:45 the staff begin a security walk. One inmate complains that the walks are too close together. He continues to argue, delaying the showers and range activities for the other ranges. The inconvenienced inmates begin to pound on their cell doors and activate their cell alarms in protest. An inmate

begins yelling, "Open the fuckin' doors, you're holding up the showers." The others soon join in, sending up a deafening chant.

There is another lock-up at 19:15, but when the cell doors are closed several inmates are still out on the range. One of them on 1L throws a half-full Coke can at the control office window. Unit staff arrive to open his cell door so he can be there for the count. He continues to shout profanities as he steps inside. By 19:25 the inmates are locked up and secured on the ranges, and the other inmates begin returning from the yard. When they are finally locked in for the count, the second shift of inmates begins pounding and banging on their doors: "You're delaying the fuckin' yard." Beginning with 2M, one range at a time is released to the yard.

The security staff at Millhaven routinely search five cells each night for contraband. This means that all cells are searched at least once during a sixty-day period, leaving fifty-nine days of relative immunity for most offenders. Tonight, the staff begin with 2M. A cell is opened and the officers instruct the inmate to step out for the search. He responds, "Fuck you, assholes, I am dumping it right now. Are you happy, you fuckin' goofs?" He dumps his homemade brew from a garbage bag into the toilet and yells, "Get away from my door, you fuckin' pigs! I am dumping it." The officers wait until the brew is gone, then signal Control to close the cell door. The inmate continues to curse the officers as they leave the range.

At 20:40, showers commence. After returning from recreation, an inmate from 1K begins yelling at Control about his cell being searched: "You fuckin' goofs, put my stuff back when you search my house! There are some of my pictures on the floor!" The inmate proceeds to Control, shouting, "You fuckin' pigs, fuckin' goofs! Who searched my cell?" The officer in Control tells the inmate that he didn't search his cell, that he should talk to the floor officers, but the inmate responds with, "Fuckin' assholes, come on out here, you fuckin' goofs," and proceeds to kick the window. "Come out here, you fuckin' pigs, and I'll kick your white asses!" At 22:50 the unit is secured for the night. The count is commenced by floor staff.

After his life was threatened four times by an inmate at Millhaven, one officer wrote out an observation report. Although the correctional supervisor in charge of the range had asked the inmate to apologize for his threatening behaviour, the offender refused to acknowledge that he had even made the threats and accused the guard of lying. The officer understood that it was part of the job to be subjected to verbal abuse from inmates, but he felt that death threats should be dealt with seriously. Sending the inmate to segregation would have sent a clear message to the other inmates that this behaviour was unacceptable. Instead, the guard was moved to a different post after his shift ended, sending a clear message to inmates that they could make threats without consequences, or so the guard in question believed.

During orientation at Millhaven, the offender is interviewed about his current offence, and the resulting report becomes part of an ever-lengthening paper trail. Part of the process compares the offender's version with the official account and then notes any discrepancies. Important information provided by the offender is verified if possible. The Statistical Information on Recidivism Scale is used to help assess the risk of future conflict with the law, and a Sexual Offence History form is also completed for all offenders. An Offence Severity Record reviews the severity of all offences on the inmate's criminal record. Staff look closely at seven areas believed to have an impact on criminal actions: employment, associates, community functioning, attitudes, marital or family situation, substance abuse, and emotional problems. The offender is allowed to telephone anyone on his authorized call list to inform them that he has been admitted to a penitentiary. To complete the process, checks for any outstanding charges are made with the Canadian Police Information Centre.

Treatment and program plans are made at the beginning of a sentence. If an offender is having adjustment problems caused by severe anxiety or suicidal reactions to incarceration, a referral is

made to a psychologist. This is also done if he has a history of persistent or gratuitous violence, is a sex offender, or is what the system calls "high needs," code for substance abuse problems or general social incompetence. Outside referrals are occasionally made to determine the overall risk posed by the inmate.

Ideally, the psychological assessments are made while the offender is still in the intake assessment unit. Testing is also done if criminal behaviour is linked to unemployment or if the person's level of education prevents him from benefiting from rehabilitation programs. Family violence assessments are done if there is a history of spousal assault, either as a perpetrator or as a victim. ("Spousal" includes heterosexual and homosexual common-law relationships.)

The orientation program also introduces offenders to the Correctional Service of Canada. Topics presented include CSC's mission statement, the Corrections and Conditional Release Act (CCRA, the law that governs Canada's prison system) and its regulations, the Canadian Charter of Rights and Freedoms, available health care services, policy for temporary absences and parole, rules governing inmate conduct (including privileges and responsibilities), program opportunities, security procedures, the case management process, institutional operations, finances, visits, the offender grievance procedure, access-to-information procedures, and the function of the correctional investigator. With the help of CSC, inmates become experts on their rights from their very first days behind bars. They are offered counselling to help them adapt to the prison environment, as well as spiritual, educational, and vocational guidance. And they are informed of their parole eligibility dates. Records are reviewed within seven days of admission to see if the offender is eligible for accelerated parole review, or APR. Those who qualify for APR include first-time federal offenders who have not committed a Schedule 1 offence (a violent crime) under the CCRA and who have not received judicial determination of parole eligibility for a drug offence. This enables a prisoner's

paperwork to be ready for the National Parole Board if he is to be released on accelerated parole after serving one-sixth or six months of his sentence, whichever is greater. Previous stints in provincial jail are not taken into account when APR is being considered for a federal inmate.

An inmate serving his first federal sentence for a non-violent crime can be out in as little as six months, even if he has a string of offences as a juvenile or time served in the provincial system. In the Ontario correctional system, reserved for those serving sentences of less than two years, inmates must earn any remission on their sentences. They must be drug-free, non-violent, and enrolled in rehabilitative programs. Offenders who qualify can be released after serving one-third of their sentences, though most are released after serving two-thirds.

The revised Statistical Information on Recidivism Scale (SIR-R1) is a tool for predicting the likelihood of an inmate's reoffending. It is completed at the beginning of his sentence. A rating on this scale is mandatory for all offenders in the federal system except aboriginal and female offenders, who have "customized" correctional systems. The inmate is incarcerated as close to his home as possible, taking into account the availability of a suitable cultural and linguistic environment and of programs and services to meet his individual Correctional Plan.

New prisoners are classified as minimum-, medium-, or maximum-security, a designation that is fully explained to them during the assessment process. Security designation is based on the risk posed by an individual inmate rather than on his offence in itself. Factors used in the security assessment include danger to the community, the likelihood of reoffending, and institutional adjustment. Minimum-security inmates are considered to pose a "limited" risk and so enjoy the greatest freedoms and privileges. Medium-security offenders are still believed to pose some threat to the community and have correspondingly fewer perquisites. But there are no armed guards inside the perimeter of either minimum- or medium-security institutions. Maximum-security incarceration is reserved

for inmates who exhibit negative behaviour and who pose "serious" risk to staff, other inmates, and the community at large. Weapons may be deployed inside the perimeter of such institutions, although every effort is made by prison bureaucrats to avoid an "ostentatious show of force." The Custody Rating Scale is a statistical tool used by the parole officer to determine the level of security for an inmate's initial placement. The new inmate will be placed in an institution in "the least restrictive environment possible," taking into account his safety and the safety of staff, fellow offenders, and the public.

Until very recently, this meant that a first-degree murderer could be sent directly to a medium-security facility like Fenbrook Institution, in Gravenhurst, Ontario – where he would have a key to his own room – within months of his conviction. On February 22, 2001, after interviews with the tearful family members of several victims, Solicitor General Lawrence MacAulay succumbed to public pressure and announced that first- and second-degree murderers would now serve at least two years in a maximum-security institution before being eligible for lower security and the greater freedoms it brings.

CSC administers the sentence imposed by the court, and the head of the service, its commissioner, reports to the public through the solicitor general. CSC managers at the regional and national level liaise with Crown attorneys, justice officials, the courts, and police.

The offender's Correctional Plan is the central document for managing his case throughout his sentence. Ideally, it outlines the steps to be taken to reduce the probability that he will reoffend. It includes both long- and short-term goals and is customized for each person. One of the tools used to develop the plan is the Offender Management System, a comprehensive database developed for CSC and the National Parole Board. The database includes sentence data, tombstone information, criminal profiles, risk assessment and risk management data, program and treatment information, and release potential.

Compared with other institutions, Millhaven is very restrictive, both in what an inmate can do and in how he does it. Although

core programs in areas such as formal education, living skills, and combatting substance abuse are offered, a lower-security institution has more opportunities and a greater variety of jobs – and much greater freedom of movement. The system is built on the notion that once an inmate deals with the reasons he was placed in "max," he will be moved to a lower-security institution.

Former CSC commissioner Ole Ingstrup brought the idea of "unit management" to CSC. Although the same concept had been tried and had failed in the United States, he firmly believed that all staff should interact with inmates. At the most basic levels, officers found the concept far better in theory than in practice. An officer who was stabbed in the back by an inmate around the time they were bringing unit management to Kingston Pen said, "There is no way they can expect me to look after a range of sixty inmates to make sure they do what they are supposed to be doing. To enforce the rules. To maybe have to go in to wrestle, fight them, and charge them, to go to court, to have them sentenced. But yet I'm supposed to sit down and say, 'Hey, buddy, now I'm here to do your case management. Tell me your story.' Sorry, it doesn't work. . . . It can't work, it didn't work, and it still doesn't work."

Under unit management, inmates deal on a daily basis with correctional officers referred to as CX1s and CX2s. There is no national standard to establish the ratio of prisoners to staff; it varies from institution to institution, as do so many other aspects of Canada's correctional system. Two factors that affect the ratio are an institution's security classification and the presence or absence of the latest electronic security systems. The CX1s and CX2s are known as "line staff"; they answer questions and listen to requests from the inmates. Each inmate is assigned a CX2, who assists with case management. The CX2, who is senior to a CX1, confers regularly with the inmate and his case management officer or parole officer and checks with the CX1 about the offender's behaviour and attitudes. Correctional supervisors (CSs or CX3s), also called keepers, are management, responsible to the administration and supervising the line staff on a daily basis. The unit manager is the administrative head of the unit,

supervising the CSs, CX1s, and CX2s as well as the parole officers. The parole officers are directly responsible to the unit manager for all aspects of an inmate's casework.

The Unit Board comprises the unit manager, the correctional supervisor, CX2s, parole officers, the case management coordinator, and the institutional preventive security officer (IPSO – an intelligence officer), as well as other support staff such as psychologists. Weekly meetings are held to review cases presented by the parole officers, who may recommend transfers, programs, visits, or any other changes to an inmate's Correctional Plan. Problems are discussed by the full team.

Millhaven's population is divided into three segments. New inmates go into the orientation population. Inmates who are frequently or constantly in trouble with prison authorities are called the "general" population. The term, introduced at Millhaven in January 1999 to rename the former "non-compliance" population, was chosen to avoid "stigmatizing" inmates. The warden explained to an inmate meeting "that this range is not intended to be punitive but to differentiate between those inmates who want to progress in the unit (do programs etc.) and those chronically finding themselves in segregation."

The third group, now called "reintegration" inmates, is those who are achieving the goals of their Correctional Plans. Based on their behaviour in the orientation process, co-operative inmates normally go from orientation directly to a reintegration range since under the CCRA, the service places offenders in the least restrictive environment consistent with their safe management. Medium-security management is the goal.

The changes to the old "non-compliance" category were presented before their implementation at one of the regular meetings the warden holds with inmate representatives. The representatives, chosen by range and by certain ethnic groups, had a variety of concerns. The inmates detected a "loss of rights" for those in the new general population, such as yard privileges with the rest of the offenders. They didn't want a strict unit where they would be

forced to participate in programs in order to get off the ranges. The inmate reps felt the unit was illegal and that it would not solve problems. To support the inmates' "code," offenders might feel they had to "act out" if they were moved to the general-population ranges. Offenders demanded that the extra funding Ottawa had designated for the changes be used for other purposes at Millhaven. The warden agreed to think about the inmates' points, promising further discussion would take place prior to implementation, but the unit was officially launched in January 1999 despite inmates' concerns.

The orientation program at Millhaven normally lasts for thirty days. It is primarily for new offenders requiring a maximum-security setting, offenders transferred from lower security after their behaviour showed a need for higher security and stricter controls, and reoffenders released from a maximum-security setting who have been sent back to Millhaven for serious parole violations or new crimes. Inmates in orientation have their movements somewhat restricted in order that staff may assess their needs and observe their behaviour.

Participants in the orientation program are each given a copy of the *Millhaven Reception Unit Offender Orientation Handbook*, which gives general information about incarceration in a federal institution, and a printed copy of the daily routine. The orientation also gives information about the maximum-security programs and regulations specific to Millhaven, as well as how to obtain access to certain types of information. All policy directives and CSC procedures are available for review in the library, which includes a section on the law. New inmates are encouraged to ask questions and submit suggestions about things that might be improved.

Inmates are told that the goal of the orientation program is simple: "To encourage and support you in participating in a Correctional Plan which will allow you to move to a lower security placement and eventually return to your community as a law abiding citizen. You are expected to demonstrate a willingness

to interact effectively, individually, and in highly structured groups, while subject to constant and direct supervision and demonstrate, through participation, your acceptance of a program plan designed to meet your individual needs, particularly those which would lead to placement in a less structured environment."

Embrace Jesus, in this case CSC's philosophy and your Correctional Plan, and you will be saved.

While inmates are being evaluated, timelines are set for transfer to their next placement. They can participate in most Millhaven programs, including courses in cognitive skills, dealing with substance abuse, and anger management. Any inmate with less than grade 10 is offered a placement in school. Federal inmates are usually the country's most poorly educated citizens: 64 per cent have not completed high school; 30 per cent have not even completed grade 8. In standard literacy testing, the average inmate scores at grade 7.5.

Meanwhile, the general-population ranges at Millhaven provide "the full range of rights, privileges and opportunities that are provided to a maximum security population," according to Institutional Standing Order 730. The institution accommodates offenders who are "unwilling to adhere to their Correctional Plan." If their behaviour interferes with the delivery of programs to other offenders or increases tension on their range, they will be placed in the general-population ranges, where controls are stricter. They can also be sent to these ranges if they are found with contraband or are physically or verbally aggressive or violent toward staff or other inmates. The purpose of the placement is to change the behaviour of disruptive inmates. About 70 to 80 per cent of federal inmates have a history of violence.

Once an inmate in a general-population range decides to co-operate in his Correctional Plan, "pre-release steps" are put in place. A meeting is scheduled to review his Correctional Plan and behaviour, and he even signs a behavioural contract agreeing to follow the revised plan. If the inmate wishes, he can participate in a program "to assist you in problem solving and in dealing with

behavioural issues that resulted in your placement to the general population." Before his transfer to reintegration, the inmate is assigned work cleaning the range, assisting the food service officer, or cleaning the administrative offices at Level D pay – $5.25 a day. If his work and attitude are satisfactory, the inmate is transferred to a reintegration range.

The routines in reintegration are a little more relaxed and open, although offenders who are late for work or programs can be locked in their cells by the staff. Range reps and ethnic reps are released on the range, and their cells are kept open during both working hours and range activities in the evening, including the range walks by correctional officers. The aim in these ranges is to prepare each inmate for transfer to a lower-security institution by meeting the goals in his Correctional Plan.

While correctional officers have their problems with inmates, offenders also have their complaints about guards and prison life in general, as minutes of Millhaven's meetings between inmates and the warden clearly show.

At a range rep meeting held on May 7, 1998, ethnic representative Edwards (first names are generally not spelled out in prison documents) claimed that black offenders felt they were being ignored. If their concerns were not addressed, he warned that "political steps would be taken." One of the issues of contention was the "issuing of hair grease and pick combs." Offenders felt that these were basic personal items, but no action had yet been taken to provide them. Correctional Supervisor G. Campbell left the meeting to check with Supply and Institutional Services. He returned to inform the meeting that picks would be issued, asking Edwards to let him know how many were needed.

The other issue raised by the ethnic rep was the problem of finding a spiritual adviser for Rastafarian offenders. Prison chaplains were responsible for this arrangement. Edwards requested that Barr Frederick, the unit manager, make the arrangements, but Officer Frederick said he could not interfere with the chaplains'

authority. Edwards would be given a pass so he could meet with the chaplains.

The inmate reps also complained that "staff are not adhering to the routine." The unit manager agreed that he would reinforce with staff the need to comply with the routine at all times. At a meeting on June 4, 1998, inmates raised the problem of poor staff interaction, primarily among female officers and offenders. Notes taken at the meeting indicated, "Communication has improved but still needs improvement."

Offenders were also asking for more variety in their meals, such as a Buddhist/vegan diet. Food complaints were a staple of every meeting. According to the inmates, meal "presentation" had slipped and the lasagna "continues to be a problem." Even the tofu "had gotten worse." Dave Curtis, chief of food services, agreed to look after getting a little more variety and also to set up meetings for individual offenders with the dietitian to discuss their needs. Offenders also requested fewer boiled potatoes and a baked potato substitute. One officer's name was mentioned at the meeting as being dishonest and "provoking offenders."

The dietitian and health care staff would not support the inmates' request for protein and amino-acid supplements, on the grounds that medical research showed that they create undue stress on the liver. Inmates argued that it was none of management's business and should be a personal choice. A similar decision was being grieved by inmates at nearby Joyceville Institution.

Inmates also felt it was taking too long to get an appointment with the doctor or dentist. (The maximum waiting period was ten days, much shorter than is often the case on the outside.) Inmates complained of the heat on the ranges and wanted cool showers during the days, even though they were allowed to purchase fans for their cells. Inmates on 1K wanted Plexiglas installed at the range barrier to keep down the noise made by guards during the evening and midnight shifts.

At the August 6, 1998, range rep meeting, management reiterated that the kitchenettes on the ranges were not to be used for

open cooking, since there were no exhaust fans or fire extinguishers. Microwaves were to be used instead. But inmate reps protested that some offenders had been allowed to cook with woks and hot plates for religious reasons. Unit Manager Bart Frederick corrected them: woks were to be used only during specific religious periods. The Food Services Department provided religious diets for every-day consumption. Offenders who did not agree with this were invited to submit a formal complaint.

Inmate reps also felt that meals were left on the food carts longer than necessary. They made some suggestions to enable everyone to get a hotter meal, and management promised that staff would be informed of their ideas. But the inmates didn't get everything they asked for: a request by inmate reps for "summer holidays" was denied as not being consistent with their sentencing. (The reps had requested a week of weekend routine, in which there would be no jobs or school, during which they could sleep in.)

At the August 12 meeting, the main population had no problem with the current mixed breakfast menu, but there were complaints from offenders on diets who said that they were receiving too many eggs. The chief of food services agreed to find a substitute for eggs and fatty foods such as burgers for those on diets. The menu for vegans was discussed and agreed to. Dave Curtis would also follow up on the complaint that vegetables were being overcooked by the institution's food service officers. Although the six-week diet menu was "yet to be fully accepted," the offender population was "almost happy" with the six-week regular menu. However, they wanted the brand of breakfast cereal changed on a regular basis – corn flakes for six weeks in a row were just too much. Blenders were approved for range kitchenettes, even though their razor-sharp steel blades could be turned into weapons.

The upcoming change from "non-compliance" to "general pop-ulation" was discussed at the August 20 meeting. The warden had to leave the meeting at 9:30 to meet some visitors from Australia who had come to tour the institution, but he promised to continue the session the following day. When the meeting reconvened, the

warden agreed to more yard time for inmates. Leatherworking and painting were offered for hobby crafts, but the inmates complained that there was no interest in such activities. They suggested wood-working and stained glass instead, hobbies that required carving tools and X-acto knives. The inmates also wanted their music room back and increased access to the common rooms for card tournaments and other social events. The warden invited them to submit a proposal.

The warden advised that new construction in the units would mean that the common rooms and kitchenettes would be inside range barriers, and therefore more accessible to inmates. (Since both milk and juice dispensers would be placed in the new kitchenettes, "brewmasters" – makers of moonshine – at Millhaven were no doubt happy about the arrangements.) The inmates also wanted TVs in the common rooms. Once again, they were advised to put their request in their proposal. The warden suggested that intramural sports tournaments would be beneficial at the institution.

It was once said of Millhaven, "A moral insanity permeates the place." One inmate was killed and another seriously injured in a series of riots in January 1997. The trouble began when violent and predatory inmates were jammed into one unit, triggering power struggles over who would control extortion and drug trafficking in the institution. Everything from changes in routine to the quality of the muffins then seemed to be enough to spark a savage incident. Appeasement was the order of the day and security at Millhaven was so lax that neither guards nor inmates could be protected.

Normally the inmates ate at 17:00, but after the rioting began on one range, Steve Gilbert, a food steward, was not allowed in until 21:00. There was water on the floor, and the acrid smell of tear gas hung in the air. The guard escorting the worker wore a gas mask, boots, and rain gear. The inmates were yelling death threats, and the steward wondered how he would get through the ranges. Suddenly Gilbert had an idea. He started singing "It's a wonderful

day in the neighbourhood" as loudly as he could while delivering meals. The guard took off his mask and joined in. The inmates stopped yelling and started saying "Please" and "Thank you" as Gilbert handed out their trays. "I get along with the inmates because they think I am totally crazy, which I am to a point," Gilbert said. As soon as the singing steward made his exit, the rioting inmates continued on a full stomach.

Kingston Penitentiary's Emergency Response Team had been doing a hostage-taking exercise at their own institution when the call for help came in at about 14:00. Suited up and ready to go, they were at Millhaven in under an hour. They could smell the sour, pungent odour of gas from outside the fences. The situation was critical. One hundred and thirty inmates on J Unit were out of their cells and doing serious damage. The power had been cut and the inmates were definitely in charge of the unit. About thirty-five ERT officers armed with tear gas, batons, and three shotguns cleared each range as they fought to take the prison back.

The shotgun is the most forbidding weapon in Millhaven's arsenal, and guards knew it carried weight with even the most violent rioter: "It's the weapon the inmates fear and respect," an ERT member said. "A lot of times on the street, it was the inmate's weapon of choice. So they know the damage that can be done by a shotgun." The inmates had ripped the sprinkler system apart and were now armed with two-inch-thick iron pipes, as well as their usual shivs or shanks, homemade weapons fashioned out of Plexiglas and other materials. They carried sharpened screwdrivers and toothbrushes with razor blades melted into the plastic. It took until 4:00 the next morning to regain control of J Unit.

Each inmate had to be subdued, cuffed, and searched before being locked in his cell. Millhaven cells have sliding "barriers" with glass windows, which inmates had smashed so that they could attack anyone walking the range. They also smashed toilets and sinks and started throwing razor-sharp pieces of porcelain, followed by volleys of concrete. Inmates had to be fed one at a time

by ERT officers going from cell to cell, a stressful and exhausting exercise made all the worse by the fifty pounds of riot equipment each was wearing and by the danger of "going down" on the slippery floors. The bizarre spectacle of armed men fighting and feeding went on for almost a month, since regular officers could not walk the ranges while the insurrection was in progress.

Inmates smashed through cell walls and then began destroying floors and outside walls. On some ranges every cell wall was breached. "You can go from number one right to number fifteen at the back, and not even step on the range. All of that was ripped out. And I'm not talking a little hole to crawl through. I'm talking the entire wall," one ERT member recalled. The pipes were also destroyed, and the water in the cells had been turned off.

Inmates were throwing their feces, as well as concrete, at the hapless guards: "It was gross. You'd walk through there, and a range at Millhaven – from the ceiling to the roof, I guess it's ten feet. A lot of spots – 1 and 2K Range were probably the worst – I'd have to bend over to walk down the range, because the debris [I was walking on top of] was piled so high. I'm six-three so I'm a fairly tall guy anyway, but still that's how much debris was out there. And there was all kinds of stuff mixed in, it wasn't just concrete. . . . It was a sewer. Burnt material, pieces of toilet, sink, everything," one ERT member recalled.

Operating in the dark, the ERT had to work by flashlight: "Anybody who turned your flashlight on was pelted with material." This included small incendiary devices made of ground match heads lit by homemade fuses. When they hit their target, they burst into flame. As in an anteroom of Dante's inferno, the yelling and screaming continued day and night.

Normally, inmates would not have been kept in such conditions, and even the rioters were surprised that the authorities didn't use force to remove them. But as one ERT member said, "What do you do with 130 inmates that are flipping out?" At one point, ERTs were called in from neighbouring Collins Bay Institution and Joyceville

Institution to help the OPP Tactical Rescue Unit extract and escort thirty of the biggest troublemakers to the special handling unit in the Regional Reception Centre of Sainte-Anne-des-Plaines Complex in Quebec, a high-maximum-security prison, or "super max," for extremely violent offenders. The rest of the inmates were moved to another range at Millhaven. TV cameras were allowed on one range at the end, but not before the day-shift ERT cleared the range of debris and water and scrubbed off areas blackened by the fires. Ottawa had stepped in by this time, and no one in authority wanted the public to see just how bad the situation was.

The riot ruined careers; Millhaven's warden, Al Stevenson, resigned. He was replaced by Lou Kelly, who later became CSC assistant commissioner for Ontario. One officer who helped quell the riot blamed the warden for not being tough enough with inmates: "Appeasement, again, is the word of the day. He wanted the institution treated in a certain way. . . . The warden didn't want to do what needed to be done – basically, lock the prison down and search it."

On-duty ERT members don't have the luxury of questioning an order. In the wake of the seemingly interminable Millhaven riot, which caused $4.5 million of damage at taxpayers' expense, one officer wondered what would have happened if inmates had been given only a litre of water a day, instead of full food services, while they were tearing the prison apart: "I'm sure after a couple of days it would have ended. How long can you go without eating?" But the team knew that if they didn't feed the inmates, someone else would get the order to do it, and there would certainly have been injuries among untrained personnel.

As late as August 1998, only ten Millhaven inmates at a time were being allowed out on a range. Promising that no further incidents would take place, disgruntled offenders demanded that this number be increased until the entire range was once again allowed out en masse.

When the warden finally decided to allow all inmates out for range activities, they responded by not returning to their cells when ordered, delaying the count. The inmates shifted the blame

to others: "Inmates believe the problem lies with the staff more than the inmates."

Management had a few complaints. It was discovered that shivs were being hidden in the fridges on the ranges at Millhaven. That way, no charges could be laid because ownership of the weapons couldn't be established. "If this continues," management warned, "fridge privileges will be removed from ranges affected." In fact, illegal weapons are a fact of life in any prison. According to a guard, "Just the other day, we had one inmate – management were going to put him in segregation because they found two shanks in his bed. He made a deal with management. He said, 'If I give you five more, will you keep me out of the hole?' . . . He went back from range to range and brought back five different shanks! They put him on his range."

By the end of October 1998, plans were being made for the inmates' annual Christmas social, in which outside visitors celebrated the season with offenders. A collection was taken up for children's gifts. Management made it clear that any inmate who was charged before the social would not be permitted to attend. A Sony PlayStation rather than a no-name substitute was approved for the social by the Program Board. Capri Pizza was caterer of choice for the festivities.

Meanwhile, it soon became clear that inmates had been reading their copies of the CCRA. They demanded full range activities to open up the institution to "the least restrictive measures," as was their right by law. The reps complained that the new population at Millhaven was paying for the behaviour of the old population who had smashed up the institution the previous year. The reps requested copies of commissioner's directives, the CCRA, and other policies for their range office in order to make their case.

Exceedingly fine distinctions were made by inmates who studied CSC's own rules and regulations as carefully as if they were preparing an appeal of their cases. They argued that putting an inmate on another range after he was released from segregation was a "punitive" rather than preventive measure, and they demanded that he

be returned to his home range. Management insisted that they had the right to move inmates they believed were causing problems, but agreed that in future inmates would be put on probation before actually being shifted to a new range. Inmates also wanted to be able to keep their cell doors closed in the morning as "a matter of personal dignity." They claimed that control officers verbally abused them when asked to close cell doors. The unit manager agreed to talk to staff about leaving the doors open just a couple of inches, which would give inmates the option of closing their door if they so wished.

Kettles had recently been allowed in segregation cells at Millhaven, in spite of the safety concerns of officers, who are routinely showered with hot water. On November 2, 1998, an inmate decided to make a statement. He threw boiling water on Officer S. Shaw. Shaw had second-degree burns on his arm because management had decided that being able to prepare a hot drink would make inmates happier. "The reason for [the inmate's] sudden violent outburst was that he had been woken up by officers performing duties on the day shift," a source at the institution said.

Judging by the nature of inmate requests at Millhaven, it often seemed that management was fielding complaints from fussy condominium owners. But events had a way of reminding officers exactly who they were dealing with. Officer Farrish, a CX1 at Millhaven, was escorting inmate Rowan to an outside court date on April 26, 1999. While they were driving back to Millhaven that afternoon after the case was remanded, the inmate began to talk about the assault on another offender that had led to his charges: "I don't fight with my fists. That guy wanted to fight me holding his fists up, but I don't fight with fists. Fuck that man-to-man shit." Farrish asked Rowan what he had done. He responded, "I led him out and stabbed him. He squealed like a pig." Rowan planned to plead self-defence: "I'll tell them he had a knife too."

Some of management's best efforts at regulating events at the prison were directed at guards. Warden Lou Kelly issued a memo declaring that staff were no longer permitted to smoke. Any officer

caught defying the order would face progressive fines of $25, $50, even $75 a day. Inmates, meanwhile, could light up at work or at school. Proper ventilation had to be installed in the inmates' smoking room. When staff asked for a smoking room of their own, they were told, "It's not in the budget."

A no-smoking range was considered at one point for Ontario's other maximum-security institution, and staff put out a petition seeking interested inmates. Out of 290 respondents, only 15 volunteered to go smoke-free. One veteran guard was not surprised: "They are prepared to be violent, I mean violent, to back up their rights. They will kill somebody to support those rights. Plus, the thing is, they know and I know. . . . doing away with cigarettes is doing away with a form of currency." Cigarettes also had a darker use at KP, as the same guard noted: "At our place, if you want to have somebody killed, you hand out a carton of cigarettes or an ounce of grass."

2

KINGSTON

Kingston Pen is known among Canada's fifty-two federal prisons as the trash heap of the system. After an inmate's trip to Millhaven for assessment, if it is determined that he is a maximum-security candidate, there are only two places in Ontario he can be assigned: Millhaven and KP. Infamous as the decrepit home of "diddlers and rats," a protective-custody environment for inmates who literally couldn't survive in other institutions, KP is a prison filled with violence, drugs, and ever-simmering racial tensions that can explode at any moment.

Spread over twenty acres, the fortress-like facility faces Lake Ontario to the south. On a typical day in 1999 there were 101 temporary detainees inside (inmates whose parole had been suspended), along with 242 maximum-security inmates, 56 medium-security offenders, and a lone minimum-security inmate. The Regional Treatment Centre at KP housed 124 psychiatric patients. Although it is within the walls of KP, the RTC is considered a separate institution.

The "main dome," as the central tower at Kingston Penitentiary is called, is the prison's nerve centre. Circular in construction, it is more than a hundred feet high and about seventy feet across. It was originally topped by a dome, which was destroyed by fire,

Four wings, each about 180 feet long, radiate from the main dome to form a cross shape. The wings have fourteen-foot-thick outer walls pierced with floor-to-ceiling windows. Three of the four wings are divided up the middle into two cellblocks each. The cells are in back-to-back rows, facing out to the common areas and the windows.

The cellblock wings are four floors high. Each floor has electronically controlled doors at both ends. At the dome end, the doors open onto four-foot-wide catwalks that run around the inside of the central tower. Stairways connect the floors on the east and west sides of the dome.

In the centre of the dome is B-1 Control, the main control centre. Originally planned to be four floors high, with catwalk access to all floors, it was scaled down to a ground-floor cage with windows all around. It controls the doors leading from the floors into the tower. Additional control stations are on the second and third floors in the corners where the wings meet the dome, and the fourth floor also has a couple.

Each cellblock is divided into lower ranges (floors 1 and 2) and upper ranges (floors 3 and 4). Cellblocks A, B, E, F, G, and H together with the main dome are referred to collectively as the "wing and cells" area. The C and D wing, built as cellblocks in 1836, was gutted after a riot and has housed offices, classrooms, and a library since the late 1980s. South of the main dome complex is a slightly smaller building known as the "shop dome," containing the prison's workshops and more program facilities and offices.

The cells themselves – nineteen to a floor, thirty-eight to a range – are only fifty feet square, ruling out double-bunking. Once considered to be the slum of Canadian prisons, KP has had its infrastructure totally upgraded. The cellblock renovations included new furnishings, fire alarms, sprinklers, and call buttons in each cell. Cell doors are more like gates, made of a grid of metal bars. Although the doors can be unlocked electronically from the range control post, they must be closed manually to re-engage the locks. Inmates have learned to block the locks with string, elastic bands, or even

socks so that they can be opened even though they appear closed.

The principal entrance (PE) of Kingston Pen is an imposing structure. A camera covers the area immediately in front of the entry door, and there is an intercom to communicate with staff in the control centre. The doors in the entrance corridor are on an interlock system. Admission and departure is controlled by the pedestrian control officer, who opens and closes the double set of doors. Weapons and ammunition for the prison are stored here in the control centre. Small property lockers for visitors are located in the corridor to the right of the control centre. There is no search room to conduct intrusive searches of visitors, but there is a walk-through scanner.

The control centre in the PE contains the monitors for the many closed-circuit televisions located in the institution. It also has a public address system to broadcast messages throughout the prison. There is a visual display board to keep track of staff as they make their rounds through an electronic keypunch system. And there are display boards for fire alarms, security-door status, fixed-point alarms, and portable personal alarms carried by correctional officers.

There are also gun racks in the PE control centre. One holds nine-millimetre AR-15s with inserted magazines, for use if an emergency arises at the PE. Another has loaded magazines stored on a shelf above the weapons for issue to inside staff or external posts. A tear-gas gun is stored with the firearms. The control centre also has a supply of restraint equipment. An electronic key safe contains keys to be distributed by the control centre. Staff punch in their codes, open the safe, and draw out the required keys, leaving an electronic record. The safe is also used to store chemical agents like Mace and tear gas.

If staff have to leave the control centre in an emergency, they can use a trap-door entrance to a tunnel. (Ironically, most of the tunnels at KP do not go under the walls but end in a dead end or in passages too narrow for a person to pass through.) There is a series of tunnels at the prison, used for electrical wiring and ventilation. Staff can also use them to escape from control centres in the

cellblocks and to get onto the roof in an emergency. The only other way out is through doors at the end of the floors, which cannot be used unless inmates are locked in their cells. Once in a stairwell, guards would have to descend to the ground floor, where a staff member outside the building would have to open the outside doors with a key. Moving firearms to the range control centres quickly and safely is a major problem at Kingston.

Visitors to the prison who expect to see Alcatraz North are in for a surprise. Instead, they will find inmate ranges with microwaves, coffee pots, toasters, hot plates, at least three public phones per range, card tables, bulletin boards, showers, washers and dryers, and one or two fridges. Light floods onto the ranges through large, new windows. Baffles on the walls muffle noise, and from 11:30 to 13:00 there is a daily quiet time on the ranges. Each cell is fitted with a desk, a comfortable bed, shelving, and a stainless steel toilet and sink. All cells are equipped with cable TV and computer hookups, but it is up to the inmate to provide his own television and computer. They are much like university dorm rooms, except that students usually don't have their own washrooms, and often have to double-bunk.

New inmates at KP are bombarded with noise, a cacophony of boom boxes, CD systems, televisions, and inmates screaming at one another in order to be heard above the incessant din. According to one guard, G Block's inmates include black and native groups that play their music of choice at competing volume levels. "Then you get a guy who likes heavy metal and he is playing his music. . . . And then they are screaming and hollering at each other, roaring. A lot of the people, the kids, the younger cons, they have one level of speech. That's high volume, that's it. It's like they are standing in a railway station and the train's going through. They are screaming and hollering at each other. . . . There are studies that support how this wears you down. The CIA used it for psychological reasons down in Panama."

Most of the inmates aren't officially allowed to cook on the ranges at KP, but there are hot plates and even some stoves. Inmates

still manage to get raw food smuggled out of the kitchen. On some ranges, people from ethnic minorities cook regardless of the prohibitions, filling the ranges with the smell of exotic spices. The official kitchen goes along with the practice because it saves staff the trouble of having to prepare special orders. "Nobody wants to challenge them. The guys in the kitchen will smuggle it out."

Thirty years ago at KP, inmates got one shower a week. They were marched down from the shops to the "horseshoe" (also known as the "car wash"), a giant horseshoe ring of showers. They came in one door and put all their dirty clothes in a hamper at a window. Then they shuffled around the horseshoe from shower-head to showerhead until they reached the other side. At a window beside the exit, they were given clean clothes and returned to their cells. A guard regulated the water; it was up to him to decide whether the showers were hot or cold.

Before modernization, the older prisons used to smell, an institutional farrago of industrial cleansers, sweat, urine, and, some guards say, the peculiar tincture of fear and rage. The majority of inmates today are much cleaner. There are four showers on each range at KP, and inmates can take a shower any time they are on the range. For those who avoid the showers, there is no avoiding the nasty boys: "These guys would go under pressure and they would wash and scrub. I have actually seen some of the heavies on the range stand right there and say, 'Ugh, bar of soap, use it. I want to see soap suds.' There is self-discipline that way." But even here, there was a business opportunity for KP's ingenious predators, as one guard remembers: "'You want to take a shower, it's a package of cigarettes. If you take a shower and don't pay me off, I'll beat you up.' We found out about that and put the kibosh on that, because you'd go in the guy's cell and the guy didn't smoke – forty-five packages of cigarettes."

Despite the renovations and the daily showers, a former officer, Dave Burke, describes another smell at KP that was beyond the eradicating powers of soap and water. "Every now and again,

depending on the weather and stuff, you'd get the odd hit of . . . I don't know whether it was rot or mildew. I don't know what it was."

Inmates meticulously watch their keepers in an attempt to master their habits and routines. They can tell when an officer has a cigarette, how many times he has coffee or goes to the washroom, and whether he reads on duty. Inmates are innovative and can make binoculars or even telescopes to facilitate their surveillance projects. From some of the cellblocks at KP, they can actually see over the walls into the parking lot to identify guards' vehicles. On the other side of the institution, they can see who goes into the Portsmouth Tavern, a favourite watering hole for KP staff. Recalls Phil Whaley, another former officer, "I remember I got a little white truck, after I didn't have a vehicle for a while, and I pulled into the parking lot. The cons, when I went in, they had me working on the same cellblock where they could see out over the walls. 'I see you got a new truck, boss.' I was standing in front of this guy's cell, I look out through this device, and there's my truck, I can see it."

Even better than the staff, inmates know how things are supposed to be done by the book and are quick to go after a staff member who steps outside the rules: "It's just a hobby with them. We watch them, they watch us. And they can tell the person that watches the cellblock from the person that sits there and reads the newspaper, puts his feet up, doesn't bother," Whaley says. The first thing inmates will do when the shift changes is look to see who is in the control office to see how far they can go. Some don't care, but most tailor their behaviour to the habits of the officer who happens to be on duty.

"Some officers are pretty stiff and enforce the rules and regulations. Some people are pretty lax, although some of the staff over the years have adopted the attitude, 'Well, if I don't bother the cons, they're not going to bother me.' Well, that's not a good idea,

because you might have an easy shift once in a while, but they are going to take advantage of it eventually," Whaley says.

Whaley maintains that the live-and-let-live attitude is the dominant philosophy at KP these days, particularly among new staff who make up about 85 per cent of KP's current roster. "Nothing against them, but they don't have any real experience, and they have watched other officers when they started and figured, 'Why should I bang my head against the wall all night long, or all week long? I'll just let things go.' The cons love that because it allows them to do various things that they shouldn't be doing. . . . Joe Blow over here, he's not doing anything, nobody even bothers him. Luckily for him or her, nothing happens. But then if something does happen, you get one of these 'please explain' letters in your file: Why was this cell door left open? Or why was that man allowed to be drunk or whatever? This person brought drugs into the range, why didn't you frisk him before he went in, because it should have been suspicious? Whatever. You stand there with egg on your face."

Asked how often the job comes down to a predictable routine, Whaley replies, "That's a really hard question because there is no 'routine.' You've got at KP 450 pretty nasty people, as you have in most jails, sitting locked up or out in their own little society. You've got all sorts of things going on, like drug deals, or I don't like the way this guy cuts his hair, or I don't like the colour of this guy's skin, or this guy comes from the East Coast and I don't like downeasters, or comes from out west."

Fighting racism is a preoccupation of Kingston's management team, given the prison's mixed population of black, oriental, native, and white offenders. Although on paper, for example, CSC has an official zero-tolerance policy for racial indignities, they are routinely treated as minor occurrences when the victim happens to be a correctional officer. As one black officer recalled when he showed an inmate the charges against him, "He called me the N-word. OK. It's a minor offence." Outraged, a fellow black officer

made the point: "What if one of us, especially a white officer . . .
called an inmate the N-word? What would happen to that officer?
He would lose his job. If that was proven, he would lose his job."

In October 1998, Monty Bourke, the warden of KP, sent a memo
to staff ostensibly aimed at fostering a more respectful environment
for staff and inmates alike. An ongoing review had shown that there
had been overall improvement, but "there is an unacceptable level
of continuing verbal and physical abuse and disrespectful behaviour
from some inmates in the population." The warden knew from staff
feedback that "the verbal and physical abuse causes emotional and
personal stress and job dissatisfaction."

Since the disciplinary process had not dealt with the problem,
Bourke asked managers to treat this type of incident "at a high
level of priority and with increased interventions and disciplinary sanctions against inmates who act in this manner." The
warden wanted reports submitted for offensive, threatening, or
abusive language or actions and assured staff that these reports
would be treated seriously. In the past, staff had put up with the
abuse, since the behaviour when reported either was ignored or
went virtually unpunished.

The memo did not have much effect. On February 24, 1999, an
officer submitted a report about an inmate. Upper G Range had
been called for "gym-up" at 20:45. The inmate left the range and
headed to the Upper F Range barrier door. He accosted two
officers and became very loud and abusive: "Fuck you, you fucking
goofs!! Suck my big black cock!!" he told one of the officers who
happened to be black. "Your wife left you for another woman.
Suck my big black cock!" As he repeated the words, the inmate
grabbed his crotch and thrust his pelvis toward the officers.
Nothing happened.

At Kingston Pen, racism is a card that inmates play with consid-
erable skill. Officer Dean Bryce, black himself, grew up in Sydney,
Nova Scotia, and tries not to let ethnic-minority inmates get the
upper hand: "I tell a lot of inmates in here, Look at me, don't give
me any of your song and dance. . . . You get a lot of these younger

– I call them inexperienced punks, black Jamaicans, they try to impress me about the ghetto, about hardships, about racism, they call for the racist card. Listen, I fought racism when they were still being thought of! . . . I said, 'Don't you even start with me, because you don't know what racism is.' Another inmate, Wesley, he's always going around saying, 'Wesley's my name, it's a slave name, a slave name.' I said, 'Wesley, I've got a son that's almost as old as you. You wouldn't even know what slavery is all about, so don't start. Every time somebody says something, you want to bring up a race card in their face. By crying wolf all the time nobody pays any attention to you.' That's the scary thing about it all. This is the management, my own personal opinion – Monty Bourke and management before that . . . the rest of them, they are afraid of the black inmate."

On October 24, 1993, twenty-three-year-old Robert Gentles died of asphyxiation on Upper G at KP during a forcible cell extraction. Before his death, if an inmate was causing a problem in his cell, he would routinely be taken to segregation by officers. Faced with the easy way or the hard way, most cons went peacefully. But because of policy changes that followed the coroner's inquiry into the Gentles affair, inmates now know that officers won't be coming down the range to enforce the rules or conduct a cell search unless permission has filtered up and down the chain of command. In the event that permission is granted, there is now plenty of time to hide evidence. Inmates also know the CCRA restrictions on the use of physical intervention. As a result, institutions have become far more tolerant of violence and drug use on the ranges, and inmates have lost respect for staff authority in the higher-security prisons.

One guard remembers the days when a respected senior inmate assumed internal charge of a range and helped keep the peace. In the wake of Gentles, he says, all that has changed: "Nowadays it's all intimidation, and brute force, and who has the most drugs to sell." As a result, front-line staff have little doubt that it is the prisoners who really run the institutions: "No two ways about it,

we can do nothing to them now. Absolutely nothing. At one point, at least we had the threat of being able to lock them up and charge them, or some type of control. Now you tell them you are going to charge them – they laugh at you."

The destabilization of the prisons after the Gentles affair has made them far more dangerous places for guard and prisoner alike than they were before. No one inside ever knows when he might become the victim of sudden violence. Inmate Alden, who struck and nearly killed Officer Dave Burke with a broom handle during a riot on Upper H at KP in August 1997, attacked his victim from behind. Burke suffered permanent damage and was unable to return to work. Alden got six months in the special handling unit at Sainte-Anne-des-Plaines for the attack and will be deported to his native Jamaica in 2003.

After he returned to KP from the SHU, Alden broke another officer's jaw and later stabbed another inmate. Officer Dean Bryce recalled hearing Alden "yapping off and yapping off." Bryce looked to see who Alden was talking to, and "Monty Bourke was standing right by his cell." Bryce could hear everything that was going on. "He was going on yapping about the lockdown, about this, and everything is unfair, and the people around here are racist. He said, 'That Officer Bryce, he's always picking on me. . . . Oh yeah, he's a racist.'"

When the warden left the range, Bryce confronted him: "I looked at him and I said, 'Hey, excuse me, sir, I see you got the lowdown on me. Yeah,' I says, 'inmate Alden here has given you the whole story. I'm picking on him and everything. Maybe I do, sir, but the problem is with him.' He said, 'What's that?' I said, 'They don't like the word no, and they can't cry racism because I'm a black officer. I'm not stepping on their side and backing them. I do the same with every inmate there. Every inmate that's there, I treat them all the same. They don't like that.' . . . This was one of [Alden's] biggest cards. I find a lot of, not all of them, use that racist card as soon as they couldn't get something done. 'You

are a racist. You do not like me because I'm black.' . . . It's used against the white officers."

Before Dave Burke was knocked unconscious by the broom handle, management had been warned in several observation reports that there was going to be trouble on Upper H Range. Guards knew that there was a volatile mix of different racial groups who had not exactly adopted multiculturalism as their guiding philosophy. The four principal camps – Canadian blacks, Jamaicans, aboriginals, with whites in the minority – were living under an uncomfortable truce. Things were so bad on Upper H that many officers refused overtime if it meant working there.

Burke recalls, "I've found that a lot of drug users, for whatever reason, especially the non-Caucasian ones, think the world owes them a living. And that's the guys we had trouble with upstairs. We had trouble with them upstairs for three or four years. And management would never acknowledge the fact there was a problem. They were scared to death of these people because of this human rights thing. . . . They would come in and they didn't know the word no. These inmates didn't want to conform with the rules because they thought they were better than everybody else. They had their little gang or posse, and they threatened everybody."

The fuse, long lit, finally exploded on the difficult range on August 27, 1997, when an inmate on Upper H was stabbed. The victim managed to lock himself in his cell and then press the alarm. The other inmates were out of their cells and became aggressive when two officers attempted to respond to the alarm. The officer in the control post saw trouble and quickly ordered backup. Two more officers went on the range to help their trapped co-workers. As per CSC's regulations, all of the officers were unarmed. Nor was help anywhere nearby. KP is the only maximum-security penitentiary in Canada that does not have weapons in the control posts overlooking the ranges.

Burke was the supervisor downstairs on the first and second floors. It was about 22:30, lock-up time, and the inmates on Lower E Range were in their cells for the night. He received a

call on the radio that there was a problem upstairs and that the duty officers needed help: "So I went upstairs. There were a bunch of officers gathered up there. Evidently an inmate had been stabbed. Now I'm not sure if they ever determined, to this day, if it was ever a real stabbing, because the guy was not seriously injured. . . . So the question remains: was this a serious stabbing, like a warning to this man because he didn't pay off drug debts or whatever, or was it a ploy to get staff on the range? I tend to believe it was a ploy. But you don't know that at the time. You have to take it at face value. . . . So I went down the range, and I was locking doors, the ones that I could. There was a commotion behind me. It started with just yelling, verbal, and it got progressively louder and louder. And then it turned physical, a little pushing and shoving. This is what I heard. I turned halfway around to see what was going on. That's all I remember."

His fellow officers managed to get Burke out, locked the range off so inmates couldn't escape, and gathered in the main dome to wait for the ERT, which normally takes about two hours to assemble, gear up, and devise a plan for controlling a situation. Before being implemented, the plan must be approved by the warden or deputy warden. The deputy warden of KP, Janet DeLaat, appeared half an hour after the trouble started. The officers were still unarmed and standing in the middle of the dome floor. According to the guards on the scene, her first, nervous words were, "Any inmate injured?"

The men who had kept the inmates from escaping were livid. There was a seriously injured officer on his way to the hospital on a stretcher, and others had minor injuries, yet management's instinctive concern seemed to be for the rioters. The guards involved in the riot found themselves remembering the first words they had heard when a new female manager had addressed the CXs of Kingston Pen and looked out over the mostly male contingent: "I don't see enough ovaries out there."

DeLaat was informed about the stabbed inmate, still in his cell. She pointed to four new staff and told them to open the barrier

and walk toward the inmates. The officers, who were "green as grass" in the eyes of their veteran colleagues, picked up batons and began walking toward the stairs as ordered. Officer Leo Prosser yelled, "Let's stop this now! We are not thinking straight here."

He and the others told the deputy warden that she would get the officers killed, and that anyone who obeyed the order at that point in time was "out of their mind." As one officer on duty that night said, "Those forty guys would have destroyed these four guys within less than ten seconds. The batons would have been taken out of their hands and shoved up their butts, to be blunt." They could also have been dragged into the showers and shivved as they came through the corridor, a dread scenario that was widely rumoured, after the incident ended, to be the inmates' plan.

The officers begged for a weapon so that they could secure the inmates in the event they broke down the range door. Management refused. Meanwhile inmates began setting fires and flooding the building from the top floors, as well as storming the door. Faced with a potential major riot, management finally authorized a rifle for KP's beleaguered staff.

According to Officer Pedro Sousa-Diaz, who handled the gun, "I really do believe . . . that if there had been a weapon on that corner, inside that office . . . there would not have been a riot. Those inmates respect force. I'm not saying you need to abuse that force, but they respect force."

It had taken almost an hour and a half from the start of the incident to get a weapon in place. Since they were vastly outnumbered, the unarmed staff had already decided among themselves to abandon the institution by running for the gate if the inmates breached the barricade on Upper H. They knew it was unlikely that all of them would make it outside alive. "I think the common person that doesn't work inside an institution has no idea what a group of these guys can do," observes Sousa-Diaz, a former football star at Queen's University and a five-year veteran of KP who has left CSC.

Finally, almost two hours after the riot started, the ERT arrived with shotguns, gas guns, and Mace. Short-handed, they asked Officer Sousa-Diaz for support as they attempted to penetrate the barricaded range. It took them almost three hours to break in and walk the range. The inmate who had been stabbed had to go through the whole riot, including a tear gas assault, before he could be removed safely for medical attention.

Dave Burke never returned to KP. "It destroyed my life enough that I didn't want any more part of that. It really did. I saw a psychologist for, I guess, about two years.... I guess it helped. I'm still alive today, I didn't commit suicide or anything." As well as permanent physical injuries, Burke suffers from a disorder common in those who return from war zones: post-traumatic stress syndrome.

For Burke, losing his job also meant losing part of the family tradition. His aunt was superintendent at the nearby Prison for Women; she had an apartment on the premises where she had often babysat Burke and other relatives. But the prison world had changed utterly since the days of his aunt.

Although he had been threatened many times and dismissed it as part of the job, this was the first time Burke had been seriously injured. "When that lad hit me and I went down, it was like reality struck here. Just like old Humpty Dumpty, cracked his shell, can't put it back together again. My world collapsed right around me. There was absolutely no way in the world I could ever rebuild that world."

Oddly enough, Burke actually had a good rapport with many of the black inmates on his range. "The night I got hurt, most of them were high on something. The next day, when they all started to sober up, [everyone could see] there was something like $100,000 damage done to the range. They said, 'Well, what went on, what did we do?' The guards said, 'Well, this is what went on,' and they said, 'That nigger hit Mr. B.? And you don't know if he's alive or dead?' They said, 'Yeah.'" White or black, an inmate will be known as a "nigger" inside if his behaviour is abhorrent to other inmates, including blacks.

"The [other inmates] were going to do [Burke's attacker] in, do him in right there. But he was gone. They had him locked up. The blacks will tell you this: there's black people who were 'niggers.'... They were like the low-gutter bottom-feeder scum of the black race. They weren't respected on that range, and they were the ones who caused all the problems. . . . My caseload were on that range. When they sobered up, they were really ticked off."

On Saturday, June 5, 1999, inmates at KP were proceeding from the yard just before 20:00 following a social. Guards suspected that several inmates were drunk and high on drugs, a feeling that was later confirmed by searches. But when officers tried to apprehend the suspects, "all hell broke loose," and staff were attacked. Within a matter of minutes there was a concerted effort on the part of the inmates on Lower B Range and Upper B, E, and F Ranges to take over the prison.

Staff were threatened and responded with a number of rounds of tear gas fired from B-1 Control, in the centre of the main dome. This cage houses the controls that operate most of the entrance and exit doors in the wing and cells area. KP's Emergency Response Team was called in when the situation began to spin out of control. The inmates refused to lock up for the 20:00 count. Instead, they threatened staff and began smashing furniture and windows on the ranges. Fires broke out and the noise levels escalated.

At first, the segregation ranges – Lower A, B, and H – did not participate. Nor did Lower F; the special-needs unit (for dysfunctional inmates) on Lower E; or the temporary detention ranges, Upper A, B, and H. Deputy Warden Alex Lubimiv had given the order to close the existing dissociation and segregation building, B-14, at the end of May 1999. Built in the 1930s, it had twenty cells, and it was directly connected to B-1 Control in the main dome.

Inmates will refer to being sent to the "hole," but the original reference is to a dungeon, long since closed, that was once used to punish unruly offenders. Until 1999, troublemakers were sent to dissociation cells ("diss" cells) in the concrete segregation building, which was above ground. Inmates were confined twenty-three

hours a day and had one hour of exercise in a segregated yard. Government projects are often behind schedule and the replacement building was still under construction when the 1999 riot broke out. The new segregation unit was scheduled for occupancy in May 2001 at a cost of $2.7 million. In the meantime, Lower H Range at KP had been converted into an interim segregation unit, with what most people would consider to be normal cells.

The ERT from Millhaven was called in to assist the KP team, and the team from Collins Bay was placed on standby. At 00:20 on June 6, the ERT was still attempting to do a count, since unarmed regular staff are not authorized to go down the ranges during an insurrection. As well as a physical count, the ERT was also videotaping and putting out the fires that inmates kept setting. At 3:25, the ERT forcibly removed five inmates from Upper F and transferred them to Millhaven. At 7:00, another three from Lower G made the short trip to the other maximum-security institution.

Brunch began at 11:00 on the 6th. By 12:30, more trouble was brewing on Lower A Range: noise, threats, and small fires. Management decided that the inmates were just blowing off steam and ordered the normal routine to resume. At 20:00, the men on Lower G refused to lock up, but after a swarm of regular staff arrived on the range, inmates apparently decided that it would be in their best interest to do so.

But on June 8, 1999, the breakfast serving commenced five minutes late and trouble started on Lower H Range, which housed segregation and dissociation cells and was home to Paul Bernardo. Six inmates were out of their cells at one time, even though it was supposed to be a lock-up range, where only one inmate at a time is allowed out. According to a number of officers, KP managers feel that inmates have a right to privileges, even when they put staff and other inmates at risk.

A female officer was in command of two male staff. The inmates threw hot water on the CX staff and tried to take over the office area and the key safe on the range. Unlike other ranges, this range has a glassed-in office at the front without security doors, earning

it the jocular name among staff of the "greenhouse." If the inmates had got the keys as well as staff hostages, they would have had access to all the cell doors, as well as the door leading to an enclosed exercise yard outside. They would also have had access to canisters of Mace, handcuffs, leg irons, and – what mattered most to KP management – Paul Bernardo.

Luckily, the staff were able to get off the range without injury, taking most of the security equipment with them. Staff from the other wing and cells areas assisted in containing the inmates. A total of twenty-four T21 gas dispersal shells were fired from 20:00 on June 5 to 14:50 on June 8. This was unheard of at KP. As one officer with more than thirty years' experience said, management took a very dim view of the use of gas: "Never, never, never use gas except as an extreme last resort!" The ERT was called back when the inmates on Lower H began to "remodel" the range. More important from management's point of view, the inmates indicated that they were going to "get" Bernardo.

When the plot to kill Bernardo became known to management, the system jumped into action. Prison authorities went through the second-floor door, ran down the range, and quickly scooped Bernardo out of his cell. He was taken to safety in the shower cell of a peaceful cellblock. Although there were about thirty-eight inmates on Lower H Range, Bernardo was the only one who was "rescued." No effort was made to remove the other inmates. The outside windows were broken, as were the shatterproof windows of the office. The washer, dryer, microwave, telephone, and everything else that wasn't bolted down was destroyed.

But by 14:30, all the prisoners were locked down, except for about forty-five temporary-detention inmates in the main yard, seventeen inmates in the visiting area, and the inmates on Lower H, who had by now managed to smash open the door to the outside exercise yard, a small, walled enclosure between the old diss cells and H Block. When the "hole" was closed at the end of May, the doors were actually welded shut and KP's Warden treated the event

as a giant leap forward for KP's otherwise inglorious traditions. But the inmates rioting on Lower H would have to be put somewhere, so the order went out for the machine shop to bring welding torches to unweld the diss cell doors. This time there were no promotional shots of smiling Monty Bourke to commemorate the event. The ERT was in the wing and cells area on standby, but Deputy Warden Lubimiv and others continued to try to negotiate with the inmates – unsuccessfully. At 17:15 the ERT moved onto Lower H to start defusing the situation and began the dirty work of moving the rioting inmates to the newly reopened diss cells.

At 17:40 an inmate was carried off the range on a stretcher and sent by ambulance to an outside hospital. The 16:30 count was called and certified correct at 18:00, but the inmates had still not been fed. At 18:15, supper commenced on the ranges, with CX staff escorting the food service officers from cell to cell. On Upper G, the staff were threatened and the inmates began hurling anything they could get their hands on at the officers. The ERT was not called, since management felt that the inmates should be "allowed to vent." As per CSC policy, a supervisor and a videographer were dispatched to record the venting. The tear gas shells in B-1 Control were restocked by the armouries officer just in case.

After the inmate supper ended at 19:00, Lubimiv ordered a staff briefing to bring them up to date on the "official version" of what had happened. These were the same staff who had been on the ranges all day. The Supply and Institutional Services staff were called in to decontaminate and clean Lower H Range. They cleared broken glass and debris and broken office furniture from the "greenhouse." About thirty inmates were still on Lower H, and the procedure took about two hours.

At 20:00 the count was taken and certified correct. The deputy warden then ordered the officers on the non-segregation ranges to release the inmate committee members from their ranges so that they could be sent down to the common room for a talk with management. Astonishingly, while the inmates took part, no line officers

who had helped quell the riot were included in the discussions.

At 12:30 the ERT was called yet again, this time to the reopened diss cells, where an inmate had set a major fire. Line staff had to get fire extinguishers from the main wing and cells area, since fire extinguishers and the main large firehose had been removed from the diss cells when the building was closed. The nurse was called, but there was no real damage except for a lot of smoke.

(Fires were no laughing matter at CSC. Inmates on a segregation range, including Paul Bernardo, launched a $400,000 class action suit against KP after a Halloween 1999 fire set by inmates was not put out quickly enough by guards. The suit alleged that KP staff took "excessive time to respond and to extinguish the fire while inmates were forced to breathe thick, noxious smoke and fumes." Each man sought $13,500 damages for feeling "trapped" and "put in fear of their lives by the reckless acts of the prison staff and officials.")

At 21:15 the ERT removed an inmate from Lower H to the diss cells and took another inmate to the treatment centre. As one of the guards left at 23:05, he heard the inmates hooting and hollering and banging in their cells. He wondered if they were watching something about themselves on TV, or maybe they were just upset at the way the hockey game was going. Eight ringleaders were sent to Millhaven.

On Wednesday, June 9, 1999, the reopened "hole" at KP was cleared of all inmates, and by 16:00, the doors were welded shut for KP's second great leap forward. The inmates were put on other segregation ranges, even though many guards believed that they were not suited for occupancy there. "They, as of 1600 hours this date, have emptied the diss cells at KP, once again filling their mandate to have the only maximum-security institution in North America without a Dissociation Cell Block Area and have once again welded the doors shut!" one guard wrote in an e-mail. The prison was quiet. Cell-by-cell feeding continued on some ranges, with few or no privileges or movement. In the peaceful ranges, the normal routine ticked along like a metronome – feeding, yard, and

gym, just as if nothing had happened. Inmates from Lower H, who had been moved to Lower A, a segregation range, after the riot, were busy flooding it at 23:00 as the shift changed.

In the end, most staff were tight-lipped about what had happened. Management made it known that they did not want to see contradictory stories in the press, just the official line; the institution had undergone a "minor disturbance." One guard admitted he was "a little worried" about the media coverage of "the worst riot at Kingston Pen since 1971." The inmates had threatened to kill guards, tried to take them hostage, and made the usual ethnic slurs against white officers. But the media had played down the riot, and "management is again trying to cover up a serious situation in order to hide their own mistakes." He noted: "How often do you hear of the Emergency Response Teams from three different prisons being called in to stop a 'minor disturbance'?"

This was not an isolated incident. On April 11, 1997, there had been a riot at Collins Bay Institution. Three hundred inmates smashed through concrete walls, lit fires, and destroyed government property. This too was reported to the media as a "minor disturbance." Sources at the penitentiary say that the warden ordered the cleaning staff to work over the midnight shift to clean up the mess before the local media were allowed in the next morning.

Despite official attempts to "spin" the media, concerned prison staff had begun releasing information about both offenders and CSC managers to the press. On October 29, 1998, KP warden Monty Bourke issued a memo to staff about "illegal disclosure of information." "This practice is in direct contravention of the Standards of Professional Conduct which states: 'Staff shall treat information acquired through their employment in a manner consistent with the Access to Information Act, the Privacy Act, the Security Policy of the Government of Canada and the Oath of Secrecy taken by all employees of the Public Service of Canada.'" The memo noted that employees who talked could be fired. As a result of two newspaper articles I had recently written, Warden Bourke had convened

a disciplinary fact-finding inquiry and had asked the RCMP to conduct an independent investigation. (I was later contacted by the Justice Department and warned that I could be charged with undermining the peace, order, and good government of a federal institution if I wrote further articles. With the support of my newspaper, the *Toronto Sun*, I continued to write stories and no action was taken by authorities.)

With the offending journalist under investigation, Monty Bourke completed his follow-up by sending an apology to inmates I had named in my articles. His memo read:

> Many of you are aware that The Toronto Sun newspaper has published two articles this week about Kingston Penitentiary. Both articles have, in my view, clearly demonstrated that privacy laws governing the sharing of offender-related information have been violated. The deputy warden and I have met with the inmate committee chairman and other inmates and we are aware of the concerns created by the articles on inmates in the population. Let me assure you that every effort will be undertaken to investigate these violations of your right to privacy. I am taking these violations very seriously and I will take appropriate action following completion of the investigation being convened on this matter. I have directed that an internal fact finding be **undertaken immediately** to investigate the breach of the Security Policy of the government of Canada and the Privacy Act.

Despite the warden's best efforts to suppress information about what was really happening in Canada's oldest penitentiary, the investigations he ordered actually triggered even more information from concerned CSC employees. Tremors were felt right across the CSC. One Millhaven guard who had worked in J Unit for ten years wrote to the author:

It's been a long time since I've seen a piece of journalism that tells it like it is. Concern: Ever since I've been in the service, security has been a steadily declining priority and quite frankly it makes me angry sometimes. Most of the administrators haven't a clue about what's going on inside and what's important. They decide the policies based on what they think they know with no input from line staff. . . . The suits put us in dangerous positions on a daily basis under the guise of "risk management" and all their other fancy terms. I think the truth is that they're all afraid to take a stand and make waves. It's about time the people knew what was going on. It's the only way change will happen.

One of the things prison authorities at KP would prefer to keep secret is the fact that prison violence is a way of life inside, making a mockery of management's vaunted claims about "rehabilitation." The union kept a record of some of the assaults against officers and other incidents at KP from August 1997 to September 1998. During the riot on Upper H Range in August 1997, numerous staff were assaulted and Officer Burke was so severely hurt it destroyed his career. The assailant got a six-month sentence, but thirty-three other inmates were involved and nothing happened to them. The same month, a food service officer was taken hostage on Upper H by an inmate brandishing a razor. The inmate was charged with assault and transferred to the designated segregation unit at Millhaven. On February 11, 1998, an inmate in the dissociation cells assaulted an officer with urine. Three fires were extinguished in his cell, and he set another fire on February 22. He was charged with assault but released from segregation on March 20, because of "improved behaviour and attitude." The officer who was showered with urine was not warned before the inmate's release.

On July 10, 1998, inmate Vernon smashed up Lower B Range after being transferred to KP from Millhaven. This was classified as a

"minor disturbance with minor damage." On July 17, inmate Bierman assaulted Officer C. Campbell on Upper G. Bierman was placed in segregation after the warden negotiated with him, and it was agreed that he could bring his TV, stereo, and other belongings. Bierman was released from segregation on August 7. There were no outside charges. Two days after the assault on Campbell, inmate Moss started to smash up Upper E. He broke a broom handle and threatened to kill any officers who came on the range. Moss was allowed to go to the yard, where he assaulted inmate Doyle. When being escorted to segregation, he put up a fight. After being locked up, he spat in the faces of Officers Clarke and Wilcox. He was transferred to Millhaven, criminal charges pending.

And the list goes on and on. According to the CSC performance report released in November 2001, major assaults by inmates jumped from thirty-one in 1998-1999 to fifty-four in 2000-2001.

For years correctional officers at Kingston have felt that security was being compromised by staff cutbacks, unmanned towers, and range walks undertaken by solitary, unarmed officers. Front-line staff have watched their numbers dwindle while those at regional headquarters grew. On September 7, 2000, Acting Deputy Warden Mike Ryan informed correctional officers at KP that nine of them would be laid off because of persistent budgetary deficits and inquired if any of them wanted to work at other federal institutions in the Kingston area.

Cost-cutting at KP extended all the way to the staff kitchen. The warden had already made it clear that inmate rations were for inmates only. Officers were strictly forbidden to consume any unused food. But the cost-cutting went further: in November 1999, Acting Assistant Warden Tim Jamieson, in charge of Management Services, sent a memo stating that because of staff cuts in the kitchen, the Officers' Mess would no longer offer hot meals to officers. As of November 29, the officers would be given soup, sandwiches, and cold salads instead.

The hot meal was a long-standing tradition in return for the understanding that the officers were on call if they were needed in an emergency during the lunch break. But the officers were the only ones losing their hot meal: there would be no change in the inmates' meal plan, including their hot lunch. And officers' individual requests for vegetarian or other meals for dietary or religious reasons could not be accommodated, although inmates' wishes were granted as much as possible.

Finally, on August 2, 2000, Warden Monty Bourke sent a memo to staff advising them of his intention to terminate seven contract employees. As a result, he had no alternative but to close the Officers' Mess entirely, effective September 18, 2000. He was prepared to offer staff a noon meal, but it would be prepared in the main kitchen with inmate labour. They would be eating the same meal as the inmates on standard inmate trays. The guards were understandably unimpressed. The last time that inmates had worked in the guards' cafeteria at KP, a number of additives of questionable nutritional value had been found in the food, including tacks, needles, rat poison, and excrement.

Clearly, Warden Bourke had not taken to heart recommendations from the report of the CSC's own Task Force on Security: "If staff are truly valued, the organization will work toward facility improvements for staff areas – e.g. fitness and training areas, briefing areas, provision for dining and work areas – to create an environment that will foster pride in one's role and enhanced self-esteem."

Although the flowerbeds inside the north gate at KP are beautifully manicured, the busiest ERT in Canada's prison system is one of the worst equipped. In May 2000 four new members of the ERT took a two-week training course at the staff college. Only one of the officers had the necessary equipment to take the course. Most of the officers bought used hockey equipment with their own money rather than go into dangerous situations without the proper gear. "We are always told that there isn't any money," one of the hockey-rink warriors observed.

3

FENBROOK

Money is no problem if a new inmate is lucky enough to be assigned to Fenbrook Institution in Gravenhurst, Ontario. Officially opened on May 7, 1998, by Solicitor General Andy Scott and CSC commissioner Ole Ingstrup, it was the first federal prison for men to be built in Ontario in twenty-five years.

The showpiece of Canada's federal prison system, Fenbrook is on the flight path into Muskoka Airport, just outside Gravenhurst. The airspace around a federal penitentiary is normally restricted, but given the prison's location, Fenbrook is an exception. As a result, the prison can muster military jets from Trenton Air Force Base should anyone try an airlift escape from Fenbrook. "In 2000, a large plane crashed in the woods beside the prison after its pilot suffered a heart attack," Warden Mike Provan says. "I worry more about a disaster like that, a plane crashing into the prison, than anyone using a helicopter to escape. But if they do, we're ready."

Deep in the heart of cottage country, Fenbrook is Canada's picture-postcard prison and the target of choice for critics who say the national corrections system has become more like a hotel chain

for society's bad boys than a network of penitentiaries for restraining dangerous criminals. Designed with twenty-five-foot ceilings in its main foyers by the architectural firm Moffat Kinoshita at a cost of over $70 million, the twenty-eight-acre prison and its grounds are nestled between an on-site natural wetland reputed to be the breeding ground of an endangered species of salamander and a dense woodlot that provides a private setting for the native healing centre that ministers to the institution's twenty-eight aboriginal inmates.

In sharp contrast to the log buildings at minimum-security Beaver Creek Institution, also in Gravenhurst, there is no doubt that Fenbrook is a medium-security federal penitentiary – at least from the outside. The administration building and main communications control post feature a double sixteen-foot-high fence festooned with rolls of razor wire and two remote-controlled gates. Although there are no weapons inside the institution, except at the main post, there is an armed mobile patrol that circles the prison day and night.

Inside the walls, Fenbrook looks more like a college campus or seminary than a federal prison. The prison itself consists of a series of buildings set around a vast central quadrangle. Footpaths link the grey, low-rise, cement-block and wooden buildings. At one end of this huge quadrangle, there is a pair of towering light standards with crosspieces near the top. Cruciform in shape, they are jokingly referred to here as the "resurrection" lights.

One of the unique features of the prison is the street signs, whose names come straight out of *Leave It to Beaver*: Tamarack Way, Forest Circle, Whitepine Lane. There are also resort-style names for each of the prison's buildings: Aurora, Juniper, Driftwood. The attractive cottage complex where inmates have seventy-two-hour family visits is called Meadow. The three units reserved for conjugal visits are joined together and there are no barriers between the residences. If inmates want to mingle at one another's barbecues, they are free to do so.

"It was my idea to give the streets names and to name the buildings," Warden Provan, known as "the mayor" by inmates, explains. "I wanted to create a sense of neighbourhood. And, believe it or not, it aids in security. In older prisons without names, various buildings have changed their purpose. If the order goes out to get to the hospital, some guards would go to the hospital and some would go to the 'old' hospital. By giving buildings a permanent name, everyone knows where they're going in an emergency."

Fenbrook's four living areas feature several large apartments shared by nine men each. An unarmed prison official occupies a desk in the foyer of each unit like a check-in clerk in a hotel lobby. Every unit has a large kitchen with a fridge, a stove, and cupboard space and a common eating area. Seventy-five per cent of Fenbrook's inmates have private rooms, with the balance double-bunking in university-residence-style units. Although Provan likes the set-up, he recognizes that there are problems. "In a traditional jail, if you do a cell extraction, you are usually dealing with one inmate. Here, you face nine, and we've got a lot of people in here who have done very, very bad things."

Inmates at Fenbrook may buy their own televisions. The living units are wired for cable, which costs inmates $6.40 per month for fifty channels, a cut-rate deal compared with prices on the outside. (Since an inmate retains the rights that every non-offending citizen enjoys, he can watch restricted movies on HBO or Cinemac and can subscribe to over fifteen pornographic magazines.) The bedrooms do not have washrooms, so inmates must leave their cells at night to use the toilet or shower.

If they want to buy a newspaper, they can get that day's *Toronto Sun* from a vending machine inside the prison walls. (The *Toronto Star* and the *National Post* were invited to have their papers on site, but they wanted to charge the prison for the rental of the newspaper boxes. Provan declined. The *Sun* provides its newspaper box free of charge.)

Fifty-three year old Provan, who started his CSC career in 1975 as a parole officer, seizes every opportunity to link healing with

punishment. It was his idea to house the segregation unit alongside the hospital and call the building Cedar. Even though Fenbrook cost about half of what it would take to build a traditional prison, the warden has been a penny-pincher in fitting out his institution, scavenging beds and lockers from a local hospital that was going to trash them. "We got beds that cost $8,000 new for $500, and the lockers for free. All we had to do was go down to the hospital and pick them up."

Other pieces of equipment, like the special "dry" cell, where suspected drug smugglers use a custom toilet to pass their stool, cost the full price: $30,000. This device, also used by customs officials at Canada's major airports, is employed when officials think a person has swallowed drugs for use or sale inside the prison. Once the inmate has had a bowel movement, the hermetically sealed stainless-steel unit provides authorities with continuity of possession of any evidence that might be obtained. (Under the old system, when evidence was manually bagged, defence lawyers often successfully argued that authorities didn't know for sure whether something had been added to the bag before the matter came to court.)

One of the newer methods that inmates at Fenbrook use to hide drugs is to swallow a two-part plastic egg suspended on a piece of dental floss tied around a back tooth. Smugglers literally pull the drug up out of their stomachs when they want to use or sell it. "If the dental floss breaks and the egg comes apart, the inmate has four minutes to get emergency medical attention, or he dies," Warden Provan says.

Although Provan is a believer in CSC's "progressive" correctional practices, he makes no bones when it comes to the grim realities he faces at Fenbrook. One of those is the institution's serious drug problem, which it shares with every other prison in the federal system, including maximum-security prisons like Millhaven and Kingston. "It's a serious, serious problem," the warden says. "Biker gangs actually compete with one another to see who will get a prison's business. I would guess that 40 per cent of our population

uses drugs, maybe more. Eighty per cent of the drugs come in the front door and 20 per cent through the back door. But as long as we're treated like just any other public building under current laws, our powers of search and seizure are limited. We need more room to get the job done."

The CCRA and the Charter hamstring the way officers can conduct search and seizure operations at federal penitentiaries. Even if there is good information that a visitor is going to bring drugs in, current laws stipulate that authorities have to prove it "beyond a reasonable doubt" before the warden will authorize an intrusive search. Front-line staff at Fenbrook estimate that drug use is actually much higher, an astonishing 90 per cent of the inmate population, with many inmates actually becoming addicted to drugs like heroin and cocaine after they are sent to prison.

Warden Provan confirms that bikers and drug dealers force people on the outside to mortgage their homes to pay for their relatives' drugs and safety inside the prison. "We've had cases like that. All you can do is refer the matter to the police. It is a terrible situation." Failing new legislation that would allow his staff to conduct "invasive" searches of prison visitors who are responsible for most of the illegal drugs in Canadian prisons, Warden Provan believes it is better to give inmates clean needles than risk spreading infectious diseases like AIDS or hepatitis C. "I lose sleep worrying about whether an inmate returning to society from prison will infect innocent people with a disease we could have prevented with a needle exchange."

At least one supporter of Fenbrook, Liberal MP Dennis Mills, doesn't agree. "After touring the prison and hearing what the warden had to say about the drug problem, I'm going to be begging the prime minister to get drug dogs into all of our prisons so that CSC's zero-tolerance policy can become a reality. I would never support giving needles to people in prison who have already ruined lives, including their own, with drugs."

Few wardens are eager to approve an intrusive search because being wrong means a lawsuit, and "CSC is afraid of lawyers," says

one officer. Drugs are smuggled in body cavities and even baby diapers. "We never search children – that's just taboo." It would also be rare for a doctor to sign for an X-ray or an intrusive search today. Even the dry cell doesn't count for much because it catches just the mule, not the supplier. If a drug dog jumps on someone, there are legal challenges and civil suits, "and if it happens to be an ethnic group of any kind, then it becomes another factor." As a result of CSC's legal constraints against searching, some drug dealers actually make more money inside than they do on the street.

The segregation units at Fenbrook can hold twenty prisoners in solitary confinement in an ultra-secure environment. Their green steel doors feature the famous Folger-Adams locks ($1,500 apiece) and are operated from a bulletproof glass control post. There is a food slot for meals and a small glass window to allow observation. Each cell has a steel bed with a blue-and-white-striped roll-up mattress, a powder blue blanket, and dark blue sheets. Also provided are towels, toothbrush, and toothpaste.

Although it is technically against regulations, Warden Provan installed stainless-steel toilets in the segregation cells to prevent inmates from doing what they did during his four years as warden of Warkworth Institution, a medium-security facility in Campbellford, Ontario: smash the porcelain toilets and use the razor-sharp shards as weapons during a disturbance. The segregation cells have two buttons on the walls, a grey one to talk to someone if a prisoner becomes depressed and a red one to signify an emergency. The cells are specially designed to prevent suicides. The sprinkler head over the cell door breaks under more than sixteen pounds of pressure. Even the air vents are specially designed, with extended inserts manufactured in a wave pattern that makes it impossible to tie a rope, bedsheet, or shoelace to them. "It's a pretty good segregation," one inmate whispered after sticking his hand out through the food slot to get attention. "I've been in quite a few. But I don't like the joint. There's nothing to do. I'm transferring out to Sask Pen."

Every Sunday, Lighthouse, the prison chapel, is filled to its capacity – fifty worshippers. The cathedral-ceilinged cedar building was

put up by Fenbrook inmates. The industrial shops, featuring towering ceilings, workshops, and huge loading docks, were also built by prisoners. Fenbrook offers private companies free space, heat, and light in the prison if they train inmates to be part of the workforce. Vintage cedar Muskoka boats, some worth as much as $250,000 apiece after refurbishing, are restored here using prison labour.

To prevent inmates from using these outside industrial contacts as escape opportunities, Warden Provan prohibits the use of large trucks to carry out the manufactured goods. Instead, he uses open-caged carts similar to airport baggage vehicles to haul the goods to trucks waiting at the sally port, the entrance to the prison. "Very large trucks have a way of concealing very small inmates when they come into an institution, and I've still got the scars on my back for an incident like that earlier in my career. I actually got the idea for the open carts by watching those little trucks at the airport loading baggage."

Public-private partnerships, so foreign to other prisons in the system, are central to Fenbrook's New Age correctional philosophy. In the shops, local boat builders produce their vessels using skilled prison labour. Fenbrook has its own dental office, staffed by an army major who works weekends on a special contract. It also has its own hospital, including a "negative air chamber" that can be used to isolate people with infectious diseases like tuberculosis, a facility so advanced that it is used by the local hospital in Gravenhurst.

Instead of setting up a prison library internally, Provan made a deal with the Gravenhurst Library, which links the prison to the outside library and teaches inmates how to do basic academic research. The link in Fenbrook also has desktop computers with most of the same features one would expect on the outside except a connection to the Internet, which would make it possible for inmates to download violent pornography.

Fenbrook has the contract to produce O'Roze birdhouses in its industrial shops; the items are then sold worldwide. Provan's next

public-private partnership is a call centre, to be located in the prison, though there will be no direct soliciting of the public by inmates. Provan hasn't specifically said who the prisoners would be calling.

These public-private partnerships provide job training but also present an image problem. Local businesses complain bitterly if a competitor gains an advantage by using prison labour, heat, space, and hydro subsidies to manufacture its products at Fenbrook. Simply put, they don't want the prison to compete with private business in the name of rehabilitation programs. Corcan, the vast prison manufacturing arm that once produced desks and other marketable items, is now a multimillion-dollar white elephant because its products can't be sold commercially in competition with private enterprise. Warden Provan does his best to avoid these built-in conflicts, but he also tries to develop good community relations through a local preference buying policy that is just as controversial within CSC.

When he staffed the prison, the warden drew heavily from the local population and even offered the twelve-week training program in Gravenhurst rather than at CSC's staff college in Kingston. (There were 700 applications for 70 jobs at Fenbrook. The total staff component is 270, including 148 guards, for 391 inmates.) When he bought fridges for his living units, he was technically required to put the request out to tender under the North American Free Trade Agreement. Instead, the warden bought locally. "I'm one of those who prefer to beg forgiveness rather than ask permission," he says.

Fenbrook has become a lightning rod for criticism of CSC, because even the most dangerous prisoners here enjoy a measure of freedom and privileges unheard of in most other medium-security prisons. In addition to having keys to their own apartments and to various doors around the prison, inmates at Fenbrook also get to choose, cook, and eat their own meals on their own schedules. Each prisoner is given $4.50 per day to spend as he sees fit at the

prison grocery store. Initially, this was another outside partnership with the IGA grocery store chain, but after the theft by inmates of $7,000 worth of goods from the store, IGA pulled out of the project. Prison staff now operate the store. There was also a Mr. Sub franchise on the premises, from which inmates in segregation could order their meals. That operation was closed down when its manager was arrested and later convicted of bringing a vial of hash oil into the prison. Mr. Sub has since been replaced with a Great Canadian Bagel franchise.

"The place is a joke to the whole system," says Glenn Copithorn, a victim of crime who was given a tour of the facility in February 2001 after his daughter's killer was sent there. Robert Appleton, who had harassed and stalked his former girlfriend before killing her, had served only four months at Millhaven before being transferred to Fenbrook. There he had kitchen privileges that gave him daily access to the same type of weapon he had used to slaughter his victim. "Where is the deterrent here? The guy who killed my daughter was put in here after just a few months in Millhaven, with access to the same type of knife he used to stab her nineteen times. My God, we treat these murderers better than we treat street people whose only crime is poverty." (After Copithorn and other family victims of crime held press conferences, Appleton was transferred to medium-security Warkworth.)

Although Warden Provan admits that the system hasn't paid enough attention to victims' rights, he doesn't think harder time for prisoners is necessarily better for society. "Look, it would be disastrous to build a whole system of Fenbrooks. Fenbrook won't work for all inmates. But it has a chance to work if offenders really want to change their lives. Can I point to any single success story proving that this place works? No, I can't. Success in this business is often a relative thing; not getting an inmate back for eighteen months instead of six months is sometimes success. But does feeding them from steel plates while shackled to limestone walls make the public any safer? I don't think so."

Despite the charge that he is running a "Club Fed," Provan says that handing "small-meal preparation" back to the prisoners is a good idea at many levels. From a financial point of view, it saves money. Now the government doesn't have to pay food service officers $46,000 a year to prepare the prison's food.

Another bonus is that the issue of "special" meal orders is now dealt with directly by the inmates themselves instead of prison staff: Muslim, native, and vegetarian prisoners buy and prepare their own food. Provan says that preparing their own meals teaches inmates a skill, makes them responsible for cleaning up, and removes one of the most volatile irritants in the prison environment: arguments over food. "If an inmate complains to me, I look him in the eye and say, 'Listen, I don't choose it, I don't cook it, and I don't eat it. That's all up to you.'"

The warden says that the small-meal preparation experiment also teaches inmates to learn to co-operate with the group. If all nine members in a unit band together, they will have a combined weekly food budget of $283.50. "It teaches nine men how to live out of one fridge. They can either have nine bottles of ketchup in their fridge, or one bottle and a lot more other stuff. It all depends on whether they co-operate with each other."

Fenbrook expects all inmates to work, and inmates who shun programs like high-school upgrading and anger management are put on the bus to more traditional institutions. But it also allows them to play. During the five to six hours of daily recreation, inmates have the use of a gymnasium that features a basketball court and floor hockey nets. Warden Provan also insisted that the gym have a stage to perform plays. An inmate painted the vast mural that acts as the backdrop for all the plays, a colourful view through Grecian columns of a bucolic scene straight out of Arcadia. "It limits the kind of plays we can put on, but I think he did a beautiful job," Provan says.

Adjacent to the gymnasium, a weight room contains state-of-the-art equipment, some of it worth $10,000 for a single apparatus.

Authorities concluded that if the equipment were cheap, an inmate who injured himself while training would have grounds for a lawsuit. But there is one important omission: there are no free weights at Fenbrook. Inmates in traditional prisons use free weights to bulk up and to settle their disputes, often fatally. Fenbrook's pressure weights are used to tone muscles rather than distort them. Protein shakes, permitted in some prisons, are prohibited here. Provan also insisted that the weight room have glass walls so that activities could be clearly monitored. In maximum-security institutions, the weight pit is usually a dank, dark, out-of-the way facility that biker-prisoners treat as their office for drug deals and other business.

(Provan approved a separate gym for prison staff as a perquisite of working in a stressful occupation where unpredictable hours are the rule. Local gym owners in Gravenhurst complained that he was taking business from them, but the warden stuck to his guns. Still, he knew where to draw the line. When the OPP asked if its officers could use Fenbrook's gym, Provan tactfully denied permission.)

Fenbrook's Visits and Correspondence (V&C) area is a large, open-air room with floor-to-ceiling windows that let in the maximum amount of light and the natural beauty of Muskoka. The plastic tables have four seats apiece, which are fixed to the tables and cannot be swivelled or moved. This was done to make it difficult for prisoners to engage in sex acts in the common area, a habitual practice in older prisons like KP, often indulged in with children playing at an amorous couple's feet.

The V&C room also has a closed visiting room for private visits of a distressing nature. Female visitors use this facility to deliver the "Dear John" message to their husbands, when they decide to move away and take the kids rather than serve out their husbands' sentences. According to Provan, "It's a pretty common occurrence, and we like to provide added security for what is a tough moment for both people."

Prisoners can have visits five days a week, and most take advantage of the privilege. The V&C room is wired for both video and

audio surveillance, and the prison's telephones are also monitored. Provan is still waiting for Bell Canada to develop the technology to prevent inmates from placing calls to third parties using call forwarding. "We tried to have a voice-over play during each inmate call, making clear that the call is coming from a federal prison, but it was struck down by the courts for Charter reasons," he says.

Since Fenbrook is initially home to all offenders from Nunavut (Ottawa is considering building a federal prison in the Eastern Arctic), it has special Inuit programs, including a sculpting shop where certified artists make their soapstone carvings, some of which sell for $20,000. The prison has a deal with a private native art co-op, which sells the works and defrays the cost of raw materials.

Provan says that the architects, who won an award for their design for Fenbrook, tried to make the inside as much like the outside at the prison, working on the theory that most of the 391 prisoners here will one day be returning to the street; accordingly, you will find job postings around the prison describing the various positions that are available and the skills needed to fill them. The warden thinks this is good practice, making inmates familiar with how to apply for a job once they are released.

Unlike traditional prisons, where every door passage is a checkpoint operated by a guard at his post, Fenbrook issues its inmates plastic keys that permit them to open doors by themselves. These keys are programmed to allow the level of access that administrators decide the inmate deserves. If he tries to use his key to enter a forbidden area, that information is recorded by computer.

Fenbrook's designers purposely built the prison so that when an inmate moves from one location to another, he must go outside. "We just felt that a lot of the pressures that build up in an institutional setting could be reduced by getting people outside on a regular basis. It really works," the warden says.

Inmates are also issued smart cards to operate the prison's vending machines. When an inmate runs his card through the slot, a video display terminal will tell him how much money he has in his institutional bank account. He then selects the item he wants – pop, a

bag of chips, a pack of cigarettes – and his account is automatically debited. Authorities then know exactly what the inmate purchased. This knowledge is useful to the IPSO, or intelligence officer. If, for example, the IPSO finds ten packs of cigarettes in an inmate's cell, and a check of his smart card transaction record shows that he didn't buy them, authorities know who might be muscling other inmates.

Despite the appearance of generous liberties, no one has ever escaped from Fenbrook, and only one inmate has tried since the facility opened in 1998. He was captured after jumping down from the prison roof and approaching the inner fence. "He was pilled up and drunk and just plain stupid. That's why he did it," Provan says. Fenbrook's unblemished security record is not an accident. The prison, which numbers eighty-eight convicted murderers among its inmates, features state-of-the-art security features, most of which are on display in the well-fortified main communications control post (MCCP).

Inside the MCCP, the operator can view every area of the prison (except the actual apartments where the inmates live), using a bank of TV monitors connected to forty cameras around the institution. Once on the location he selects, the officer can use a telephoto lens to zoom in tightly enough to make personal identifications. The officer in the MCCP can also locate a guard in the institution by receiving signals from his portable personal alarm, a cellphone-sized Global Positioning System locator carried by all Fenbrook staff that works in every building in the prison. At maximum-security Kingston Penitentiary, for example, the older personal alarms that staff carry work only in the building where a guard is assigned. If he is taken hostage and moved to another part of the prison, his personal alarm will not register his actual location.

If an inmate touches one of the two fences that surround Fenbrook, he triggers an alarm and his precise location will be indicated on TV monitors. The windows of the inmate living quarters have electronic screens that set off an alarm in the MCCP if they are forced open. There are also perimeter motion detectors that set

off an alarm should a prisoner manage to breach either of the two fences. Once the cameras pick him up, the scene is digitally recorded at the main post for future reference.

The standard-issue weapon here is the nine-millimetre AR-15 rifle. (This weapon became the norm after a riot in British Columbia in the '90s laid bare the problem of not having a uniform weapons policy. When officers were given ammunition to reload during the disturbance, it didn't fit their rifles.) The mobile officer also has a sidearm, a .38, for his personal protection. The armoury, which is located at the main post, has shotguns that hold eight shells and gas. "I know we've got them, but I'm not really up on that stuff," Warden Provan says.

One thing Provan is up on is history. When Fenbrook was under construction, he put a number of items in a time capsule to be opened by his successors in the job a hundred years from now. Included in the message to the future is a pair of handcuffs, keys, and the magnetic cards inmates use to make their way around the institution. The warden also put in a letter to the men and women of the next century in which he tried to explain the mission of the era in which he and his staff lived and worked: "We tried to build a system on justice, humanity, and the rule of law."

Although one prison chaplain literally kissed the ground when he was transferred to Fenbrook, it has not been the instant hit with inmates that one might have thought. One inmate who doesn't much care for what Fenbrook has to offer is Bill Hobson, a strapping six-footer with a long record beginning at age sixteen and a reputation as one of the system's tough guys. His longest prison term was four and a half years for a hundred break-and-enters. Hobson, who was paroled in 2001, has also been convicted of extortion and possession of a deadly weapon. The thirty-eight-year-old from Orillia, Ontario, was sent to Fenbrook after being convicted for driving while under suspension. Although he was offered a twenty-three-month sentence in provincial jail, he asked for a longer sentence that would qualify him for a federal institution.

"I knew if I did a provincial bit, I'd do all twenty-three months. I wouldn't do a provincial bit ever. And I wouldn't do one in the States either. I did a bit in Florida and got whacked in the head on the first day for not walking down the lines they got painted on the floor. And the food! Reheated beans three times a day. We got luxuries in the federal system, they got nothing."

When Hobson arrived from Millhaven's assessment unit, he was expecting a job placement in a welding shop. Not only was there no job, there was no welding shop. Instead, he says, Fenbrook's top brass, including the warden and deputy warden, dragged him into a room fifteen minutes after he arrived and told him that he should never have been sent there in the first place and that if he stepped out of line just once, he would be going back to "the Bay." (Collins Bay is known affectionately by its alumni as "Gladiator School.")

Although Hobson enjoyed the baseball, in-line skating, and food at Fenbrook, he found the people "sneaky" and the staff "fuckin' little punks" compared with the "solid" cons and "professional" staff at more traditional pens. He thought that Fenbrook staff, including the warden, "played favourites" and demanded that inmates "bow down and kiss their asses."

While at Fenbrook, Hobson took an anger management course that actually made him angry. "They didn't have enough paper for me to write down everything that made me mad. Them courses are useless anyway. They don't work because they try to shove them down your throat. The only reason guys do them is for parole. And they wonder why guys flip out when they do all the program shit and then get turned down by the parole board."

Hobson was so unimpressed by what he saw at Fenbrook that he wrote a letter to his friend Chris Leech, a lifer at Joyceville, and warned him to withdraw his application to transfer to the Gravenhurst prison: "There was no consistency in how they ran the place, except for one thing. They consistently tried to provoke me so they could put my ass on the bus to another pen. For a long time, I tried hard not to react, but in the end it was too much.

They want every con to say 'Good morning' to them and I said nothing. One day I said 'Ah fuck,' and that was it. I was on my way to Collins Bay. I was never so glad to get to a place in my life."

After being paroled, Hobson got a job at a lumberyard and found a relationship with "an angel" of a woman. He credits turning his life around to a personal decision, not CSC's programs. "I was in the can and just looked at myself in the mirror for three days and said, 'Why am I putting myself through this?' I was just sick of it. And the next time I got out, I wasn't looking to get even for them putting me in, I knew I had done that to myself. I just decided to put it behind and build a new life."

Another Fenbrook inmate, Howie Hart, has even less use for CSC's premier institution than Bill Hobson. Jailed for break, enter, and theft, Hart describes himself as "a con's con" who knows that his job is to serve his sentence and a guard's job is to keep him inside. But Fenbrook's young, inexperienced staff break the cardinal rule of the joint by getting "personal" in their constant lectures and arguments with inmates. With 75 per cent of the staff under the age of thirty, Hart says it is a major problem.

"I wasn't one of those who attended Sunday school on the outside, so I say things my way. Around here, they make you feel as though you're always swearing in front of your mother. It's like a daycare centre for two-year-olds. My caseworker isn't even twenty and she's a rude, snotty power-tripper who makes everything personal. I say 'fuck' and she says, 'You shouldn't talk like that, blah, blah, blah.' This place is for goody-goodies, rats, and ass-kissers. If you open your mouth, they just back the truck up. Next stop, the Bay."

Hart is particularly critical of the inconsistency with which he says Fenbrook's rules are enforced. "Charlie, on my range – they let him drink all day and just argued with him about it. Core guards like they got at the Bay, KP, and Joyceville would have taken him to seg[regation], that's that. But here they didn't even search his cell and Charlie kept drinking. Half an hour later, they came

back when he was off the range and took the knives off the rack in the kitchen and took his brew. When Charlie came back, he flipped. When they finally took him to seg, they didn't even cuff him like they're supposed to for everybody's protection. After I reoffended the last time, I should have reapplied to go back to William Head," an institution in Victoria, British Columbia.

The reason Hart came to Fenbrook was to be closer to his three children, aged seven, four, and three. But although he has taken programs, Hart claims that even that worked against him. As a result of taking courses to boost cognitive skills and help him with his substance abuse problem, he says that he was fired from a prime job, in the shop that makes O'Roze birdhouses, for missing too many workdays. He is also angry that management slipped a pedophile into his range and never told anyone what the man had done. "I got kids coming to the socials here and they fuckin' well should have told me. I guess it's just as well for that guy's sake."

If Hart, who had served two years at Fenbrook as of May 2001 and had ten months to go before release, is cynical about CSC's real goals, he has more reason than most for his doubts. Before leaving William Head, he realized that he was in no shape for the street and asked authorities to keep him beyond his statutory release date: "I had been doing heavy drugs inside and was wired, man. I knew I wasn't ready to get out and told them I worried about reoffending. I wanted programs for a month to clean up. What did they do? Kicked me out on my stat release date, get the fuck out. Here at Fenbrook, I've seen them return a guy to the street straight from segregation, and he wasn't in there for his own protection. Whatever it is, that isn't rehabilitation."

To get even with Fenbrook's "Sunday school" regime, Hart refused to sign behaviour contracts and "pissed dirty" (meaning traces of drugs showed up in his urine) six months in a row to express his views about "getting jacked up every day by the coppers." Authorities here have threatened to transfer him, but so far he has not made the trip to Collins Bay or Joyceville. What is

his bottom line for the time he has spent in one of the system's showcase institutions?

"I feel more bitter getting out this time than I did the last time. The way it works, you're mad at them for putting you in here, and when you get out, now it's your turn to get even. You know, it's kind of a reoffend-and-catch-me-if-you-can type of thing. It is wrong for them to generate this hate in me for them."

4

NATIVE JUSTICE

The numbers hint at the enormity of the social failure. Aboriginal people account for just 2 per cent of Canada's population but 15 per cent of the federal offender population. The national incarceration rate for the general population is 118 per 100,000; the native ratio is 735 per 100,000. In the prairie provinces native incarceration numbers are even higher, with aboriginal offenders accounting for over 40 per cent of the inmate population. At Saskatchewan Penitentiary in Prince Albert, 90 per cent of the inmates are aboriginal, mainly Cree. An astonishing 95 per cent of male aboriginal offenders have been adopted or otherwise removed from their birth homes.

Most aboriginal inmates are young males from urban areas who are addicted to chemical substances. They have experienced violence and abuse in their own lives and passed it on generously. Over 80 per cent of federal aboriginal offenders are sentenced for violent offences, compared with 68.2 per cent of the general prison population. Often these offenders have been raised in foster homes or group homes, disconnected from their culture. According to Health Canada, aboriginal children are twenty-five times more likely to suffer fetal alcohol syndrome than the world average. Up to 90 per

cent of female aboriginal inmates have suffered physical or sexual abuse, a statistic that mirrors other social disasters, including the fact that up to 90 per cent of child and teen prostitutes in Canada are aboriginal.

Bridging the Cultural Divide, a report by the Royal Commission on Aboriginal Peoples, concluded that the Canadian criminal justice system had failed the aboriginal peoples of Canada, mainly because of the fundamentally different world view that aboriginals hold about justice and how it is achieved. Although aboriginal elders began entering Canadian penitentiaries to conduct traditional ceremonies in 1972, the same year corporal punishment was abolished in prisons, until recently native offenders were treated like any other offenders in the CSC system. Donald Marshall, the Mi'kmaq wrongfully imprisoned for eleven years for a murder he did not commit, was held in maximum security at Dorchester Penitentiary in New Brunswick with other lifers subject to the same rules. Even when early aboriginal programming was offered, it was often conducted by elders of a completely different culture. Elder-assisted parole hearings started in the CSC's Prairie Region in 1992.

Traditional teachings stress respect, honesty, and caring, but research into the cultural reality of Canada's native population has shown very high rates of early drug and alcohol abuse, appalling and often brutal family backgrounds, and crippling poverty. CSC believes this history has been compounded by the prison environment. The social environment of a prison is an alien culture for almost anyone, but for aboriginals, often far from home, the food, the language, and even the climate may be far different from anything they have ever experienced. On the other hand, some native inmates, like Donald Marshall, have observed that conditions on many reserves are not all that different from life in prison.

On August 8, 1997, the Samson Cree Nation held a special ceremony to honour Commissioner Ole Ingstrup for his work in establishing Canada's first aboriginal minimum-security institution. Ingstrup was given an honorary title: Chief Spotted Eagle.

He believed that natives require a more spiritual treatment program than other inmates receive. Programs were created specifically for natives in jail because programs designed for whites were not working.

CSC management believes that aboriginal offenders respond better to programs developed and delivered by the aboriginal community, an apparently enlightened view that could equally be viewed as passing the buck. It has developed holistic "culturally appropriate" substance abuse programs, native liaison services, and spiritual programs, as well as special elders programs and post-release services. In fact, many aboriginals find their native cultural roots for the first time while they are in prison.

A glaring problem with the special-treatment approach is that there is no one aboriginal culture. Cree, Sioux, and Dene, for example, all have their own distinctive traditions. What if an inmate does not belong to the tribe offering a particular program? There appears to be a blending of different traditions that has, in effect, corrupted authentic tribal traditions rather than incorporated them into correctional programs.

A number of CSC facilities are operated specifically for aboriginal inmates in full partnership with aboriginal communities. Most staff are aboriginal, and the facilities operate "on the basis of Aboriginal ethics, values and principles," a philosophy that is built into the CCRA and the mission statement. According to Patricia Monture-Angus, a Mohawk originally from the Six Nations Reserve near Brantford, Ontario, and a lawyer who teaches native studies in Saskatchewan, natives use violence as a survival mechanism in prison. They see a guard's uniform as an "offensive symbol" of colonial oppression and react to the history of that white oppression — an observation that could be true, but applies equally to blacks, South Asians, or other minority groups with a history of oppression.

At the International Indigenous Symposium on Corrections held in March 1999 in Vancouver, Ingstrup outlined some of the things CSC had accomplished that gave him the most pride.

Okimaw Ohci, the aboriginal women's healing lodge in Maple Creek, Saskatchewan, topped his list as "a successful integration of aboriginal approaches and modern corrections."

The Okimaw Ohci Healing Lodge was the first federal prison run by native people. Small and community-based, it is a minimum- to medium-security institution for women, set in the Nekaneet First Nation reserve in Cypress Hills. Known by the Cree as "the place where the thunders are made," the 160-acre setting is breathtaking. Opened in the fall of 1995, the lodge has no fences or barbed wire, and inmates can roam the poplar forest. There is a library, a ceramics studio, and a whirlpool tub to relieve stress. The twelve cottages have alarms that go off if a door is opened at night. It costs over $100,000 per year for each of the twenty-five to thirty "residents." The lodge also has facilities for ten children up to age four, who attend a daycare centre while their mothers participate in programs.

The idea behind the lodge is to promote responsibility, self-sufficiency, and a supportive community based on "positive and ongoing relationships between staff and offenders." About 23 per cent of federally sentenced women are aboriginal. Sixty per cent of the staff at Okimaw Ohci are of aboriginal descent, and there is a strong emphasis on aboriginal culture and spirituality. The sweat lodge and prayer are a major part of the healing process.

Mornings begin with the fragrance of sage, sweetgrass, and cedar as an elder prays. The belief is that the women are spiritually unwell and that the community must work together on their behalf to heal them. The National Parole Board has elder-assisted hearings to make sure band members are sensitive to native language and culture. There is no warden, nor guards, rather a "mother" and "sisters." Staff are ordinary people from the community, not recruited from CSC. Under Section 81 of the CCRA, non-native offenders can also be sent to the reserve-run centres. One of them was Jo-Anne Mayhew, a middle-class white woman given a life sentence in Nova Scotia in the mid-1980s for the murder of her husband. At P4W, the old Prison for Women in Kingston, Mayhew had been an advocate for aboriginal women.

Released on parole in 1994, she ended up back in the federal system at Okimaw Ohci. She was granted a royal prerogative of mercy in 1998 but died six months later of Lou Gehrig's disease.

On October 5, 2001, two women escaped from Okimaw Ohci after hitting a staff member over the head with a makeshift club as she did her routine check of their residence. Renée Ascoby and Myra Bird were the first escapees in the custom facility's six years of operation. Using the "sister" as a hostage, they forced their way into the main administration centre. Holding a knife to the woman's throat, they forced a staff member to open the cash box, then locked the staff in a small room, after failing to obtain vehicle keys from another employee, who had managed to lock herself into an office and sound the alarm. The two offenders then fled on foot into the woods surrounding the lodge. They were recaptured the following day by the RCMP, hiding in a house on the Nekaneet reserve. CSC is investigating the incident.

Commissioner Ingstrup was also very proud of Pê Sâkâstêw, which means "new beginning where the sun comes over the horizon." Designed for forty inmates and twenty parolees of native descent, it was the first prison of its kind for native men in Canada. Just outside Hobbema, Alberta, a First Nation community, the $9-million institution with a $2.2-million annual operating budget aims at the successful reintegration of male native offenders through holistic, culturally based programs. Similar lodges are being developed in British Columbia, Saskatchewan, and Manitoba. CSC selected the world-famous native Canadian architect Douglas Cardinal to design the Ochichakkosipi Healing Lodge on the Ojibwa reserve in Crane River, Manitoba. The first phase opened in February 2000, although with only nineteen beds in temporary buildings. Built of locally harvested logs, the completed institution will look like an eagle from certain angles. Constructed on a peninsula, the centre will blend into the surrounding natural environment.

In his speech at the indigenous symposium, Ingstrup vowed, "We do not intend to graft a twig of aboriginal restorative justice

onto the tree trunk of traditional European or Western corrections. Instead, we intend to support the growth of a better way from the seed of aboriginal traditions." Under the legislation governing CSC, the solicitor general can make agreements directly with aboriginal organizations for the delivery of correctional services. CSC is increasing the aboriginal component of its staff, including wardens, to give the service a better understanding of indigenous cultures. When he moved to Canada in 1983, Ingstrup said, he became very interested in what was happening in the aboriginal community, particularly in corrections. "The times I worked with aboriginal people are some of the most precious in my career." His one objective was to make sure that as few people as possible returned to an institution after they were released. In fact, one of the corporate objectives of CSC is to "significantly increase the number of aboriginal offenders safely and successfully reintegrated."

Ingstrup felt that although CSC is at the tail end of the criminal justice system, it could address the overrepresentation of aboriginals in our federal institutions by making sure they are not reincarcerated because of technical violations of parole (drinking, drug use, or associating with known criminals) when they have not actually committed new offences. In effect, this amounted to ignoring offences that would cost other parolees their freedom. Despite all the special programs, aboriginal parole officers, and special healers, as well as helpers in the community, the large number of repeat native offenders is increasing by 16 or 17 per cent per year.

In September 1996, a new provision, Section 718.2, was added to the Criminal Code. It required judges to consider "all available sanctions other than imprisonment that are reasonable in the circumstances" for offenders. Judges were to pay "particular attention to the circumstances of aboriginal offenders" when sentencing. This was widely interpreted as an attempt to compensate for the overrepresentation of aboriginals in the penal system. The Supreme Court of Canada upheld this provision in 1999 and again in 2000, which angered some victims of crime in the very community it was designed to appease.

Lawyers for Jamie Gladue, a young woman found guilty of manslaughter in the stabbing death of her husband, Reuben Beaver, argued before the Supreme Court that her original trial judge should have taken her native heritage into account when determining her three-year sentence. Gladue had stabbed her husband during a drunken party to celebrate her nineteenth birthday, because she suspected him of sleeping with her sister. As Beaver bled to death, Gladue is reported to have boasted, "I got you, you bastard." (The British Columbia Supreme Court had rejected her argument because she did not live on a reserve. However, the British Columbia Court of Appeal ruled that it didn't matter if the offender lived on or off the reserve, but it also ruled that her heritage was irrelevant.) *Gladue* was considered the first test case of the new law. In April 1999 the Supreme Court of Canada ruled that the trial judge had not given due attention to the "Indianness" of Jamie Gladue. She served six months for manslaughter before being released.

In the *Gladue* case, the Supreme Court clarified Section 718.2, suggesting that judges should sentence aboriginals in a different way. Restorative justice programs would bring offenders and community leaders together to address the crime. The Supreme Court called on judges to make a special effort to deal with the problem of the high number of aboriginals in prison by considering alternatives to jail whenever possible. While everyone applauded the intent, few bothered to note that the landmark case would in effect give Canada a racially based, two-tiered justice system in which different races would receive different penalties for the same crime. It was one of the most important decisions for Canada's penal system since the 1980 *Solosky* case. The Correctional Service of Canada claimed that in *Solosky*, the Supreme Court had affirmed for the first time that imprisoned persons retained all their rights other than those they were expressly or implicitly deprived of by law.

The decision flowed from a case in which Billy Solosky, a federal inmate at Millhaven, asked the Supreme Court to prohibit prison officials from searching his possessions, including letters

from his lawyer. Solosky had already had his case dismissed by the Federal Court. In fact, the Supreme Court too dismissed Solosky's appeal, ruling that "even giving full recognition to the right of an inmate to correspond freely with his legal adviser, and the need of minimum derogation therefrom, the scale must ultimately come down in favour of the public interest." As a result, Mr. Justice Brian Dickson ruled that letters between inmates and their lawyers could be inspected for contraband by CSC officials and read to determine if, in fact, the letters dealt with the seeking or giving of legal advice. Dickson also declared, "I do not think it is open to the courts to question the judgment of the institutional head as to what may, or may not, be necessary in order to maintain security within a penitentiary."

But CSC seized not on Dickson's actual ruling but on a single paragraph of judicial ruminations he had noted along the road to finding that Solosky, as a convicted offender, did not in fact have all the rights of an average citizen when it came to the absolute privilege that exists between solicitor and client. In giving his reasons for dismissing Solosky's appeal from the Federal Court, Dickson mused, "One may depart from the current concept of privilege and approach the case on the broader basis that 1) the right to communicate in confidence with one's legal adviser is a fundamental civil and legal right, founded upon the unique relationship of solicitor and client, and 2) a person confined to prison retains all of his civil rights, other than those expressly or impliedly taken from him by law. . . ."

Although Dickson, with the concurrence of Mr. Justice Willard Estey, went on to dismiss those propositions in his ruling, senior CSC management used the *Solosky* decision to extend rights to prisoners that the court had expressly limited. Eighteen years later, in its internal magazine, *Let's Talk*, CSC was still misstating what the Supreme Court had actually ruled. "In *R. v. Solosky*, the Supreme Court further illustrated its willingness to interfere with correctional decisions when it stated that persons confined to prison retain all of their civil rights, except those necessarily limited by

the nature of incarceration or those expressly [or] implicitly taken away by law." It was a strange interpretation of *Solosky*, but it fit perfectly with CSC's consistent policy of extending prisoners' rights under the guise of following the law.

But not everyone agreed with the courts' most recent attempts to assuage white guilt over treatment of First Nations people. An editorial in the *National Post* opined, "Criminals should not be sentenced on the basis of statistics or skin colour. Nor is the criminal justice system biased against natives. Natives may suffer a higher rate of incarceration, but they also commit disproportionately more crime than all other ethnic groups. Dealing natives what are effectively 'get-out-of-jail' cards merely lowers the cost of going to prison for native criminals while encouraging anti-native irritation among other Canadians."

Section 81 (1) of the CCRA has guided many correctional services programs for native offenders in recent years. It reads: "The Minister, or a person authorized by the Minister, may enter into an agreement with an aboriginal community for the provision of correctional services to aboriginal offenders and for payment by the Minister, or by a person authorized by the Minister, in respect of the provision of those services. . . . The Commissioner may transfer an offender to the care and custody of an aboriginal community, with the consent of the offender and of the aboriginal community."

This section of the CCRA allows the reserves to sign individual custody release plans and to be paid by the federal government to place federal inmates under house arrest on the reserve or under twenty-four-hour monitoring. Even first-degree murderers can apply to serve their sentences on a reserve, since there are no restrictions in the agreement. CSC simply does a risk assessment to determine if an offender is eligible. The transfer can take place even though an offender has been sentenced to a specific time in prison without parole. Some reserves are in cities, and police officials worry about bringing potentially dangerous offenders into

urban centres. Courses and counselling available in prison may also not be available on the reserves.

The first Section 81 agreement was signed in April 1999 between CSC and the Alexis First Nation in Alberta, allowing for the transfer of aboriginal offenders to the First Nations community. Since the creation of the new territory of Nunavut on April 1, 1999, there has been an exchange-of-services agreement for the custody and community supervision of federal offenders in the new territory or territorial offenders in federal facilities. There are about seventy offenders from Nunavut serving federal sentences in the south, as well as thirty-six under community supervision. In July 2000 a memorandum of understanding was signed between CSC and the Nunavut Department of Justice to enhance delivery of correctional services in the territory. The aim was to repatriate offenders so they could serve sentences in their home communities.

In September 1999, Solicitor General Lawrence MacAulay announced the legal transfer of correctional services to aboriginal communities throughout Alberta. The agreement between CSC and Native Counselling Services of Alberta (NCSA) under Section 81 allowed the aboriginal communities to take responsibility for aboriginal offenders, including full custody. Those placed in the Stan Daniels Healing Centre in Edmonton under various forms of conditional release would be supervised by NCSA staff. (Normally the National Parole Board decides on the conditional release of federal offenders, and CSC supervises them.) Programs and services would be developed based on a combination of proven correctional methods and traditional aboriginal healing processes. The Alberta signing was followed by a national conference entitled Aboriginal Corrections in Transition, "as we are at the point in time of truly moving corrections for aboriginal offenders into aboriginal communities," according to the CSC press release.

In September 2000, MacAulay announced that CSC had been granted reserve land on the Beardy's and Okemasis Reserve, near Duck Lake, about ninety kilometres north of Saskatoon. CSC would construct and operate a healing lodge for forty aboriginal

men serving federal minimum-security sentences. Responsibility for the care, custody, and release of offenders would be transferred to the reserve community.

Lance Regan Shipman was stabbed to death by his common-law wife, Susanne Joan Riley, in 1994. Riley pleaded guilty to manslaughter in 1996. The Crown noted that her criminal record included a previous stabbing, and asked for a five-year sentence. But Mr. Justice Gordon Thompson of the Ontario Court General Division gave Riley a suspended sentence that included healing circles with the residents of the Walpole Reserve near Sarnia, Ontario. The killer was under supervision in the community for three years but did no jail time after the sentence. A native healing circle kept her out of prison. The slain man's native relatives were furious and hinted that they would seek their own justice.

Deanna Emard, a Metis woman, killed her husband with a butcher knife in January 1997. During sentencing in January 1999, her lawyer asked for a suspended sentence or a conditional sentence to be served in the community under Section 718.2 of the Criminal Code. However, the victim's sister, who was part Haida, said, "Alcohol is not an excuse and neither is being a native. There should be justice for everyone – not one system for Indian and Metis people and one for white people." The Crown had asked for a two-to-three-year sentence. Emard received a conditional sentence of two years less a day, meaning she would not go to jail as long as she abided by the rules imposed by the judge.

Fourteen-year-old Steven Herman, a volunteer with Teenagers Against Drunk Driving, was killed by a drunk driver while walking home from a bowling alley in Thompson, Manitoba. Trevor McKenzie, the eighteen-year-old driver, was convicted of impaired driving causing death in January 2000. Although the crime carries a sentence of up to fourteen years, McKenzie was given a twenty-month conditional sentence to be served at home. His lawyer had referred to the section of the Criminal Code urging judges to consider alternatives to prison for aboriginal offenders. The victim's

father felt there should have been some jail time and said, "It doesn't make sense. Why are there two standards? A treaty card is like a get-out-of-jail card."

Things had clearly gone too far. In February 2000, in the case of James Warren Wells, the Supreme Court of Canada unanimously agreed that Section 718.2 does not give aboriginal offenders an automatic pass through the prison system. It was a welcome clarification. Wells was seeking a conditional sentence, based on his aboriginal background. He had sexually assaulted an unconscious eighteen-year-old girl after an evening of drinking. He showed no remorse, had a serious alcohol problem, and had two prior convictions for assault. Wells had been given twenty months in jail rather than a conditional sentence. In upholding the lower court's ruling, the Supreme Court concluded, "It will generally be the case . . . that particularly violent and serious offences will result in imprisonment for aboriginal offenders as often as for non-aboriginal offenders." The court decision did not throw much light on why a male rapist got twenty months but a female murderer got a conditional sentence of two years less a day.

Sometimes a judge chooses to reject aboriginal status as a reason for limiting punishment. In August 2000, Mr. Justice Ralph Hutchinson of the British Columbia Supreme Court gave Katherine Sam a ten-year sentence for manslaughter in the fatal abuse of her two-year-old stepdaughter, Mary Anne Louie. The child had suffered one hundred bruises, human bite marks, and three fractured ribs before she died in 1995 after months of abuse, mainly by Sam. Although Sam, a member of the Tsartlip band at Brentwood Bay, British Columbia, drank excessively and was abused by her own mother, the judge found "no special circumstances in this case that require the sentence to be moderated by reason of her aboriginal status." David Louie, the girl's father, was given a six-year sentence for manslaughter. In his case, the judge found that Louie's aboriginal background as a member of the Chemainus First Nation, which included alcoholic parents and a

criminal record for sexual assault, was relevant. Louis did nothing while Sam actively abused his daughter for six months.

In December 2000, James Albert, the former grand chief of the Council of Yukon First Nations, was given a two-year conditional sentence for the rape of a five-year-old boy in 1967. Then twenty-four, he was babysitting the child when the crime occurred. Albert pleaded guilty to the rape.

In May 2001, the Manitoba Court of Appeal rejected the argument of systemic discrimination by three members of the aboriginal gang known as the Manitoba Warriors. Their lawyers had argued that they too should receive special consideration in sentencing because of their native status.

A study published in the *Saskatchewan Law Review* in March 2001 by two prominent criminologists, Dr. Philip Stenning of the University of Toronto and Dr. Julian Roberts of the University of Ottawa, argues that special sentencing provisions for natives were based in part on the faulty assumption that natives received stiffer sentences than non-aboriginal offenders charged with comparable offences. In fact, studies in British Columbia and Ontario have shown that aboriginal offenders generally receive shorter sentences, even when their offences are serious and they have previous criminal histories. Stenning says, "There are other factors that have led to aboriginal incarceration, and to attempt to respond to aboriginal over-incarceration by tinkering with sentencing principles is missing the main problem."

Stenning and Roberts argue that other groups such as black immigrants face similar circumstances, including high unemployment, substance abuse, and lack of education. To single out aboriginals is to ignore the problems of these other groups, an inherently racist act in itself. Because the victims of native offenders are often native themselves, lenient sentences also deny the victims fair justice. Stenning goes even further and says there is a problem with the policy-formulating process in Parliament and with the Supreme Court's interpretation of the statute. He

told the *National Post* that government-funded research is ignored during the process: "It reflects the fact that research is not considered important in policy making unless it happens to support the position the government wants to put forward. To some extent, we are in an era of political correctness, when it is political factors that determine legislation and research plays no significant role."

5

PRISONS IN PINK

Work gangs from Kingston Penitentiary began building the Kingston Prison for Women, known as P4W, in 1925, quarrying the stone from the present location of Queen's University's football stadium. A separate institution from KP, P4W opened in 1934 with a price tag of $374,000. The first calls for its closure came just four years after it opened its doors. The end finally came as a result of *Creating Choices*, a 1990 report by the Task Force on Federally Sentenced Women, which recommended closing the antiquated facility. In its place, the report's authors advised Ottawa to build four regional institutions and a healing lodge for aboriginal offenders for Canada's female federal offenders. Half of women sentenced to federal terms were then serving their time in provincial institutions under exchange-of-services agreements between the two levels of government.

Although it fluctuates, the number of women who commit crimes that call for a federal sentence is rising overall. CSC's 2001 performance report predicts that the number of female offenders will increase by 31 per cent over the next eight years. As of April 2001, 880 female inmates were under federal sentence in Canada, 372 of them incarcerated in federal institutions. At one point in

2000, there were more than 500 women in federal custody, compared with just 210 in 1990. When P4W was in full operation, the number of inmates ranged from 100 to 140. By 2000, the average cost per female offender had risen to $115,465 per year, although it levelled off to $110,473 in 2001. About 28 per cent of women are serving sentences for murder; 52 per cent are in for crimes involving violence, assault, or attempted murder; 12 per cent have been sentenced for fraud and theft; and 8 per cent are doing time for drug convictions, the fastest-growing crime category.

Creating Choices also provided the philosophical basis for the Correctional Service of Canada's new approach to female offenders serving federal time. Members of the task force, established in March 1989 by Commissioner Ole Ingstrup, came from the Canadian Association of Elizabeth Fry Societies, the Aboriginal Woman's Caucus, CSC, and other organizations sympathetic to women offenders. The task force consulted individuals and organizations across Canada, including female offenders themselves, paying particular attention to the special needs of aboriginal women. The new model treated female offenders very much as social victims, and programs that were introduced in the wake of *Creating Choices* were entrenched in Section 77 of the CCRA in 1992.

The guiding statement of the task force was: "The Correctional Service of Canada, with the support of communities, has the responsibility to create the environment that empowers federally sentenced women to make meaningful and responsible choices in order that they may live with dignity and respect." Meaningful and responsible choices were clearly defined: "Women need options to make responsible choices. Dependence on alcohol, drugs, men and government financial assistance has denied women the opportunity and ability to make choices." While the changes recommended by the task force percolated through the system, serious problems continued at P4W. Staff had done their best, but they were pushed to the limit by a difficult offender population in an aging building with a crumbling infrastructure.

George Scott, a psychiatrist hired by CSC in 1960 to plan and organize psychiatric systems in Ontario penitentiaries, described the special challenges of the female offender in his book *The Psychodynamics of the Prisoner*, published in 1979: "The woman offender, by nature, seems to be a creature of hate, rebellion, conflict and selfishness. . . . Her feelings of hate are usually so overpowering that she will try any method to relieve her chronic anger. . . . Because her compounded emotions react violently to frustration, she will resort to self-mutilation, self-destruction, and violence, if her needs are not met by the medical department." Scott saw most inmates as criminally "ill" victims of society.

On February 22, 1991, inmate Marie Ledouxe discharged herself from the Regional Treatment Centre at KP and returned to P4W. (Under the Mental Health Act, people cannot be hospitalized against their will unless they are deemed to be a danger to others or themselves, a finding with a very high burden of proof.) Ledouxe had been sent to the RTC after an attempted suicide. Although she was monitored around the clock with a television camera, Ledouxe, a Cree from Alberta, received no counselling from either a psychiatrist or a native spiritual leader. Despite suffering from drug and alcohol problems, depression, and stress, she told the psychologist who tried to convince her to stay at the RTC that she wanted to leave. Four days later, Ledouxe hanged herself in a private family visiting unit at P4W during a visit with her father.

Four aboriginal women had killed themselves at the prison since 1989. A fifth had survived an attempt in the fall of 1990 but remained in hospital with serious brain damage. In 1988 Marlene Moore, a former candidate for dangerous-offender status, was found hanging from the frame of her bed in the prison hospital. It was never determined if her death was murder or suicide.

In an attempt to deal with rising violence, a separate unit designed to isolate aggressive, predatory, or manipulative inmates was opened on B Range at P4W in early July 1991. Even though these inmates still had jobs, visits, yard time, and their normal programs, Don Bailey, a lawyer who worked in the women's prison,

said this unit violated their rights, and he threatened that inmates might launch a court challenge against CSC. Bailey also claimed that the unit violated the spirit of *Creating Choices*. He said that the twenty-two women assigned to the unit were "as much the victims as the victimizers." The Canadian Association of Elizabeth Fry Societies supported Bailey's views, which soon became the central theme of CSC policy toward federal female offenders. Bonnie Diamond, head of the association, believed that the aggressive women were the ones who actually needed the most rehabilitation and that new types of programs should be delivered in as pleasant an environment as possible.

But the creation of the special unit for violent women was already having beneficial effects at P4W. The rest of the inmates were now living in relative peace, moving around the institution without fear of being bullied or assaulted by the "heavies." The administration hoped that the new range would also curb the use of drugs and weapons, both of which were very serious problems in the institution. In the weeks before B Range opened, there were six assaults, five attempted suicides, an escape attempt, and twenty slashings at P4W. Staff blamed the assaults on the heroin, cocaine, and Quaaludes that had been smuggled into the prison with apparent ease.

In 1990 the federal government announced that it would close P4W by September 1994. Accepting the recommendations of the task force, it planned to build the five new smaller prisons across the country so that offenders would be closer to their homes and families. The estimated cost of the new institutions was $54 million. But P4W would not disappear into Canadian penal history gently.

At 5:30 on the afternoon of Friday, April 22, 1994, six inmates who were being taken from B Range to the prison hospital for medication attacked four female guards. Tensions had been high for a month because the flow of drugs to the prison had been interrupted by a security crackdown, and the women had switched to homemade brew, which was later found in their cellblock.

Kathy Vance, the officer in charge of B Range, held a bachelor's degree in women's studies and criminology. She had joined CSC

specifically to work at P4W. Inmate Brenda Morrison struck Vance several times. Vance was then stabbed with what she believed was an HIV-infected syringe. She was punched and kicked by another inmate, Ellen Young, who told her she was going to "kill you." Young then asked her fellow inmate Joey Twins for a pair of scissors, "so I can stick her." Another guard, Linda Boston, knocked the scissors away as she tried to rescue Vance.

Brenda Morrison was now kicking Vance, in a martial arts move. Susanne Fabio, a guard who was also trying to help Vance, was grabbed by Twins and told she was going to be her hostage out to the front door. Twins, who was serving a life sentence for second-degree murder and had a violent and troubled past, was an influential inmate and was considered the boss on her range. At one point inmate Young seized Officer Fabio and told the two inmates who were hitting her to "grab the telephone and we'll string up the bitch right here." Fabio was dragged by her hair as the inmates held her arms.

Meanwhile the hospital nurse had called for help and Officer Gerry Gillis used Mace to free Fabio. He was kicked in the knee by Joey Twins. More guards arrived, and the women were finally subdued and locked in segregation.

Five guards had been assaulted. Linda Boston, who feared for her life, was bruised and bitten on the hand; another officer had torn knee cartilage and blood clots. One guard would have long-lasting injuries. The six inmates would later plead guilty to a variety of charges and receive sentences ranging from sixty days to twenty months.

By Sunday, the situation inside P4W had escalated dangerously. Both inmates and guards were angry and afraid. Three inmates already in segregation were slashing themselves, and four attempted suicide. The noise of the women yelling obscenities was constant. They threatened to kill staff, Karla Homolka, and other protective-custody inmates, whose cells were inside the segregation unit. Joey Twins yelled out that Homolka should hang herself.

The women began to scream, "Riot, riot, riot!" The guards worried the sound would spread through the air ducts to other parts of the prison and incite the inmates. Late on Tuesday night, Warden Mary Cassidy called in the Emergency Response Team from Kingston Pen. In the end, a four-day uprising at P4W, in which prisoners attacked guards, threw urine at them, and set numerous fires, led to the strip-searching of eight inmates by a male ERT looking for drugs and weapons. (A razor blade attached to the handle of a toothbrush was a favourite weapon.)

P4W's female riot squad had been disbanded in 1992, and neither male nor female officers at the prison had been trained to handle violent women. CSC bureaucrats believed that women were more likely to harm themselves or use verbal abuse against regular guards. Cost-cutting was another factor. ERT members are volunteers chosen from regular prison officers and specially trained to handle violent situations like hostage takings, cell extractions, and riots. Their ten-week training course is repeated annually. Helmets keep the identity of ERT members secret, for fear of reprisals against the officers and their families. If they are on normal duty when called, another officer has to take their place. Many incidents happen at night or on weekends, so there is also the question of overtime pay.

Female guards and the riot squad strip-searched the eight inmates in segregation, recording their actions on videotape according to CSC policy. Most of the women removed their own clothes as ordered, before the squad entered their cells. (The CCRA defines a strip search as "a visual inspection of a naked body.") But Brenda Morrison refused and was forced to the floor screaming, then shackled. A female guard named Tracy Bertrim started cutting off Morrison's pants with a special hooked knife, and two ERT members began pulling off her T-shirt, finally cutting it off with the same knife. Morrison later testified that she considered the strip search a criminal sexual assault, and that she suffered flashbacks as a result of the search. Two weapons were found in the cells.

It was impossible not to be horrified by the videotape of the strip search of Morrison, which CSC fought in court to suppress. National CSC headquarters was so concerned about the explosive nature of the incident that "someone," who was never identified, deleted the reference to male ERT members seeing the women naked from a draft of its internal investigation report. The warning "Questions will undoubtedly be raised about having male staff members restrain nude females" disappeared from the 1994 report, as did the mention that the search was videotaped. There were striking differences between the whitewashed CSC report, used to support denials that anything went wrong at P4W, and the one done by the independent Office of the Correctional Investigator in 1995.

As part of damage control, CSC argued that the tape should be kept confidential, "out of respect for the privacy of inmates." The leaked video was shown in February on CBC-TV's *the fifth estate*. The inmates had agreed to the broadcast. Members of the ERT were immediately vilified as inhuman. The fact that CSC had no all-female ERT was seldom mentioned by the press. Rather than identifying a blatant policy failure, the media adopted a Hollywood storyline in which all inmates were viewed as victims, all guards as brutes. The public outcry over the videotape of the strip search shook political knees all the way to Ottawa, which came up with its own emergency response to the incident at P4W.

On April 10, 1995, Madam Justice Louise Arbour of the Court of Appeal of Ontario was appointed to head the Commission of Inquiry into Certain Events at the Prison for Women in Kingston. The mandate of the commission was to investigate and report on the incidents at P4W beginning April 22, 1994, and to make recommendations as to the policies and practices of CSC in relation to the incidents. The commission had a budget of $3.3 million, with an additional $275,000 set aside to fund groups and individuals granted legal standing.

During forty-three days of judicial hearings at Westlake Hall in Kingston, twenty-one witnesses were heard. The first session

convened on June 28, 1995, and final oral submissions were heard January 15 and 16, 1996. Both inmates and CSC staff wept on the stand as they recounted what they had been through. Tom Dafoe, the coordinator of the ERT, testified that all strip searches are humiliating: "It's humiliating for one human being to have to do that to another human being." He said the squad hated being called to P4W because they found it hard to use force against women. He said the men tried to treat the women more gently than they would a male inmate. Dafoe testified this was the first time the team was asked to be present during a strip search of women.

Arbour also toured other women's correctional facilities across Canada. There were rumours that she was so touched by the plight of the women that she lent her credit card to staff to purchase Christmas gifts for the child of an inmate who testified at the inquiry. But a spokesperson for Arbour denied the allegation, saying it was inquiry staff who bought the girl clothes, a doll, and a Nintendo game after taking care of her during the proceedings.

In the second phase of the inquiry, Arbour held nine days of round-table policy discussions. The commission met with CSC staff, inmates Joey Twins and Brenda Morrison, and correctional experts from across Canada and abroad. Arbour presented her commission's findings to Solicitor General Herb Gray on March 28, on time and within budget. The 300-page report contained more than 100 recommendations. Gray asked the deputy solicitor general to convene a senior-level response group and report to him within six weeks.

The federal minister made the report public on April 1, 1996. It was a scathing if highly subjective indictment of CSC policies, and Gray offered the women involved in the riot at P4W "a heart-felt apology for what they have endured." The CSC commissioner, John Edwards, resigned the day the report was made public. The chairwoman of the P4W inmates' committee during 1994 said the women were "happy" with the "thorough and professional job" done by the inquiry. The eight inmates launched civil suits against CSC, seeking "hefty" compensation.

The report of the Arbour commission had the most significant impact on corrections thinking since the introduction of the CCRA in 1992. One of the major issues under the judicial microscope was CSC's compliance with its own policy and the law. Arbour concluded that CSC in fact broke the law in its treatment of the women. She called the strip search "cruel, inhumane, and degrading." Arbour wrote in her report that CSC had a "deplorable defensive culture. Too often the approach was to deny error, defend against criticism, and to react without a proper investigation of the truth." She found that up to 80 per cent of female inmates had a history of physical and sexual abuse and needed women-centred therapy and training.

After the release of the Arbour report, Nancy Stableforth was appointed the first deputy commissioner for women in CSC history. She has functional authority over all matters pertaining to women offenders and reports to the commissioner of CSC, who in turn is accountable to the solicitor general of Canada.

Neither Arbour nor the press paid much attention to the other women who inhabited P4W, including female guards. Correctional officers were devastated by the Arbour commission's one-sided view of the P4W riot and the press coverage that painted guards as sadistic "knuckle-draggers" trailing a ring of keys and a bad attitude behind them. Mary Vincent, an officer at P4W from 1978 to 1991, retired from the Correctional Service of Canada in 1998. After reading several articles in the *Kingston Whig-Standard* about the closure of the Prison for Women, she tried to balance the public record with an account of her own experiences.

Among her allegations, made in an article published in the *Whig-Standard*, Vincent claimed that P4W was a time bomb because it was the only federal prison for women, which meant that first-time minor offenders were housed with hardened murderers and other violent offenders. Because there was no possibility of involuntary transfer to another prison (a threat used against male prisoners), women inmates could behave with greater impunity. Many of them slashed themselves and guards.

As for the women guards, CSC seemed not to care much about their needs. Like much of society, CSC seemed to regard female offenders as victims, less dangerous than male inmates, and their guards as "matrons." It took years for emergency lighting (standard equipment to prevent guards from being trapped among inmates in the dark if there is a power failure) to be installed at P4W. Vincent concluded: "I hope Corrections Canada doesn't make the same mistakes with the new women's facilities. After all, it wasn't the building that was the problem, it was the people responsible for its direction."

Vincent's fears proved prophetic. It was one thing to see female offenders as victims, quite another to live with the harsh reality that some of them were very dangerous people. The first female offenders were transferred out of P4W in November 1995. But as late as December 1997, there were still seventeen women classified as maximum-security inmates at the prison. That left ninety employees staffing the prison at a cost of $300,000 a year per offender, an annual cost of $5.1 million.

Theresa Glaremin had actually stomped someone to death with her boots: she began serving a life sentence at P4W in 1998 for the 1997 murder of Lyn Larose. Fellow prisoners had labelled Glaremin a rat, and she believed another inmate, Tammy Lynn Papin, had poisoned her pet fish, "my two little boys," with bleach. After spending the night of April 6, 1999, in a rage over her dead fish, Glaremin decided to get even. Armed with high spike heels and a pencil, she attacked Papin early the next morning, as soon as the cells opened at 7:00. Papin, who was still in bed, was beaten and stabbed with the pencil, and Glaremin threatened to kill her. In November 1999, Glaremin was convicted of assault with a weapon and uttering a death threat; she was sentenced to an additional five months, to be served concurrent with her life sentence.

On May 8, 2000, Theresa Glaremin was the last woman to be transferred out of P4W, protesting to the end that she didn't want to go. She was sent to the new women's prison in Kitchener, Ontario.

The Kingston Prison for Women finally closed its doors for the last time in the summer of 2000. The July 6 closing ceremony, viewed as a kind of triumphant step forward in Canadian corrections, was attended by Ole Ingstrup and Lawrence MacAulay.

The five new regional facilities that replaced P4W had no maximum-security units. They are now fully operational and accommodate minimum- and medium-security women from across the country: Nova Institution for Women in Truro, Nova Scotia; Joliette Institution in Joliette, Quebec; Grand Valley Institution for Women in Kitchener, Ontario; Okimaw Ohci Healing Lodge in Maple Creek, Saskatchewan; and Edmonton Institution for Women in Edmonton, Alberta. The women live together in houses in small groups, cooking and taking care of their own housekeeping needs.

Front-line workers hired to work at Grand Valley (GV) were put on the payroll on January 2, 1996. They were screened to meet the new philosophy of the service and took a ten-day course in women's issues. Many had worked at shelters for battered women. The institution was scheduled to open in April 1996, but the opening was delayed until October, so employees were deployed elsewhere in the interim. According to Grand Valley warden Marie-Andree Drouin, most of the new prison's "clientele" would be coming from P4W, so GV employees had a "corporate obligation" to assist Kingston during the transition.

CSC wanted to send the GV employees on five-week stints to P4W, but staff resisted because they thought this would endanger their relationships with the female inmates once they came to GV. At P4W, they would be wearing uniforms and turning keys, whereas the front-line workers at GV were trained to consider themselves helpers rather than guards.

For the twenty-four prisoners at GV when the institution finally opened in 1997, there were about fifty unionized "primary workers" (CX2s) and eight managers, plus another twenty employees who worked as computer experts, as psychologists, and in other capacities. Only in hindsight did CSC realize that the kinder and

gentler prisons that came out of *Creating Choices* failed utterly to address the special needs posed by the 10 per cent of federal female inmates who are extremely violent. In fact, 75 per cent of maximum-security female inmates are serving time for violent offences. Experience has shown what Mary Vincent knew so well, that these particular offenders are hard to manage no matter where they are incarcerated.

The very violent offenders spent much more time in segregation at GV for disciplinary reasons arising out of escape attempts and substance abuse problems than the general prison population. And despite all CSC's programs, these inmates retained severe anti-social attitudes. In the philosophical euphoria that greeted the design of the new prisons, authorities tragically lost sight of the fact that women were now increasingly involved in violent crimes.

CSC's move to the new, prisoner-friendly institutions quickly turned into a public relations disaster. A number of highly publicized escapes by dangerous women made it painfully clear that the new facilities were grossly inadequate for maximum-security and so-called "special needs" offenders. Female front-line staff had warned their managers that the new prisons would not work for the small number of women who needed higher security, but their concerns were ignored.

A first-time visitor follows James Street as it curves past neat suburban houses on the edge of Truro, in the rural heartland of Nova Scotia. The Canadian flag flaps in the March breeze, and at first you are not sure if you are on the right road. Nova Institution is architecturally striking, dove grey with white trim and skylights. Surrounded by landscaped lawns, picnic tables, and acres of woods, it looks like a resort rather than a prison, the Fenbrook for women of Canada's penal system. There is a convenience store across from the visitors' parking lot, which is almost full. On closer inspection, one notices the mesh fence topped by barbed wire and the security cameras. In fact, the original plans called for a rose hedge to surround the institution.

Visitors let themselves in through the institution's front doors and enter a pleasant reception area. Recently delivered cartons of toilet paper are stacked to one side, and inmates and their carefully boxed and labelled effects enter Nova through the same doors. A display case offers an array of inmate crafts for sale: mittens, a beautiful black doll, and a teddy bear. A metal plaque with a quote from Goethe commemorates the official opening of Nova on October 27, 1995: "Treat people as if they were what they ought to be and you help them become what they are capable of being."

There is a constant flow of traffic through the reception and security area of the main complex; the Xerox representative is followed by the men who have come to inspect a new twenty-eight-bed housing unit before it opens. A large contingent from the Salvation Army is scheduled for an evening tour. The atmosphere is friendly and relaxed. Notices with the words "Out of Bounds" are taped beside the exit doors, as if to remind inmates that they are not to wander across the street to the convenience store. People who enter Nova must pass through an AM SCAN machine, similar to the search technology at every airport. All parcels and briefcases are searched or scanned. Sometimes the body scanner beeps for a wristwatch, sometimes it doesn't.

A sunny, pleasant visiting area is just past the security desk. Visitors come Tuesday and Thursday nights and on weekends. Large, brightly coloured toys litter a children's play area in one corner. A security camera in the ceiling is covered by a half-dome that makes it look like a modern light fixture. There are no ostentatious shows of security or surveillance here. Inmates take turns having individual family visits in a private house on the property.

There is a full-sized gymnasium with volleyball nets, and a white piano someone has donated in the corner; a fully equipped workout room used by staff and inmates; a chapel; a computer-equipped schoolroom; and a hairdressing salon. Cuts and perms are free every six weeks, but colouring is $15, about three days' salary for most

inmates here. Nova is structured to mirror community living as closely as possible, so prices for these beauty procedures in Truro are posted on the salon door.

The institution can hold forty women and it is full, even though a couple of inmates are on sixty-day unescorted temporary absences (UTAs) in the community. Some are double-bunked or housed in children's playrooms, even in segregation cells if necessary. Springhill Institution, the men's prison built near the community that suffered one of the worst coal mine disasters in Canadian history, is the Regional Reception Centre for women. They are sent to Nova as soon as a "bed" becomes available.

Staff here believe in their mission to restore damaged women and get them back into society in the shortest possible time. There are fifty-five staff, eight of them male. All are intelligent, friendly, and carefully chosen. Nova cost $7 million to build and has a $4.5-million annual operating budget. The budget will increase when new staff are hired to work in the twenty-eight-bed row house that will accommodate both medium- and minimum-security women.

Given the abusive backgrounds that many of the women share, the easy camaraderie with male primary workers comes as a surprise to visitors. Like the female staff, the men are role models for women who may never have known a man who was actually nice to them without wanting something in return. Jeff Rix has a degree in psychology and worked at the Nova Scotia Hospital with mentally ill patients before coming to Nova in 1997. Compassionate and intelligent, he wants to make a difference. At Nova, he has seen first-hand just about everything he once read about in his university textbooks. About 75 per cent of the women at Nova suffer from substance abuse and the lifestyle that goes with it.

When asked about slashing, a form of self-abuse unique to female offenders, Rix closes his eyes for a few seconds, as if struggling with images too grisly to recount. His answer is professional, but he clearly understands the pain. He confides that even after

hours, he tends to socialize with fellow employees. No one else could possibly understand what they see during their shifts – things a visitor with a printed itinerary will certainly never see.

There are four inmate houses in addition to the new building. The rooms have the feel of a relatively new college dorm, with blond wooden furniture, an abundance of personal belongings, and large windows. Normally each woman has her own bedroom with her own key. Smoking is allowed in private rooms, but not in the common areas of the house. The no-smoking-in-bed rule is strictly enforced. There have been too many panicked calls in the middle of the night to put out mattress fires. Female inmates have extraordinary input into their lives behind bars. There is a house representative for each unit, a native sisterhood chair, a black culture chair, a French liaison officer, an inmate chair, and a secretary.

Houses 2, 3, and 4 are medium-security; House 1 is minimum, where the women have more freedoms and privileges, such as seventy-two-hour passes in the community instead of the forty-eight hours that medium-security inmates receive. Knives are locked in a metal box on the kitchen counter. (During the day, the knives in the minimum-security house remain unlocked. In the medium-security houses, the box is opened only during meal preparation.) Using a personal identification number, inmates can make calls from a telephone in the common area of the house, which is bright and comfortably furnished.

The women share normal household chores, although the best cook usually prepares meals for the house. Supper in House 1 smells good tonight: beef burgundy "without the burgundy," one woman quips. Chores run smoothly here, where most women know they will soon be released. They simply want to do their time, mind their own business, and get out. Household jobs are a constant source of irritation in some of the other houses.

There is a mother-child program at Nova that allows women to keep their children with them up to age four. Today there are no children, but officials say the program has worked well in the past. Two women are pregnant, but they will be out on parole before

they deliver. Many of the inmates are single mothers, so a parenting skills program is offered to help break the criminal cycle and reduce recidivism. There is also a successful canine program where the women train dogs to work with handicapped people, a job skill some of them have built on to find work in the community.

Programs are holistic and women-centred. Core programs offer formal education, living skills, and assistance in coping with personal abuse, trauma, and substance abuse. At the heart of rehabilitation is the so-called "cognitive skills" program. "What or how an offender thinks, views the world, understands people, values and attempts to solve problems are factors that play an important role in criminal behaviour," CSC policy says.

Jeff Rix, Warden Mary Ennis, Assistant Warden Genevieve Butterworth, and incoming warden Gizele Smith attend the graduation of three women from the cognitive skills program. The graduates seem genuinely pleased with their certificates and the small fuss that is made over them. The program was delivered in thirty-six two-hour sessions over eleven weeks. It included group exercises, board games such as Scruples, and debates as well as assignments.

One young woman about to return home to Dartmouth, Nova Scotia, after being at Nova for two years said the program had taught her to take control and to think before she acted impulsively. But she was fully aware there were "a lot more challenges out there than in here."

Asked what the biggest problem is when doing time, Connie Penny – serving a sentence for break and enter, fraud, forgery, and assault – says, as many inmates do, "Doing time! It's the lack of freedom. It's the boredom. It's seeing the same old faces every day, not being able to go for a walk if you want to go for a walk to the store. The disrespect from certain staff, that you have to take it from them and smile about it because you are the inmate and they are the staff, when on the street I wouldn't put up with someone talking to me the way some of them talk to me. There are some staff here who are extremely ignorant."

The enhanced-security unit (ESU) in Nova's main building has locked front doors and is used as a reception area for new inmates while they are assessed, as well as for segregation. It also houses women who turn themselves in at Nova after jumping parole, arriving by taxi rather than risking being picked up by police and sent to Springhill or a provincial institution. In the ESU, women are let out of their cells only when two staff are on duty.

Penny feels two male staff should not run the enhanced unit (nor should a woman go on an escorted temporary absence [ETA] with only one male staff person) because of the potential for abuse by the guards. But she realizes that that is only half the potential problem. "There is [also] the potential for the woman to say one male staff raped her while the other one kept lookout. . . . It's nothing to give yourself vagina bruising. You get a banana, and you jab yourself hard enough. It's a disgusting way to do something, but it's a fact. . . . We had a woman that tried to say another woman raped her, and that's how she went about it. She took the banana and jabbed herself."

The ESU at Nova features a common room overlooking a walled courtyard available for exercise, but most inmates would rather watch soap operas than use the yard. Meals are prepared in the unit kitchen. Equipped with a sink and toilet, the rooms are of painted cinder-block construction and resemble conventional prison cells. Although there are food slots for those in segregation, flowered curtains cover the door windows when an inmate needs privacy.

One cell is wheelchair-accessible, and there is a dry cell where inmates are placed if they are suspected of "hooping" drugs. (Males "suitcase" drugs; females have two orifices to "hoop" drugs.) Penny says, "There's drugs here . . . everything from hash, speed, crack cocaine, and heroin. Needles have come in." They have the bleach program, but "we use our bleach for laundry." No one wants to signal they are using drugs and be targeted by the urinalysis program. "You know what you can and can't get away with with certain staff. Some staff, they walk in and they smell weed in the house. As they are leaving, they tell you, 'Open the windows.'"

In Penny's opinion, "They are too lazy to do the paperwork, or they are high themselves. We have one staff member here – we know he gets high. Nobody wears sunglasses at nine o'clock at night." According to Penny, all the illegal drugs at Nova are brought in by inmates and visitors. "It comes in, they are never going to stop it from coming in."

She is adamant that none of the staff would ever bring in drugs, not one. Despite monthly house searches, the drugs are well hidden. "They tore apart [the house of] one of the main dealers here, but they didn't find nothing. They had the dogs in, the dogs are stupid! They are not going to find it." Nova has a machine that detects drugs, "but they don't use it," Penny explains. Asked why, she replies, "I think they like having that power of doing the strip search."

Although there are women at Nova who did time in the old P4W, "it's a whole new generation of people doing time now, it's not like it was ten years ago." A rat or a cell thief would have been badly beaten at P4W, but Nova is more relaxed. Still, a thief or a rat will do hard time. Notes will appear on your door, threats will be written on your mailbox, pieces of cheese may even be taped to it. People threaten to beat you. "You are tormented. It's a daily thing." Women routinely break down and cry over "the treatment."

But, Penny says, "a lot of things fly here. . . . The women are not less violent, they just don't act on it as much any more." She agrees this is "probably" because the programs are working. "A lot of the times you get such a close connection to your primary worker, if you have a good one, that you don't want to disappoint them. If I disappoint my worker, my worker gets mad at me, and I don't like when she's angry with me. . . . I like the approval I get from her. . . . It's like my friend is mad at me. I hate it."

As at all prisons in the system, certain inmates run things at Nova when staff are not present. Some are long-term inmates from P4W and, as Penny knows, not to be trifled with. "That's just how things go. If this person tells you to fuck off and to shut up, well then that's what you do. You don't answer them back and walk away from them."

A Nova inmate once threatened to kill another in a letter sent to her mailbox. "We all know who done it. We know who put it there, but nobody dares to say who. You don't want nothing to do with it. . . . It doesn't involve us."

Asked about the most valuable thing she has learned at Nova that would help her to adjust to life beyond the barbed wire fence, Penny says, "Honestly, coming back." She explains that she was fast-tracked back to the street under the accelerated parole program for first-time offenders. "So I had a very bad attitude. 'I'm going to get out, you can't do nothing to me.' So I would tell staff off, I would curse them. Charges – like I had two or three charges a week, and I just didn't care. Unless I got into a physical altercation, there was nothing they could do to me. I could have a dirty urinalysis, and they couldn't do nothing to me unless I was in a physical fight. I refused programs. They used to come wake me up, used to tap on my door, 'Are you supposed to be some-where?' I'm like, 'Yeah.' 'Are you going to go?' 'Does it look like I'm going? Goodnight.' And I'd go back to sleep . . . as long as I wasn't violent. I got out and I had a very bad attitude at the halfway house, 'You can't do nothing to me, ha, ha, ha, ha.'

"And they sent me back. Now I have to work for it. I have to do programming. I have to be respectful to staff. It made me put things in a different perspective." Asked if she would have avoided running into problems if the system had been stricter in the begin-ning, Penny replies, "Yes, exactly."

Nicole Duguay is another minimum-security inmate at Nova. A francophone raised in Bathurst, New Brunswick, she had "good parents," and her children, aged fourteen, thirteen, and five, are with her mother. Divorced in 2000, she chose the wrong new companion and ended up with twenty-three charges of credit-card fraud. Unlike most women at Nova, who have served time as juveniles or in the provincial system, Duguay was in for her first offence. The judge wanted to give her thirteen months of provin-cial time, but her lawyer requested a technically longer federal

sentence because she would actually be out sooner and be offered better programs in more congenial surroundings. The lawyer was right. His client went on accelerated parole and would serve six months before being released on June 22, 2001.

Many women (and men) will request a longer sentence just to get into a federal prison. Someone sent to a provincial jail for fifteen months could actually spend more time in jail than a woman sentenced to a two-year federal term. In a provincial jail most inmates are released at the two-thirds mark, but in the federal system, you can be out at one-third or even one-sixth of the sentence, depending on your offence and behaviour inside. Duguay transferred to Nova from Saint John Provincial Jail in New Brunswick on January 8, 2001, and recalls, "It was a very nice day." Brought in through the front door, she was placed in the same room used for our interview. As the van pulled up, her first impression was, "Oh my God, this is nice. . . . Very different from provincial, very different. . . . I was in a provincial where it was all dirty, and you arrive in a place like this. I'm, like, amazed."

Before, her perception of prison had been based on television. It was a bad place where they beat people up, killed people. But as she came through the front door of Nova, she found herself wondering, "Is this a jail? I didn't know what to think." She passed through security wearing clothes issued by Saint John Provincial Jail. Two female officers strip-searched her and gave her gym pants, a T-shirt, sneakers, underwear, a bra, socks, and a coat because it was winter. There was also a supply of toiletries for the new client.

Duguay spent almost two weeks of orientation in the enhanced-security unit, waiting for her paperwork to be completed. With no drug or alcohol addictions and no abuse history, there wasn't much to do. "The staff were so good to me upstairs." But Duguay still feels they put her in the wrong house since her paperwork wasn't done. She was put in House 3, a medium-security unit, "with lifers that killed." Her primary worker fought to get her out. "I was in a bad house. They are evil in there."

Asked what the biggest adjustment was for her when she came into the system, Duguay replies, "I'm not even adjusted yet." She explains the other inmates pick on her constantly. "They wrote me letters," she says. The words "Rat. I'm going to kill you, you French bitch" were scrawled on her mailbox. She does not know why. "It's probably because I'm different than them. They have all kinds of abuse and all that in their life. . . . All the girls that had abuse, they are all together. . . . They say I am spoiled rotten by the staff. They don't like that."

Duguay feels she is at risk because of her lack of criminal background, and that the women should have more supervision. There is a phone downstairs in her house, but if a fight starts upstairs there are no emergency call buttons. Inmates can lock their doors from the inside, but the lifers know how to open the doors. "There is a lot of harassment: 'I'll kill you, and beat you up.'" The threat wears you down even if it's not carried out. Duguay says there have been "quite a few" beatings, but no one wants to talk about it. "Instead of just leaving the house to ourselves, they should have a staff in the house with us. . . . The medium ones are bad – oh my God, they are bad, believe me, they are bad. . . . They are evil, because they think evil. There is one that has AIDS there. When I first came in, the two weeks I was in House 3, they wanted to poke me with her dirty needle. You don't know what I've been through. In three months it's very hard for me, very hard. . . . I pity them how they think so evil."

Duguay says things are easier in House 1. "We are different from the other ones because we don't think like them." Nicole avoids socializing in the evening, because there is too much backbiting gossip that can lead to violence. There are a lot of "couples" inside, even people who would normally be heterosexual on the street. "I've seen it all, I really did see it all, in here. . . . Like the lady, a sixty-year old lady going to a twenty-three-year-old's bedroom, and have sex and you hear them. . . . They have sex, they get a girl, usually it's her and another one, they are like the boss for the gay ones." The older woman is the one in charge. The younger woman

must co-operate, "or else, like, 'I'm going to kill you, like the girl I killed.' It's threats like that."

On September 20, 1996, CSC officials announced that Nova and Edmonton Institutions for Women would no longer house maximum-security inmates. (At that time, the other new prisons for women were not yet fully operational.) Nova had maximum-security inmates when it opened in 1995, but two violent situations in a year had forced the federal government to turn it into a medium/minimum institution. Staff were spending so much time and effort trying to control the maximum-security population that they had little time to offer programs to the other inmates.

CSC's decision to consider all women a low risk for violence after *Creating Choices* was published turned out to be an arbitrary and unsubstantiated policy preference that had nothing to do with realities inside. On September 4, 1996, six female offenders had trashed one of the four inmate houses at Nova. A toilet bowl was ripped out, flooding the premises; a mattress was set ablaze, and windows and furniture were smashed. The rampage lasted for over a day because prison officials in the post-Arbour era were afraid to use what might be viewed as undue force to restore order. An all-female extraction team eventually removed the women, and four were sent to a special women's unit at Springhill Institution. (Since 1996, CSC policy has prohibited male staff from strip-searching females.)

CSC made plans to build a new five-bed maximum-security unit as well as an eight-bed house to shelter inmates with mental health problems at Nova. Originally scheduled for completion in the fall of 2001, the two houses are expected to be ready by January 2002 at the earliest, a full six years after Nova opened its doors. The new secure units will share support and administrative services, but they will have their own program areas. In contrast to practice in the main complex, inmates will move out of the units only under staff supervision. Thirty new employees will be hired to staff the two units.

Maximum-security women's units are now temporarily located in Springhill Institution in Nova Scotia, the Regional Reception Centre in Sainte-Anne-des-Plaines, Quebec, and Saskatchewan Penitentiary in Prince Albert. In British Columbia, the provincially run Burnaby Correction Centre for Women accommodates women offenders of all security levels under a special federal-provincial agreement.

The units that house a small number of female offenders in male prisons have made the delivery of programs difficult and expensive. If the inmates have to be moved out for health care or other reasons, part of the men's prison sometimes has to be shut down. Since many of the women have suffered abuse from males, it is not ideal for them to be in a male institution, even if the two populations don't mix.

CSC plans to build units at four of the five regional women's facilities to house maximum-security inmates. The government has spent $5 million to add a maximum-security wing at Grand Valley Institution in Ontario that will help boost the capacity of the institution from 72 to 111. The other new "max" housing units will cost an estimated $7 million and house about thirty women. This is in addition to the $54 million originally spent on the five new institutions.

Many female inmates suffer from severe mental health problems, having grown up in foster care, group homes, and detention centres before entering psychiatric hospitals. The new women's prisons are ill equipped to handle these difficult inmates, who have the potential to harm themselves or others. Sometimes it is not possible to provide alternatives such as care in a psychiatric hospital. Frequently the women refuse treatment, which is their right under the CCRA.

Nancy Stableforth, deputy commissioner for women's corrections, knows that there is only so much the system can provide. "Someone who wants to seek treatment voluntarily is one thing, but very often we're talking about involuntary transfers. You can't put somebody involuntarily in a mental health institution." Accordingly, another $5 million will be spent to construct houses

for about thirty-five women with special mental health needs. Specialized staff will be on hand for support and intensive supervision. In addition to capital costs, the Intensive Intervention Strategy will cost about $9.3 million a year to operate, actually $2.3 million less than it cost to house maximum-security and special-needs women in P4W and the special women's units in men's prisons.

In February 2001 the Office of the Correctional Investigator, which looks into prisoners' complaints, tabled its 1999-2000 report in the House of Commons. The report maintained that conditions for women serving time in men's prisons were brutal and discriminatory. About thirty women classified as maximum-security prisoners were being held in Saskatchewan Penitentiary, Sainte-Anne-des-Plaines, and Springhill, transferred after a series of escapes and a murder at the lower-security institutions. Ed McIsaac, the office's executive director, said, "The housing of maximum-security female offenders and those with mental health concerns in male institutions was totally inappropriate, and it's still going on." He said that the institutions were underfunded in the mental health, programming, and treatment areas. All the women did was eat and sleep in austere and isolated conditions, and there was little access to programs that would help them get to lower-security institutions.

In March 2001, the Canadian Association of Elizabeth Fry Societies, along with aboriginal and women's groups, chose International Women's Day to launch a human rights complaint against the federal government on behalf of women housed in men's prisons, alleging discrimination based on sex, race, and disability. Ironically, it was the triumphant philosophy of these same groups that dominated the thinking of *Creating Choices* in 1990. One of those triumphs was to persuade the federal government not to build high-security facilities into the new prisons that replaced P4W. It was a mistake that guaranteed maximum-security female offenders could not be housed in places like Nova, and one that cost taxpayers millions of dollars that might otherwise have been spent on programs.

The virtual absence of internal and external security at the new prisons was the direct result of pressure from the Task Force on Federally Sentenced Women, which was dominated by women's groups and agencies like the federally funded Elizabeth Fry Society. They believed not only that all female inmates were victims of society rather than convicted criminals, but also that these female offenders could be rehabilitated and restored if they were simply treated with dignity and respect. At the time that the federal task force presented *Creating Choices* to government, CSC was run exclusively by males. Well-placed sources in CSC confirmed that no male manager wanted to risk his career by offending powerful feminist groups in Ottawa. Accordingly, CSC ushered in a new regime for incarcerating female prisoners that ignored the reality of the hard-core offenders the system had to deal with.

The first six months of operation of Edmonton Institution for Women (EIFW) after it opened in November 1995 were a nightmare for CSC: one inmate was murdered, and there were assaults on staff, suicide attempts, and seven escapes of medium- and maximum-security inmates within eighteen days. Three convicted murderers were among the flock of escapees. Solicitor General Herb Gray finally ordered twenty medium- and maximum-security inmates temporarily transferred to provincial jails after the breakout of three women on April 30, 1996.

It was a humiliating moment for a service that claimed protection of the public as its first priority. Warden Jan Fox of EIFW said that the women lived in houses with unlocked doors because of fire regulations, although an alarm sounded when the doors were opened. Even though all escapees were recaptured, seven out of twenty-eight inmates had managed to break out of prison with ease, an astonishing 25 per cent of the total prison population. People in Edmonton joked that traffic signs should read: "Slow, prisoners escaping."

CSC had to close down the new facility for all but five low-risk inmates in May 1996 to upgrade security. EIFW reopened in

September of 1996 with a fence that was increased from six feet to more than eight feet, and topped with new razor wire. Officials added a motion detection system, more lighting, and more security cameras. The cost to taxpayers of the retrofit for the brand new $5.4-million institution was $440,000. Maximum-security inmates would not return until a separate unit was built for them. The new "mini-max" is scheduled to be completed within the institution by January 2002, although recent criticisms may speed things up. In the meantime inmates have been sent to special units at Saskatchewan Penitentiary in Prince Albert and the Regional Psychiatric Centre in Saskatoon, both specially renovated to accommodate female offenders at a cost of $510,000.

Tammy Lynn Papin, serving time for robbery, was one of the women who escaped from EIFW on April 30, 1996. While at P4W in September 1988, Papin had pleaded guilty to assaulting two female correctional officers and uttering a death threat against one of them. She was given an additional seven months. Shortly after her escape from EIFW, Papin, age thirty, was charged in the death of a fellow Edmonton inmate, Denise Leanne Fayant, a twenty-one-year-old Cree woman, on February 29, 1996. After the death and escapes, some maximum-security inmates were even sent back to P4W, which had been scheduled to close in 1996. Papin was one of them.

Fayant had repeatedly told CSC staff that she feared for her life if sent to Edmonton Institution. She was in fact murdered just thirty hours after her arrival. Fayant was found strangled behind her bed, with a bathrobe sash around her neck; she died two days later in hospital. For two months after her death, prison officials insisted Fayant had committed suicide. It was a convenient, if false, account of events.

The police conducted an independent criminal investigation of their own after a tip to a radio program and came up with a very different version of events. Inmate Natalie Dubreuil pleaded guilty to killing Fayant and received six and a half years in jail in addition to the seven and a half years she was serving for robbery and

aggravated assault. It turned out that Dubreuil had strangled Fayant with a piece of sinew probably meant to be used for a craft project. Papin, an accessory, got three years for using a bathrobe sash to make the death look like suicide. Fayant's parents sued CSC and the Justice Department in 1997. The government settled out of court with the Fayants in December 1999, burying the details of the arrangement in the terms of the deal.

Denise Fayant's murder seriously called into question CSC's entire philosophical approach to handling female federal offenders. In February 2000, Judge Albert Chrumka of the Alberta Provincial Court released a damning report after examining the circumstances of the fatality.

Fayant was a maximum-security prisoner serving two and a half years for aggravated assault, uttering threats, and assaulting a police officer. At the time of her sentencing she was pregnant, and her son was born at the Regional Psychiatric Centre; he was two years old when she died. Chrumka concluded that Fayant was the victim of an "untested concept to manage federally sentenced female inmates," the victim of *Creating Choices*, the ten-year-old report of the Task Force on Federally Sentenced Women. He also concluded that Fayant's death was avoidable.

Chrumka wrote, "The process failed tragically and inhumanely. The evidence demonstrates a lack of forethought, a lack of administrative accountability and a callous and cavalier approach within the Correctional Service of Canada which cannot be condoned or tolerated." CSC unrepentantly denied that it had been callous or complicit in Fayant's murder. "We did not foresee the impact the maximum-security inmates would have or the resources they would require." At the time, CSC believed Fayant could be held safely in the enhanced-security unit at EIFW.

The emphasis at the five regional centres for women, including the healing lodge in Saskatchewan, was on rehabilitation, not punishment. Fayant was transferred to EIFW even though the warden at Edmonton knew there were violent offenders in that institution who hated Fayant and had threatened to kill her because she was

regarded as a rat. Fayant allegedly also had poor hygiene and would slash and burn her arms with cigarettes and shove her seared flesh into the faces of other inmates. The warden at the time told the inquiry that she had accepted assurances from the women that they would not harm Fayant.

Fayant had been subpoenaed to testify against her fellow inmate and former lover Natalie Dubreuil in a serious assault case. The two women had originally been incarcerated together as young offenders. They had participated in a conflict resolution session while they were at the Regional Psychiatric Centre, awaiting the opening of Edmonton Institution, but Dubreuil had still assaulted Fayant. Fearing for her safety, Fayant had requested she be placed anywhere but Edmonton. But this was contrary to the new CSC policy of placing female offenders as close as possible to their communities.

At its opening in 1995, EIFW's rated capacity was for fifty-eight women. Six units were designed to include infant children who would participate in the mother–child program. Because the facility is close to a residential area on the outskirts of Edmonton, community-based programs and services would be used as part of the plan to reintegrate the women. When it was being built, citizens were told that only 10 per cent of the women would be maximum-security. Six months after it was opened, fifteen of its twenty-eight inmates were classified as maximum-security.

The design of the facility, based on the *Creating Choices* recommendation, envisaged maximum-security women mixing with the other offenders in the belief that rehabilitation would be improved if they were treated with respect. But a pre-opening audit of the institution done by CSC between September 25 and 29, 1995, showed security concerns.

Although the concept satisfied the program and case management needs of minimum-, medium-, and maximum-security inmates, as well as the security needs of minimum- and low-medium-security inmates, the audit report noted "a more controlled inmate movement process is strongly recommended to enhance

detection." On the copy of the document released in response to an access-to-information request, a passage about higher-security inmates has been blacked out by CSC.

Medium- and maximum-security inmates would make up more than 50 per cent of the EIFW population, higher than estimated by *Creating Choices*: "This is a concern. Possible solutions were put forth in an effort to minimize the risk to the community while preserving the basic philosophy behind the design, keeping in mind that community support has been gained through much effort. . . . An escape could have a very negative impact on those efforts and the Edmonton Institution for Women."

Most of the staff were recent graduates of the Correctional Officers Training Program. Twenty-eight front-line staff were carefully hired from among 556 applicants. Non-violent crisis intervention would be used, although staff would also be trained in the use of tear gas, pepper spray, restraints, and control holds.

Judge Chrumka recommended that a commission that was totally independent of CSC be created to investigate inmate complaints, with a representative in each correctional facility. Segregation facilities were necessary for the protection of inmates, he found, although they should not be punitive in any manner. The judge also reminded CSC that "the prison administration is exclusively in control." He wrote, "Inmates ought not to be seen by other inmates as seemingly or actually exercising control within the institution."

Three meetings had been held with the inmates, including Dubreuil and Papin, and they promised prison officials that they would give Fayant another chance. Within hours of the last meeting, the unfortunate victim was strangled.

Chrumka ended his seventy-three-page report with the admonishment that members of the CSC ought to be compelled to read the transcript of his inquiry. On February 29, 2000, CSC responded, rejecting the judge's demand for an independent commission to investigate inmate complaints. Nancy Stableforth, the deputy commissioner of CSC, said there was already an independent Office of

the Correctional Investigator to look into inmate complaints. Like other institutions, Edmonton Institution for Women also has a Citizens' Advisory Committee (CAC), which oversees the running of the prison and hears inmate complaints. The CAC has a locked box near the guards' office for inmate complaints, and members also take phone calls. New inmates are told how to contact the Office of the Correctional Investigator and the Citizens' Advisory Committee in an information kit given to them when they arrive.

While CSC agreed with Chrumka's recommendations that segregation not be punitive, and that maximum-security inmates should be separated from the other women, prison bosses said they would not compel staff to read the transcript of the inquiry, although it was available if they wanted to do so.

Although the mission statement of CSC calls for the "safe, secure custody of offenders," and a provincial judge had found that officials had failed in that duty, CSC's own internal inquiry concluded that staff were not to blame for the incident. In fact, EIFW warden Jan Fox was named director for the parole district of northern Alberta and the Northwest Territories. Deputy warden Karen Smith-Black was promoted to warden at Grand Valley Institution for Women in Ontario, and Rémi Gobeil remained deputy commissioner for the prairie region. Nobody in CSC was taking it on the chin for the murder of Denise Fayant.

In 1993 Karla Homolka made one of the most reviled plea bargains in Canadian history and was convicted of two counts of manslaughter for her role in the abduction, rape, and murder of fifteen-year-old Kristen French and fourteen-year-old Leslie Mahaffy. Homolka's legal negotiations with the Office of the Attorney General in Ontario ended in a disgraceful twelve-year sentence. The sentence was all the more revolting because it also covered her role in the rape and death of her fifteen-year-old sister, Tammy, on December 24, 1990, after she had doped the girl with sleeping pills and Halothane. Within weeks of killing Tammy and getting away with it (neither Homolka nor her husband, Paul

Bernardo, faced charges in that crime), Homolka wrote to a friend about her grieving parents, who wanted Karla to postpone her wedding. "Fuck my parents. . . . They are being so stupid. Only thinking of themselves." Her statutory release date was July 6, 2001. Her full sentence expires on July 5, 2005.

Under the current system of justice, Karla Homolka was eligible for parole in July 1997 at the one-third mark in her sentence. She did not apply. While at P4W she had a hot cup of coffee thrown at her, and several inmates spat on her to show their disapproval of her ghastly crimes. But her stay in Kingston was relatively uneventful, even though the other inmates hated her. She was employed as a cleaner on the segregation range at $6 a day. Homolka had to be segregated from the rest of the population for a couple of years, but things settled down after the warden warned the other women that anyone who harmed Homolka would be shipped to a maximum-security institution. After spending the first four years of her sentence in P4W, Homolka was transferred to Joliette Institution in Quebec.

Compared with the daily regimen of Paul Bernardo (who insists it was Homolka who killed the two teenaged girls), Homolka's treatment by CSC is a perfect illustration of the dark side of the correctional system. Bernardo is in solitary protection twenty-three hours a day, except for occasional trailer visits with family, friends, and, as many guards claim, women. He has no birthday cakes or dress-up parties with other inmates. He lost his final appeal to the Supreme Court in September 2000 and has been declared a dangerous offender. He will probably spend the rest of his life in prison.

Homolka got different treatment from the very beginning of her legal odyssey. To bolster her credibility as a witness during Bernardo's trial, Crown Attorney Ray Houlihan portrayed Homolka as a battered, traumatized victim. Homolka made her infamous deal under Ontario attorney general Marion Boyd, when the NDP was in power. Boyd was known as a strong defender of battered women. Social workers and staffers at shelters have perpetuated the myth that women who commit crimes are victims of

the men who "made them do it." A prison system that focuses only on "rehabilitation" and ignores the public's sense of justice will be criticized. But even CSC can't take the heat when it comes to Homolka, if only because the public knows the case so well.

Joliette Institution, which is in a residential community seventy kilometres northeast of Montreal, opened in January 1997. It was designed for eighty-one women. Inmates move relatively freely behind a fence more than eight feet high, topped with razor wire. As at Nova, the main building includes a visiting room, an administrative area, an admission and release area, space for programs and school, a gym, a library, a workshop, and a chapel. The enhanced-security unit also located in the main building has two sectors: "1700" houses new admissions and women with mental health problems, and "1600" can accommodate six women in administrative segregation. The ESU yard has both a six-foot fence and a ten-foot fence.

Women at Joliette live in five semi-detached housing units. Each contains eight bedrooms with ten beds, and the houses function independently of one another. The rooms where inmates live resemble a college dormitory. With a fixed budget, inmates order their own food and cook for themselves. They also do their own laundry and housekeeping. Although classified as a multi-level institution, Joliette looks more like a traditional low-medium-security institution – minimum security with an alarm system.

The warden, Marie-Andrée Cyrenne, reports to the regional deputy commissioner for Quebec on operational issues and to the deputy commissioner for women for specific issues relating to women. There are about sixty employees, including twenty-eight primary workers (CX2s), who work on both security and case management. There is a community reintegration manager as well as two parole officers who work at the institution. Forty per cent of the staff are bilingual, but only 16 per cent of the inmates are English-speaking.

During the first six months of operation, the institution ran smoothly. The relationship between staff and inmates was open and

friendly, and there were no major security or disciplinary incidents. But a few inmates began to arrive who were more aggressive and resisted authority. There were threats, assaults, harassment, and finally gangs who wanted control on the inside. Behaviour that was easily controlled at the Regional Reception Centre had a very negative impact on the women at Joliette, where there was neither the physical security nor the staff to manage the rowdier inmates.

Instead of having relaxed and friendly relations with inmates, the exhausted and stressed staff had to concentrate on security. A staff member was assaulted in August 1997, and even though Joliette had been open only for a brief time, an inquiry found "signs of discouragement, burnout and/or questioning of career choice, particularly among Primary Workers." On July 1, 1998, the local union sent an official letter to the warden outlining staff concerns about the behaviour of certain inmates and the lack of human resources.

Warden Cyrenne responded that she was "aware of the fact that interventions relative to certain inmates have not always produced expected results and that their problems can present a challenge for those who are more comfortable with an intervention based on a helping relationship-type intervention." She acknowledged that the institutional environment "has been tense for some time" but did not agree that the troubled atmosphere had been created by a minority of truculent inmates. "I believe rather that the tension . . . is also due to other factors, such as the tendency towards emotivity which is right away more present among female inmates." She encouraged staff to continue expressing their concerns but didn't respond to their call for changes.

At Joliette, even the most difficult cases were managed at the lowest security level possible in order to respect CSC's mission statement and the CCRA. The only "safety valve" was the reception centre in a men's maximum-security prison. The RRC, the maximum-security unit for women in Sainte-Anne-des-Plaines, serves as a reception unit for the Quebec region. It also has the country's only special handling unit for women. The women's unit is located away from the main part of the institution, and every effort is made to

limit contact between male and female offenders. The RRC yard even has a canvas cover to ensure privacy. But staff who believed in "helping" were reluctant to send women there, because they believed the reception centre was too restrictive and Joliette was the better place for women with severe behavioural problems.

Staff at Joliette were ostensibly hired because they were sensitive to women's issues. In fact, since most federal female inmates are high-needs and low- to medium-risk, staff were selected based on their ability to ensure that inmates live in a community-like environment with programs for the specific needs of individuals. Many primary workers had worked only in the community, not for CSC. They believed they were there to "help" the inmates; security was very much a secondary issue until the environment inside began to deteriorate.

In August 1998, twenty-two of the total population of sixty-four women then at Joliette were in for homicide, attempted murder, or manslaughter. Four had been sentenced for sexual offences. Over 20 per cent were doing life or indeterminate sentences. Although drug use was not necessarily more widespread at Joliette than at other federal institutions, the impact was greater because of the smaller population. Staff members often smelled pot in the units and witnessed women smoking drugs – a problem that became more obvious on evening shifts. Staff suggested more planned evening activities. As in other institutions, even though staff knew certain inmates were regularly using drugs, the consequences were so minimal and ineffective that they felt there was no point in intervening. Urinalysis was made more difficult by Charter challenges, and Joliette lacked the staff to do frequent searches.

Rampant drug use dragged a trail of dreadful problems in its wake. A February 2001 study of inmates at the Edmonton Institution for Women found that twelve of the sixty-seven inmates tested positive for HIV/AIDS and fifty tested positive for hepatitis C, a disease that can be just as deadly. Most of the women would be returning to the community and could spread the diseases to others.

(There have been repeated calls for a needle exchange inside Canadian prisons. Bleach, which supposedly kills HIV but not the hepatitis C virus, is already located in several discreet locations within federal prisons, but successive solicitors general have been reluctant to agree to a needle exchange because they fear it would appear that CSC was condoning the use of drugs. Judging from the numbers coming out of prisons like Matsqui Institution, a medium-security facility for male prisoners in Abbotsford, British Columbia, an estimated 50 per cent of inmates are injecting heroin. As well as posing a crime and health problem in Canadian prisons, needles used to inject drugs are also popular weapons.)

On August 17, 1998, at 21:00, the inmates at Joliette were returning to their units at the end of their evening activities. The outside yard normally remained open until 22:00. At 21:08 three female inmates climbed over the fence, triggering the alarm. The security camera showed that the three women were assisted by a fourth inmate as they made their escape. Three staff members ran to the yard in an attempt to foil the escape. Four minutes later an alarm went off in another sector, where the fourth inmate was making a futile attempt to get over the fence.

She was pursued back to her housing unit by prison staff. When the primary workers tried to get her to accompany them to the enhanced-security unit, she refused. Other inmates in the house were told to go to their rooms. After being shown a gas cylinder, the woman grabbed a pair of scissors and threatened staff and the other inmates in the house. The primary workers left at her insistence, and the inmate barricaded the doors of her house.

Only six staff members were on duty at Joliette that night, which, though a surprisingly small number to run an institution designed for eighty-one inmates, complied with standards: an assistant team leader at the operational office; three primary workers at reception, at the main communications and control post, and in the administrative segregation sector; and two more primary workers with multiple duties related to activities and case management. Although there was an alarm button in the would-be

escaper's house, no staff were designated to supervise the unit for over an hour.

The acting warden was notified, other inmates were told to return to their housing units, and backup staff were called in so an official count could be done. An hour later, at 22:30, the team leader entered the unit, believing he could convince the inmate to move to the enhanced-security unit. The woman was hiding two wooden shivs behind her back as they talked, but after half an hour she agreed to go to the ESU. At first she refused the mandatory strip search; she reluctantly removed a third wooden shiv from her sock. After fifteen minutes of cajolery, she finally consented to allow a strip search.

The three women who had escaped were recaptured by the Joliette police at 21:55 and returned to the prison, and by 1:05 the transfer team from the Regional Reception Centre had arrived. At 4:22 the three escapees were strip-searched on videotape prior to their transfer to the RRC, where, after being examined by a nurse, they were escorted to their cells at 6:00. By 9:30 Joliette had resumed normal activities, and meetings with inmate representatives were held.

The board of inquiry looking into the escapes found there was sufficient information to have had at least two of the four inmates reclassified as maximum-security prior to the escapes. The board questioned the quality of the security classification rating evaluations carried out at the RRC and also questioned the placement of two of the four women at Joliette.

In January 1998, the last of the maximum-security inmates at the RRC had been reclassified as medium-security and transferred to Joliette. Since the RRC unit was now empty, it was temporarily closed. It had to reopen in the early hours of August 18, 1998, following the escapes at Joliette.

The board of inquiry found that a great deal of effort had been put into managing the four women at Joliette rather than transferring some of them to a higher-security institution: "As a result, the rest of the population suffered consequences in several regards."

Once again, reality did not match policy, putting everyone at risk. The board concluded that even though the RRC was not the ideal solution, it was the only alternative available. It was preferable to strictly supervise some inmates with serious behaviour problems "rather than letting the environment of a centre as open as Joliette institution deteriorate."

Drug use had also increased when the four women involved in the escape attempt came to Joliette, significantly increasing the number of violent incidents. The board believed that the women should have been transferred to the RRC well before the escapes. In their finding about the appropriateness of the placement of the four inmates in Joliette, the members wrote: "The Board perceived that there was pressure not to reopen the RRC and although the pressure was not formal, it was present and seemed to have had an influence on the decisions made regarding the maximum security classification ratings of the inmates."

In fact, the board found: "Security classification rating assessments produced by the RRC did not adequately detail the actual behaviours of, or risk posed by, these inmates and, in certain cases, relevant information was minimized." At Joliette several interventions to manage the disruptive inmates had taken place, but few were documented in reports. Staff believed they could have managed the difficult inmates if they had static security measures such as the ability to lock doors, as well as additional staff. Ideally, the women who could not function among the others would have a more secure unit on the same grounds. Although the board found that the staff at Joliette had responded well to the incidents, it made several suggestions for improvements, including assigning someone to supervise the unit where an armed inmate had threatened staff and other inmates, and then barricaded herself inside.

Most French-speaking neighbours in the community of 18,000 that bordered Joliette Institution had never heard of its most famous inmate, Karla Homolka. In August 1999 Homolka's case management team did not recommend her for parole. Three recent psychological assessments revealed that she was still presenting

herself as "strictly a victim," that she needed to connect emotionally to the violence she had committed as well as she did to the
violence she had suffered from Bernardo, and that her desire to
be released on parole "could be interpreted as showing a lack of
deeper understanding of the impact of her offences on society."

Medical experts were also concerned about her willing participation in the violent sexual assaults. Psychological tests showed she
displayed sexual interest in both adult males and females as well as
a variety of fetishes. In fact, Homolka was widely reported to be
having a lesbian relationship with another Joliette inmate said to
be in line for a $1-million inheritance.

Homolka had kept the surname Teale (a serial killer in the 1989
film *Criminal Law*), the name Bernardo legally changed his name to
four days before his arrest as the "Scarborough rapist." In May 1995,
Dr. Angus McDonald, a psychiatrist who had interviewed her for
two days, had described the Barbie doll with the bad eyes: "Karla
Homolka remains something of a diagnostic mystery. Despite
her ability to present herself very well, there is a moral vacuity
in her which is difficult, if not impossible, to explain." It was also
noted by her case management team in 1999 that despite an anger
management course and group therapy sessions, Homolka could be
angry and defiant when she did not get her way.

At his trial for obstruction of justice for withholding the tapes
of French's and Mahaffy's grisly ends for sixteen months,
Bernardo's former lawyer Ken Murray testified that as he watched
the infamous recordings for the first time in June 1993, he realized
Homolka was a sexual sadist. "There was a look of feral joy in her
face." He saw Homolka "as an initiator, a person in control. . . .
This was someone who is not afraid of anybody. This is someone
who was far more involved than any of us believed."

In November 1999, a *Toronto Star* crime reporter, Michelle
Shephard, obtained Homolka's application for passes to Maison
Thérèse Casgrain, a halfway house and former convent in a lovely
residential area of Montreal close to Westmount. There were three
schools in the area, including an all-female high school. Homolka

said she wanted to live in Montreal after her statutory release in July 2001. The paper printed the story before a publication ban went into effect later the same day.

The ban was issued by the Federal Court's chief clerk after instruction from the court's regional director, Monique Giroux. Homolka's life inside prison was protected by the Charter and by privacy laws. Ironically, it was harder for the families of her victims to protect the rights of their dead daughters. It was not until December 2001 that they succeeded in having the videotapes of their daughters destroyed.

Homolka's five-page handwritten application gave details of her rehabilitation, how she wanted to take a parenting course because she hoped to be a mother one day, and how the program called "Improving Your Inner Self" had deeply affected her life. As she wrote, "I learned to get rid of my mistrust, self-doubt, misplaced guilt, and defence mechanisms. I am now completely in touch with my inner feelings. My self-esteem is now quite high," as her long, self-centred letter made abundantly clear.

She was currently involved with the "Survivors of Abuse and Trauma" program: "This program has enabled me to better deal with the physical, sexual and psychological abuse that I suffered. It has also helped me to lose my mistrust and self-doubt." The three-part program included awareness, group therapy, and support groups. Not only by her own account but also according to CSC standards, Homolka was a model inmate: she integrated quickly once placed in the main population, performed required and voluntary programs such as anger management and self-esteem training, and completed a bachelor's degree in psychology. She had also been respectful to staff and completed her Correctional Plan. She had "behaved impeccably" and had never once received an institutional report.

Homolka's application included letters from two jurors in the Bernardo trial who had obviously bought the Crown argument that Homolka was a manipulated, controlled, and battered victim

of spousal abuse who was coerced into participating in unspeakable acts because of fear for her own life. The Crown had needed to portray her as a victim in order to use her as an effective witness against Bernardo, and CSC programs reinforced that image.

The warden of Joliette had turned down Homolka's application for passes to Maison Casgrain, and Homolka had appealed the decision to the Federal Court of Canada. In her lawsuit against the federal government, Homolka claimed that Warden Cyrenne had violated her Charter rights by rejecting her bid for temporary release, "in a perverse or capricious manner." On November 18, 1999, she withdrew the appeal, two weeks after news organizations published the details.

On Friday, October 6, 2000, Homolka was transferred to the Regional Psychiatric Centre in Saskatoon, a 206-bed maximum-security psychiatric facility, where she was to undergo a forty-five-to-sixty-day assessment. The facility is surrounded by two steel fences topped with razor wire, and motion detectors that trigger lights and alarms. Armed guards patrol the perimeter. Homolka was placed in room E-20, a special segregation cell away from other inmates in the twelve-bed women's unit. E-20 is also used for quiet time and transition, but it is staffed twenty-four hours a day, seven days a week, so that all patient activity is monitored. The Saskatoon centre was one of four institutions in Canada that did in-depth psychiatric evaluations for CSC and the only one with a secure women's unit.

The decision to transfer Homolka was made just five days after the September 22, 2000, edition of the Montreal *Gazette* printed photos of Homolka and Christina Sherry, another sex offender, partying and vamping it up in evening dress at Joliette. Sherry was doing five years for kidnapping and sexual assault causing bodily harm. Sherry's accomplice, Tracy Gonzales, sentenced to eight years for her part in the same crimes, was also at Joliette.

One photo showed the three women laughing and opening cards and presents behind a huge birthday cake at a party in the

prison lounge. The two other women actually had a lot in common with Homolka: both had lured young girls to an apartment where the girls were tortured, raped, and forced to become a man's sex slaves. The man, James Medley, received a twenty-six-year sentence and was declared a dangerous offender. (The photos were sold to the *Gazette* by a former inmate at Joliette for $500.)

Douglas French, Kristen French's father, said that Homolka could never be rehabilitated and that institutions like Joliette "shouldn't even exist." He declared, "It's a disgrace to Canada." Homolka shared a comfortable house with other women, had the key to her own room, prepared her own meals, wore her own clothes, and could wander the spacious grounds freely. CSC said the photos created a distorted view of life inside a women's federal prison, but in a rare move issued an apology of sorts: "CSC certainly regrets the distress it must have caused to the families of victims."

The whole country followed Homolka's every move behind bars. Canadian Alliance leader Stockwell Day demanded in the House of Commons that Prime Minister Jean Chrétien personally guarantee that Homolka would never have another prison party like the one depicted in the *Gazette* and the *National Post*. Chrétien turned the matter over to Solicitor General Lawrence MacAulay, who said: "I'm not standing in the House to defend Karla Homolka. What I am defending is the system that works to protect public safety better than any other. Correctional Services Canada has a job to do. Offenders are punished and attempts are made to rehabilitate. That is the mandate."

It was a remarkable statement coming from the solicitor general of Canada. The word "punishment" had been erased from the CSC vocabulary years before, as a throwback to the days when convicts lost their rights as citizens after their convictions. But this was such a hot political issue that even the minister was prepared to make an exception in Homolka's case.

Homolka had gone to court to fight her transfer to Saskatchewan, her lawyers arguing that her life would be in danger if she was moved to the women's unit in Saskatoon. Homolka wrote in her

affidavit, "I am convinced that the proposed transfer will put in peril my life and personal security. . . . I have been the victim of several death threats in the past and that is why the authorities agreed to my request to be transferred to the Quebec Region." She noted that the transfer would also cut her off from visits with family and friends. An e-mail from the Elizabeth Fry Society supported Homolka's claim, since the organization had received information that inmates in the Saskatoon facility were telling staff they would kill her.

Once she arrived at the Saskatoon enhanced-security unit aboard a private RCMP plane (the trip cost taxpayers $20,000), Homolka refused to undergo psychiatric evaluation. Her daily behaviour was watched closely. Homolka's lawyer at the time, Marc Labelle, said that CSC had violated its own rules when it moved Homolka to Saskatoon. He was right. According to both commissioner's directives and the CCRA, the service has to have the consent of the inmate before it can transfer him or her for psychiatric evaluation. Section 28 of the CCRA says CSC has to consider several conditions, including "the person's willingness to participate in those programs."

Homolka had been enrolled in the "Intensive Healing Program" without her consent, and she had made it clear she would not participate in it. Commissioner's Directive 803 reads: "The consent of the offender must be obtained for: all medical procedures; all psychiatric and psychological assessment and treatment. . . . Consent shall be voluntary, informed and specific to the assessment, treatment or procedure."

A spokesperson for CSC, Michèle Pilon-Santilli, denied that the service was in violation of any directives, even though Homolka had refused consent. If she didn't want to participate, the assessment would be based on her institutional behaviour. Marc Labelle complained that Homolka had been threatened with a move to a maximum-security prison if she did not co-operate with the assessment, coercing her into co-operating "a bit."

Homolka had also refused to participate in psychiatric testing at Joliette, claiming she had not been assured that the results would

be kept confidential. An August 2, 2000, report by Dr. Hubert Van Gijseghen said that although Homolka had refused to meet with him or participate in tests, he had examined her file: "The portrait that emerges . . . is that of a very articulate, manipulative person, who is fairly egocentric if not narcissistic." The doctor recommended a serious evaluation of Homolka.

Solicitor General MacAulay claimed there was nothing political about transferring Homolka to Saskatchewan for assessment. In a scrum after Question Period, he told reporters, "This was a decision made by Correction Services Canada, of course not a decision of mine. It's normal process. . . . I didn't do it. If somebody did it for election reasons, it wasn't me. It's a normal process that takes place. This is not a unique thing. This is something that happens on a regular basis."

But many Ontario MPs were worried that the Homolka photos would hurt the Liberal Party in the coming federal election and wanted the government to appear to be hard on Canada's most despised female inmate. It was known that MacAulay had called the CSC commissioner the day that the photos were published. Ontario premier Mike Harris labelled the Homolka case "a tremendous failure of the federal justice system." Harris's minister of correctional services, Rob Sampson, said that the Liberals' policy should be consistent with punishment, not just when there was public pressure and an impending election.

CSC received thousands of letters, faxes, and e-mails from people who were outraged about Homolka's case, approximately the same volume of correspondence it got about the serial child murderer Clifford Olson. In a rare move, CSC decided on December 29, 2000, to recommend that Homolka not be released on her statutory release date because she was still too dangerous. CSC decided to transfer Homolka after three months in Saskatoon to the Philippe Pinel Institute, a psychiatric hospital and research centre affiliated with the Université de Montréal, for a treatment program. The institute was known for treating troubled teens, survivors of abuse, and sexual offenders.

On Wednesday, January 3, 2001, Karla Homolka was moved from the Regional Psychiatric Centre in Saskatoon to the Pinel Institute. Once again, Canada's most infamous female inmate was flown by private RCMP aircraft. Again, she refused psychiatric evaluation and therapy from specialists in criminal sexuality at Pinel. Homolka wanted to return to Joliette, and Marc Labelle said that his client would launch a Supreme Court challenge if she was sent anywhere but back to the Quebec prison where she felt safe. Labelle believed CSC had caved in to public pressure and was not treating Homolka fairly.

According to CSC policies, he was right once again. Under the CCRA, security levels and parole recommendations are based on an offender's behaviour while in CSC custody, not on the severity of his or her crime. Only 223 of the 4,758 offenders eligible for statutory release in 1999, a mere 4.6 per cent, were referred for detention by CSC. The comparable figure for women is even more revealing; a mere 1.6 per cent are referred for detention beyond their statutory release date. Most of them were detained by the National Parole Board. A special detention hearing before a panel of three parole board members had to be held for Homolka before April 2001. In the end, she decided not to attend.

On March 8, 2001, the NPB denied Homolka's statutory release. In a three-page letter addressed to Homolka, the board said she was likely to repeat her "monstrous and depraved" crimes: "The fact that you continued your crimes after the death of your sister, which occurred while you sexually abused her, clearly shows that you have difficulty mastering your violent sexual impulses to the point where you put other people's safety at risk."

Even though Homolka has been held past her statutory release date in July 2001, the decision must be reviewed annually. Failing all forms of early release, she will have to be freed in July 2005, when her warrant expires. Homolka reportedly plans to leave the country.

Tim Danson, a lawyer for her victims' families, has suggested that Parliament pass a new sexual predator law to extend imprisonment indefinitely for those likely to offend again. He supported the

parole board's decision but not before saying that "Karla Homolka could be as dangerous in July of 2005 – or even more dangerous than she is today." Legal experts doubt a new law is possible. Under the Charter, once people have served their time, they can't be punished again, since it would be a violation of their rights.

Sometimes the most eloquent critics of Canada's "women-centred" prison policies are the women themselves. Veronica Brown was jailed for robbing Toronto cabbies and stores at knifepoint or with a meat cleaver or gun to maintain her $1,000-a-day crack habit. She was sentenced to fourteen years for several robberies in 1992, but the sentence was reduced to eight years on appeal. She skipped parole twice in 2000, once in January and again in September. Her parole officer had asked for a urine sample.

Knowing Brown to be violent when using drugs, Detective Constable Douglas Ducharme of the Toronto–York Region ROPE (Repeat Offender Program Enforcement) unit had tried to find her three times. Ducharme said that absolutely nothing the system had done had worked to reform her. "They have put her in programs, tried to get her jobs, and given her chance after chance, but it has all blown up in their face." Brown was finally caught in November 2000 after she and a friend grabbed a man's genitals as a unique means of forcing him to hand over his wallet.

Brown and a friend, Sherri Dorsey, had taken off while on an unescorted family visit to Toronto during the Thanksgiving 2000 weekend. They were roommates at Grand Valley in Kitchener. Brown and some of the other women had complained about conditions at the new women's prison. There was badminton, baseball, bingo, tennis, and houses for family visits, but Brown said that P4W had actually offered more programs and vocational training.

At P4W women could see a psychologist whenever they wanted. In the final days at P4W, there were eighty staff and only seven inmates, so these women had a hard time adjusting to independent living at GV. As in the real world GV was supposed to emulate, the women now had to make appointments to see health care professionals and wait, just like citizens on the outside.

Brown complained that problems arose because the women were not evaluated properly. People with all sorts of different convictions were housed together, and not everyone could live in that kind of structure. If the conflicts continue, some women feel there could be a riot similar to the one at P4W in 1994. But they say it would be worse, because although Grand Valley has the same kind of inmates as the ones who rampaged at P4W, the new jail has far less security to keep them in check. The primary workers don't wear uniforms, so it would also be hard to tell the difference between staff and inmates in the general chaos of a riot.

Brown and Dorsey were known to associate with high-level crack dealers in Toronto. Dorsey had numerous convictions for trafficking as well as robbery, stretching back fifteen years. She was two-thirds of the way through a two-year sentence for trafficking and obstructing police when she walked away at Thanksgiving.

Do CSC's new women-centred policies rehabilitate female federal offenders? When officials at Nova Institution were asked about recidivism rates, it was clear the question made them uncomfortable. Headquarters would have to answer that question since there were so many ways to interpret the statistics. Staff acknowledged that many of the same faces kept turning up. One woman about to be paroled told her primary worker, "I'll see you when I come back." For some women who commit federal offences, the new prisons designed especially for them are a step up.

Despite obvious evidence that there are serious problems inside CSC's kinder and gentler prisons for women, bureaucrats not only are congratulating themselves, they want the same concept brought to prisons for male offenders. According to the report of the Task Force on Security released in late 1999:

> CSC has enjoyed remarkable success in the management
> of facilities for federally sentenced women. The design
> of these facilities has demonstrated the viability of the
> multilevel concept being proposed by the task force.
> Further, inmates are housed in small units that mirror

> community standards. Again, this is consistent with the
> Task Force recommendations for housing male offenders.
> The Task Force also notes that the role of Primary
> Workers in these facilities closely approximates our
> vision of the role we are proposing for CO 2's [CX2s] in
> male institutions.

The task force recommended that CSC use the lessons learned from the women's facilities in the development of plans for men's facilities and that CSC's national recruitment strategies and staff training follow the requirements for primary workers in the women's facilities. There is only one problem: since 70 per cent of federal male inmates are serving time for violent offences, how can giving them greater freedoms result in anything other than greater risk to the public for a very uncertain return on rehabilitation programs, just as it has in the women's prison system?

If the experience of the other women in Canadian prisons – female correctional officers – is any guide, applying principles developed in the prisons for women to men's institutions will be a disaster. Female guards, who are grossly abused by inmates on a regular basis, know that male prisoners push the envelope at every opportunity when they sense weakness in the system.

PART TWO

The Game

6

OLD AND NEW

The countries bordering on Hudson Bay might serve as an English Siberia, where we might hold our convicts, instead of hanging them by thousands at home, or transporting them to corrupt the natives of our colonies. Convicts should always be sent to a country barren, and in a manner uninhabited, because there they cannot corrupt by their bad example; are secure from their former temptations; and must be industrious – and consequently have the best chance of reforming and growing good.

   – *The Gentleman's Magazine*, November 1754

Penal thinking in Canada has come a long way in the last 250 years, all of it in one direction: the expansion of prisoners' rights. The term for people imprisoned in this country has changed over the decades to reflect the custodial fashions of the day: "convicts" until 1914, "prisoners" until 1939, then "inmates," now "offenders," in some cases "clients," and perhaps soon even "guests."

The softening of the jargon has gone hand in hand with how justice administrators viewed crime itself; originally as sin, then sickness, and now social disorder, making of the lawbreaker a victim in his own right. This changing attitude within the system has led to a clash between the rights of the offender and the rights of the community he offended against. According to polling by Ipsos-Reid, an astonishing 80 per cent of the public currently believes that the justice apparatus, including the shadowy domain of the national prison system, doesn't work.

Crime and punishment have always been emotional subjects. The public has been concerned about the nature of the prison system since the publication of *The State of the Prisons in England and Wales*, by the Quaker reformer John Howard, in 1777, when convict gangs ruled the prisons and typhus or starvation frequently ended the suffering of inmates. Details of the horrors of the prison system in Howard's day led to the establishment of the first "penitentiary houses" in Britain in 1779.

Since criminal behaviour in the eighteenth century was seen as sinful, these wholesome houses of "penance" would, in theory at least, keep hardened prisoners from reoffending but would also reform their evil ways. The diet was crude, the labour hard. Inmates wore uniforms intended to aid in their discovery if they escaped, but also to humiliate. Yet if a prisoner's conduct was satisfactory, he was progressively given more comforts, an early variation on the notion of earned remission.

During the early nineteenth century in Canada, municipalities ran local jails. The public had lost its taste for banishment, transportation, and hanging, but overcrowding and frequent escapes led people to believe that crime was out of control. In 1831, a report to the House of Assembly of Upper Canada by Hugh Thomson and John MacAuley recommended that a penitentiary be built. As the name implied, Thomson believed it "should be a place to lead a man to repent of his sins and amend his life." Rehabilitation through work, reflection, and religion was the order of the day, with deterrence as an added benefit.

In 1832, the government bought one hundred acres of land on the shores of Lake Ontario overlooking Hatter's Bay and built the country's first penitentiary at Portsmouth. (Originally called the Provincial Penitentiary, it was formally renamed Kingston Penitentiary at the time of Confederation in 1867.) On June 1, 1835, six inmates were admitted and assigned numbers. At the time, KP was one of the largest buildings in British North America. By 1845, the original residents had been joined by 494 additional prisoners. Then, as now, the reality was the same: build a prison and they will come.

These first Canadian prisoners were expected to quarry, haul, and lay the limestone from the site to expand the penitentiary, and to work to provide life's necessities. The convicts laboured six days a week from dawn to dusk. It took ten years to build the original wall around the prison grounds. In 1849, private businessmen began setting up operations inside the prison to employ convict labour at about thirty cents a day. The prisoners' earnings went to defray the cost of their incarceration.

The inmates were employed as shoemakers, tailors, and cabinet-makers; they also manufactured small farm implements. Thomson and MacAuley had toured prisons in the eastern United States and decided that the system at Auburn Penitentiary in New York State would be their model for the new Canadian prison. Kingston prisoners worked in silence at hard labour. They ate in a common room, also in silence, and talking was punished with the lash. Singing, dancing, running, and jumping were also forbidden. The punishment for laughing was six lashes with the cat-o'-nine-tails. Barking like a dog earned you bread and water instead of regular rations. At night, prisoners were confined in separate cells, dark cubicles only thirty inches wide, with a bucket for slops. When new cells were constructed at Kingston Pen in 1885, they were sixteen square feet.

Perhaps to ingrain a new respect for authority, inmates were given the job of manufacturing the scarlet uniforms for the North West Mounted Police when the national police force was created in

1874. But after 1883, "the Pen" was no longer allowed to compete with private industries. Something else had to be found for the men to do, so their labour was used to expand the prison and provide government with needed products such as mailboxes and metal desks. They also manufactured and repaired mailbags for the Post Office. Confinement and reform continued to be the twin objectives of prison philosophy. The first part was easy: KP's three-foot-thick stone walls and daunting gun towers meant that there were few escapes.

In the early days, Canada's first federal prison got celebrity raves. Charles Dickens visited KP in 1842 and was impressed by what he saw. In his *American Notes* the famous author wrote, "There is an admirable gaol here, well and wisely governed, and excellently regulated, in every respect. The men were employed as shoe-makers, rope makers, blacksmiths, tailors, carpenters, and stone cutters; and in building a new prison." In England, Dickens had visited his own imprisoned father daily for several months in 1836 to bring him food. The elder Dickens had been sent to debtors' prison and suffered conditions far less congenial than the ones afforded the inmates of Kingston Pen.

But there were dissenting views of KP. In 1849 George Brown, the editor of the Toronto *Globe*, wrote a scathing condemnation of Warden Henry Smith's administration of the prison. Brown con-demned the practice of corporal punishment, particularly for women and children, and his report resulted in the warden's immediate resignation, although Smith could claim he was only following the harsh prescriptions of the legislature. The same could not be said for his brutal son Frank, who was employed as a keeper in KP's kitchen. Frank shot arrows at prisoners for target practice, spit into their open mouths, used convict labour for his own benefit, and routinely assaulted female convicts. After Brown's exposé, the younger Smith was dismissed along with other sadistic prison officials.

Yet at the height of the *Globe's* revelations, an editorial in the *British Colonist* warned against what it called "the march of refined

benevolence," turning prisons into palaces. Life was hard and often pitiless for most people on the outside, and William Lyon Mackenzie warned that a prison sentence must not become preferable to a convict's civilian lifestyle. In the wake of Brown's muckraking, legislative changes were made to reduce the power of the warden, and from that point on, authority inside KP's walls was shared with a board of inspectors.

Under Donald MacDonell, the new warden, punishments were halved and softened. For breaking the rules, convicts now went on bread-and-water diets for a day or suffered confinement in a dark cell. It was a decided step up from the "cats." The rule of silence was still in effect at KP, but it was hard to enforce as long as "criminal lunatics" were sent there for restraint if they could not be managed by their families. Twenty-one lunatics were confined in the basement of KP's dining hall. They were sent to Rockwood, the new permanent asylum, in 1862, although the institution was not formally opened until 1865. Rockwood was later renamed the Kingston Psychiatric Hospital. The entire four-storey hospital, which accommodated three hundred prisoner-patients, was built with convict labour.

Under Kingston Pen's third warden, James Ferres, convicts could gradually earn privileges. Those who behaved themselves were housed in KP's west wing, which was kept lighted until 9:00 p.m. They were also allowed to walk in the prison yard for an hour on Sundays. Occasionally they could write more than one letter every three months, the normal quota. The Penitentiary Act of 1868 allowed earned remission for the first time, so if he behaved, a convict could shorten his sentence by five days a month. In 1870, only 17 of the 241 prisoners released had failed to earn some remission of their original sentence. After a full day's labour, the prisoners were also offered fourteen hours a week of education in a classroom, a welcome change from twelve hours in a cell barely wide enough for a fold-down bed.

In 1871, John Creighton was appointed KP's fourth warden and began a series of his own reforms. They were tempered by his

friend and mentor Sir John A. Macdonald, who believed that reformation was worthwhile but secondary to the primary purpose of a penitentiary: punishment. Under Warden Creighton, model inmates might get a coal oil lamp in their cell until 9:00 p.m. Creighton also replaced the lash with solitary confinement.

As the number of convicted criminals grew, so did the Canadian prison system. Saint-Vincent-de-Paul (since closed) was built in Quebec in 1873, Stony Mountain in Manitoba in 1876, British Columbia Penitentiary in 1878, and Dorchester in New Brunswick in 1880. All were modelled after Kingston Penitentiary. For the most part, prisons are society's unnoticed institutions, but that changes dramatically when there is a bloody riot or a spectacular escape. At 3:00 p.m. on the afternoon of October 17, 1932, KP inmates gathered in the main dome, the control centre of the institution, to protest against their living conditions. They wanted cigarette papers and more recreation. The peaceful protest turned ugly after Acting Warden Gilbert Smith called in the military. Guards were taken hostage in the mailroom, but the incident was defused when the warden agreed to relay inmates' complaints to Ottawa.

Three days later, convicts again began demonstrating in their cells. The troops returned and guards were issued firearms. Despite the fact that all the inmates were locked in their cells, shots rang out behind Kingston's forbidding walls. One inmate with a bullet in his shoulder lay in his cell for twenty hours before his wound was tended to. Seven shots were fired into the cell of Tim Buck, the leader of the Canadian Communist Party, who was serving a four-year sentence for sedition. Questions were raised in the House of Commons, and twenty thousand people signed a petition demanding the repeal of Section 98 of the Criminal Code, which had been used to imprison Buck. He was paroled in 1934.

During the Depression, inmate riots and strikes focused national attention on penal philosophy and led to the formation of the Royal Commission to Investigate the Penal System of Canada, under Joseph Archambault. The commission's 1938 report set a

direction for Canadian corrections that emphasized crime prevention and rehabilitation. The Archambault commission made a
novel recommendation: that punishment be eliminated in prisons.
Discipline was to be strict but humane.

After World War II, the prison population increased and
the overcrowding led to several major disturbances. By 1954 the
inmate population of KP had reached almost one thousand, part of
a growing trend toward overcrowding and unrest in North
American prisons. On Friday, August 13, of that year, a fire started
in the attic above the main cellblock. Though the rumours were
never proven, it was widely believed that the fire had been set to
facilitate a mass escape. The cupola of the main dome was damaged
and had to be demolished. Fire damage made the cells uninhabit-
able, so prison authorities housed inmates in KP's shops. Two days
later, the penitentiary erupted. Twenty-five fires were set and the
inmates went on a two-hour rampage that was finally stopped
by the army. Although public opinion was generally on the side of
the administration, people were ready for reforms that would
address overcrowding, including the segregation of the most dangerous offenders from the general population.

The Fauteux committee, established by the federal government
to examine prison conditions, released its report in 1956. It saw
prison as not just a custodial facility but a place where the attitudes
and behaviour of prisoners could be improved. More emphasis
was placed on training and education to fill the time and to
improve the inmates' chances of success in the outside world.
Inmates continued to be employed as cleaners, plumbers, and
groundskeepers to keep the prison running.

The worst riot in KP history began on April 14, 1971, when six
guards were taken hostage and the inmates took control of the
main cellblock. The uprising lasted five days. While inmate leaders
negotiated with prison authorities, the cellblocks themselves were
destroyed. The hated bell that rang several times a day to regulate
convict life was smashed to bits. Inmates broke into the protective-custody range, binding and torturing sexual predators and

informers in the centre of the main dome. Two of the torture victims died, but after a tense standoff, the guards who had been taken hostage were released. The exhausted inmates finally surrendered and were taken to the new maximum-security facility west of Kingston, near Bath – Millhaven Institution. There was irony in the way the outbreak ended. Fear of being moved to the new prison, with its state-of-the-art security infrastructure, had been one of the major causes for the riot in the first place.

After the riot, Kingston Pen became the reception centre for federal inmates destined to serve their sentences in Ontario. All inmates were assigned a security classification before being transferred to the appropriate institution. Inmates were assessed to see what treatment and vocational training would give them the best chance to succeed after their jail time was over. The prison was renovated to give inmates more space to socialize. By the early 1980s, parole officers were making the assignments of inmates to the appropriate institution, so KP changed yet again, from a reception centre to a multi-level institution. Today, Millhaven is the reception centre for new inmates coming into the federal system in Ontario.

In the past, prison society was ruled by a strict inmate code of behaviour. New inmates who failed to conform to the code were harassed and beaten. "Brew" was the drug of choice in the Atlantic region, heroin on the West Coast. Once the two cultures began to mix, the character of the prisons changed. By the 1970s, the number of drug convictions had exploded. Drug dealers and gang members paid no heed to the convict code or to the prison hierarchy that once kept things relatively stable inside. The new kids on the cellblock were usually young, violent, and unpredictable. Worst of all, they saw prison as an excellent market for what they had to sell.

Canada's modern preoccupation with rehabilitation had begun with the Archambault commission, although it wasn't until 1971 that rehabilitation without punishment became official policy, under

the Liberal solicitor general Jean-Pierre Goyer. Under Canadian law, loss of freedom is considered the punishment. The focus is on the inmate, not the harm he has done.

In a speech to the New Brunswick John Howard Society in May 1974, Goyer said "rehabilitation rather than punishment" must become the goal of our penal system. This would involve both effort and risk, "but it can help make our society a more humane and comfortable one in which to live." It was the intention of the Trudeau government to upgrade the quality of prison life to preserve human dignity and encourage inmates to take a more positive attitude toward life. Inmates weren't the only ones who needed to change their attitudes. If the new philosophy was to work, Canadians at large would have to see offenders as citizens and members of society rather than felons. It would be a hard sell.

The Kingston riot of 1971 was followed by a period of unrest and disturbances at other prisons. The majority of the violent riots, strikes, hostage takings, and murders were in the maximum-security institutions. The sheer volume of these outbursts was striking. From 1932 to 1974, there were sixty-five major incidents at federal pens. But in the troubled year 1975-1976, there were sixty-nine major incidents. And during a one-week period from September 27 to October 5, 1976, three institutions – Laval, British Columbia Penitentiary, and Millhaven – exploded, with over $2 million in damages. At one point, in March 1976, the government announced plans to build twelve new smaller prisons. Arthur Trono, head of the Canadian Penitentiary Service in the Ontario region, said it would probably be five years before the prisons would be ready for new inmates.

Faced with a national uprising within Canada's prisons, Solicitor General Francis Fox ordered an all-party parliamentary investigation into the penal system, and in 1977 a parliamentary subcommittee, chaired by Liberal MP Mark MacGuigan, issued its findings. The first recommendation stated the obvious: "A crisis exists in the Canadian penitentiary system. It can only be met by

the immediate implementation of large-scale reforms. It is imperative that the Solicitor General act immediately on this Report as a matter of the utmost urgency."

The report offered sixty-five recommendations for reform. On August 5, 1977, Fox announced that he had accepted fifty-three of the recommendations and tabled a detailed response to each recommendation in the House of Commons. Fox said that the other recommendations required further study because of their far-reaching implications.

Fox also endorsed all thirteen principles spelled out in the report as general statements of philosophy, attitude, and policy. Within four years, the Trudeau government had implemented most of the MacGuigan report's recommendations. They included the upgrading of qualifications for correctional officers, employment of women as guards, a grievance system for inmates, and elected inmate committees. Democracy had arrived in the restless colony of the prison world. Gone were the days of inmates marching in military-style lines wearing neat government-issue clothing and speaking respectfully to the men who guarded them.

According to the MacGuigan report, society had spent millions of dollars to create and maintain "the proven failure of prisons." With a recidivism rate of 60 to 80 per cent, authorities argued that incarceration had failed to correct the offender or provide permanent protection to society. Probation and parole were suggested as less costly alternatives to building more prisons.

Evidence heard by the committee convinced its members that the custodial staff were also prisoners of a bad system. Staff perceived themselves as having fewer rights than inmates, and their self-image was poor. They blamed their poor community image on the media. But MacGuigan's committee believed that some guards were actually responsible for inmate violence. It went so far as to blame a Millhaven officer, Bernard Evans, for inciting a 1976 riot at the prison that cost taxpayers $200,000. The committee reported that Evans had said, "Come on girls, pick up your skirts and pull it. No stabbings in the yard tonight – the blood bank is running low."

The committee's statement was false and slanderous, but for seven years, the unjust conclusion went unchallenged by anyone other than its victim. In October 1983, the Public Service Commission Appeal Board finally upheld Evans's complaint that his career had been ruined by a false accusation made by the committee. Suspended and told he would never work inside a prison again, Evans had been confined to a meaningless desk job at Ontario regional headquarters. The towering bear of a guard had never been formally notified of the accusation against him nor allowed to defend himself before the parliamentary subcommittee.

Another guard, Clyde White, who still worked at Millhaven, testified before the appeal board that he was the one who had made the remarks the subcommittee blamed for sparking the riot. Two other officers backed up White's testimony. The only thing Evans had said was: "Clear the yard." (Neither the guards nor their union believed that the remark had sparked the riot, and they claimed that prison officials had been warned twenty-four hours before the smash-up that there was going to be trouble.) Evans had to take his complaint all the way to the Supreme Court of Canada before he was vindicated, because none of the appeal bodies would question the veracity of the MacGuigan subcommittee's findings. It took an order of the Supreme Court to have the case examined by the appeal board and for Evans to be cleared.

In 1978, Donald Yeomans, a sound and principled manager, was recruited from the Anti-Inflation Board to modernize and take control of what was being described by top-level bureaucrats as Canada's semi-feudal prison system. The new commissioner changed the name of the Canadian Penitentiary Service to the Correctional Service of Canada, and he began to reorganize the service and institute new policy directions and accountability procedures. During the late 1970s and early 1980s, prisons were still run along military lines, and security was still more important than inmates' rights. But dramatic changes were on the way.

John Braithwaite, a legendary name in corrections, worked at headquarters at a variety of jobs. A thinker and a good speaker, he

was plugged in to a number of international correctional organizations. His book *Crime, Shame and Reintegration*, published in 1989, had a major impact on correctional thinking. The book looked at alternative correctional methods, including "reintegrative shaming."

Braithwaite's theory was that the community shames the offender but then immediately re-embraces him into the law-abiding society. In effect, the offender is forgiven and reintegrated, since it is the behaviour that is deviant, not the person, who is essentially good. Braithwaite believed that if you make a person an outcast, he simply rejects the people who stigmatized him, and the shame no longer matters. Braithwaite wrote that prisons had traditionally been "warehouses for outcasts." Instead, what was needed was social bonds that tied the offender to people in his community. Although the benefit to the offender was obvious, Braithwaite didn't give much thought to how his law-abiding victims would feel about the new relationship.

On the evening of Wednesday, September 15, 1999, Trevor Whitehouse, chief of the marine International Safety Management Code Compliance and Audit for the Coast Guard, was working late on an external audit for Lloyd's Register. From the office he was using on the second floor of the South Side Base building in St. John's, Newfoundland, Whitehouse had an excellent view of the harbour and the Coast Guard wharf. At 6:15 p.m. he saw a strange sight: a large party of well-dressed men and women crossing the wharf to board the Coast Guard vessel *J.E. Bernier*. Whitehouse was advised by a Coast Guard official that the local director general of the Department of Fisheries and Oceans was hosting a dinner party aboard the ship. Shortly after the guests had filed up the gangplank, the *Bernier* steamed to Freshwater Bay and took a cruise in the waters around Cape Spear. Although it was partly cloudy, the evening was warm and visibility was good. With the winds light at fifteen knots, it was the perfect night for a sea junket. But who, Whitehouse wondered, were these people? And

what were they doing aboard a vessel designed for search and rescue rather than marine soirées?

The next morning Whitehouse decided to conduct a spot audit of the *Bernier* before returning to Ottawa. He met with the superintendent of the Coast Guard Regional Operations Centre and asked for copies of the *Bernier*'s tasking, its sailing orders, and the vessel position report for the previous evening. He also requested the passenger and crew manifest. Sailing orders showed that the *Bernier* had been tasked to primary search and rescue status in Area 33, a patrol sector from Cape Freels to Cape Race. The ship was also to carry enforcement officers from September 10 to September 20 for middle-distance fisheries patrol.

But the *Bernier*'s orders had been amended on September 13, and the ship was directed to St. John's to prepare for what was obliquely referred to as "Wednesday evening activities." Since the amended sailing orders did not include details of the "work" to be done or the number of passengers on board, Whitehouse issued a non-conformance notice to the Newfoundland region of the Coast Guard.

When the operations centre tried to get information about the passengers, it was initially rebuffed by the executive assistant to the regional director general. But on September 16, a list of the dinner guests was belatedly supplied. Since it is mandatory to file passenger manifests with the marine superintendent prior to any Coast Guard sailing, Whitehouse issued a second non-conformance notice. A Coast Guard vessel is also required to report its position at 8:00 and 20:00 each day. At 20:00, the ship reported its position as secured alongside Pier 31 in St. John's. But the *Bernier*'s log revealed that it was actually still at sea and did not tie up at the wharf until 20:25. Whitehouse issued a third non-conformance notice in connection with an event that was getting stranger and stranger the more deeply he looked into it.

Of the twenty-four guests aboard the *Bernier*, it turned out that twenty-two were senior officials from the Correctional Service of Canada. Given the vessel's tasking, that was unusual enough. But

the meal that was served that night on the helicopter flight deck of the *Bernier* was not normal fare either. Four on-board staff were added to serve a feast of lobster, shrimp, crab, cod tongues, fresh salmon fillets, and prime rib roast. Guests were served fresh Newfoundland lobster tails as appetizers, while the crew got the legs and claws. Even though the *Bernier* should have been "dry" because it was on search and rescue duty, the commanding officer had approved the serving of wine and beer with his guests' meal. The total cost of CSC's ocean-going picnic was $9,820.37, over $400 per guest, excluding the cost of operating the ship.

While CSC brass were nibbling on their lobster tails aboard the ship that would normally have been on search and rescue (SAR) duty, a man was swept from the rocks and drowned in Bonavista Bay Harbour, ninety nautical miles from St. John's. Fortunately, another Coast Guard vessel, the *Cape Roger*, had returned from fisheries patrol to St. John's for repairs while the *Bernier* was acting as a floating night club. En route to its patrol assignment, the *Cape Roger* was assigned primary SAR coverage during transit. The vessel was ordered to respond to the SAR incident in Bonavista and arrived shortly before 24:00 that Wednesday night to assist in recovery of the man's body.

Though the drowned man's life could not have been saved by the *Bernier*, Whitehouse, the inquisitive auditor, was sufficiently upset by the manner in which the vessel had been taken out of service that he sent a "protected" memo to the commissioner of the Coast Guard on September 20, 1999. After laying out the details of the incident, he delivered the bottom line: "It is inappropriate for non-mariner staff, or staff acting without marine management advice, to task or assign work directly to a Coast Guard ship. The Fleet Safety Manual does not permit such activity."

The federal minister of fisheries and oceans, Herb Dhaliwal, who was also responsible for the Coast Guard, reviewed the embarrassing report and reluctantly agreed with Whitehouse. The minister emphasized that no lives had been put at risk by the CSC junket,

but he admitted that the incident pointed to "shortcomings in the manner in which operations were authorized and conducted." The man at the centre of the political storm was Joe Price, DFO's regional director general for Newfoundland, who had organized the spree. Price, once a Liberal MP, had been CSC commissioner Ole Ingstrup's assistant commissioner for corporate development at Ottawa headquarters until 1998 and wanted to show his former boss a good time. It was Price and John Adams, the commissioner of the Coast Guard, who actually wrote the report of the incident that went to the minister.

In a November 29, 1999, memo to his regional directors, Adams wrote, "Involvement of ships and aircraft in promotional activities not directly related to the mandate of the Coast Guard and the Department have the very real potential for becoming a black eye. Notoriety is something we can do without."

Adams's concerns proved prophetic. The story of the *Bernier*'s frivolous voyage broke on December 4, 1999, in the St. John's *Telegram*, and the political opposition in Ottawa had a field day at the government's expense. In the aftermath of its massive involvement in search and rescue activities following the crash of Swissair 101 off Peggy's Cove, Nova Scotia, in 1998, the Coast Guard had faced major budgetary difficulties. Headlines like "Prison Service Bureaucrats Took Vessel Off Search and Rescue" made Minister Dhaliwal's day in the House of Commons on December 9, 1999, a miserable one. He was forced to admit that the party aboard the *Bernier* had grossly violated existing Coast Guard guidelines and that the party arranged for CSC brass by Price, and paid for by taxpayers, was totally unacceptable. "I have been assured by the department that something like this will not be repeated again," the beleaguered minister told the House.

Quickly christened the "Booze Cruise" by the pundits, the voyage of the *Bernier* was interesting for reasons other than breach of Coast Guard procedures or the squandering of taxpayers' money. It was also the first time that many Canadians had heard the name

Ole Ingstrup. Yet Ingstrup, an increasingly imperial career bureaucrat, had already left a deep – and controversial – mark on his adoptive country.

A Danish émigré, Ingstrup played the key role in transforming the Canadian prison system from the old penal model of incarcerating felons for the protection of society to reintegrating them into the community as quickly as possible, regardless of the crimes they had committed. This enormous shift in national public policy, with its implicit disregard for victims' rights and for the public's growing exasperation with official coddling of violent criminals, was accomplished with virtually no public debate. Such sweeping reforms were possible largely because Ingstrup and his political masters operated in the deep shadows of Canada's Charter and privacy legislation, as well as the Official Secrets Act.

In 1983, when John Braithwaite learned that a group of senior CSC bureaucrats were organizing a tour of prisons in Scandinavia and the United Kingdom, he suggested they contact Ole Ingstrup for a tour of a Danish prison. Ingstrup had an impressive CV, including a degree in philosophy and a doctorate in law. He had been a director of prisons in Denmark and had also represented the Danish Ministry of Justice on the European Committee on Crime Problems, a committee of the Council of Europe in Strasbourg, France. He was a member of the European Prison Management Committee and had been president of the European Committee on Prison Leave and Prison Regimes.

Ingstrup was soon recruited to a contract position at CSC headquarters in Ottawa. He immigrated in 1983 and began his career in North America as a special adviser to the head of corrections, Donald Yeomans. Yeomans hired the likable young man to rewrite directives and set the groundwork for a mission statement. Ingstrup played the Ottawa game very well and married Senator Jean Marchand's only daughter, Marie-Eve. The personable newcomer made an immediate impression on Tom Epp, the director of administration at CSC headquarters. Although he found Ingstrup charming and a "decent chap," he was struck by an odd constellation

of traits: although Ingstrup was highly intelligent, Epp remembered that the young man espoused his views in an oddly detached way. "There wasn't any passion." Still, their first encounter was "entirely positive."

The psychiatrist George Scott, author of *The Psychodynamics of the Prisoner*, had begun the trend toward seeing all criminals as sick, not sinful – the origin of the view of the criminal as victim. After interviewing more than twenty-five thousand criminals over a thirty-year period, Scott saw the majority of inmates as emotionally abused members of a "battered underclass" who had rarely experienced social equality or love in their lives.

The prisoners he interviewed were angry but didn't know why. They hated their families, society, and themselves. Many were actually more secure in prison than they had ever been in their lives. According to Scott, most Canadian inmates suffered from some sort of mental illness and had no real emotional attachment to anyone: "Their lives are basically self-centred and they devote their time to maintaining their own little worlds."

In the 1970s, the Correctional Service of Canada began to manage some institutions on the basis of the "living unit" concept. Non-uniformed correctional officers (living unit officers) worked in offenders' living units to provide both security and case management. Uniformed correctional officers manned the institutional, "static" security posts. By the mid-1980s, the "unit management" model had replaced the traditional prison model. In federal men's prisons, each institution was divided into units that house a group of inmates, whose number varies from institution to institution. A team of correctional officers and other professional staff work with the same group of inmates. Female facilities use a modified version of unit management based on a "women-centred" approach to corrections. CSC believes that these approaches promote reintegration. The traditional custodial setting has become more relaxed, and the 1980s brought a hitherto unheard-of privilege: after 1983, inmates were allowed private family visits that lasted up to forty-eight hours.

In 1984-1985, both the Treasury Board Secretariat and the solicitor general's office wanted a review of the correctional service because of nagging budgetary problems. The government's dilemma was stark and inescapable: the offender population was growing at a time of severe financial constraints, and something had to be done. Canadians were offending in ever greater numbers; a lot of the crimes were associated with drug trafficking. Sexual abuse cases also began to be prosecuted more vigorously once the public became aware of them, adding to the number of federal prisoners. Between 1945 and 1986, the prison population tripled. Overcrowding and violence, coupled with the dramatic increase in drug use, had created a crisis. CSC recognized that it needed to re-examine its management philosophy and style in light of the Carson report, released in December 1984. The Carson Advisory Committee on Prison Management had been appointed by the Liberals in July 1984 but released its report under Tory solicitor general Elmer MacKay after the Mulroney government came to power.

Chaired by University of Ottawa professor John Carson, the committee stressed the need to reduce prison violence. Many of its fifty-six recommendations emphasized the importance of finding alternatives to prison and doing more research into the causes of violence: "Our federal penitentiaries will face an accumulation of more long-term, more violent and disturbed offenders. As the struggle for survival in prisons becomes more acute, violence-prone attitudes and behaviour may be intensified. In the long run, protection of society is not served if some offenders are changed for the worse by the conditions of imprisonment."

Overcrowding and double-bunking had intensified all the normal tensions of doing time. The explosion in drug use among the prison population increased violence and suicides in every prison in the country. Carson recommended a crackdown on illicit drug use through searches, urine or blood tests, and severe disciplinary measures.

Rhéal LeBlanc, the Tories' new CSC commissioner, was from Alberta and proud of his western roots. He was brought in to be a

reformer and an organizer, and he set out to run the prison system like a business. Unlike others who had held the position, LeBlanc never tried to play the Ottawa game by becoming part of the Glebe and Rockcliffe Park smart set.

The new commissioner was faced with a virtual moratorium on building more prisons as a possible solution to rising inmate populations. By the early 1980s, it cost $200,000 to build a single prison cell, and the annual operating costs were "staggering." On July 10, 1985, Elmer MacKay told a criminal justice congress in Vancouver that prisoners who did not pose a violent threat to society were being held in prison too long: "This is especially so in view of the huge cost of maintaining inmates in prison when they could be safely maintained in the community. It costs one-tenth the money to give effective street supervision than it does to hold an inmate in prison unnecessarily."

MacKay indicated that violent crime was low in Canada, about 8 per cent of all reported crime, and that less than 15 per cent of prisoners were in for violent crime. MacKay claimed that 70 per cent of all paroles were completed successfully. In the wake of the minister's remarks, CSC bureaucrats also concluded that there was just too much incarceration. Liberals had wanted fewer people locked up for philosophical reasons, Tories for fiscal ones, and there was a man from Denmark who could help both.

On the face of it, it is odd that Canada looked to Denmark for a new vision for its prison system. Denmark is a small country, not quite the size of Nova Scotia, with a relatively homogeneous population of just over five million people. It has a long democratic history, European big-government traditions, and very little social tension. Bicycle thefts account for one-fifth of all reported criminal offences. Only 3 per cent of criminal code violations are for violent crime, and only 1 per cent for sexual offences. (Today in Canada, by contrast, approximately 70 to 80 per cent of federal offenders are in for violent crime, according to CSC's statistics.) The Danish prison population has remained stable at about 3,300 for the last twenty-five years, despite a doubling of crime over the same

period. Denmark uses custodial sentences only when absolutely necessary. This differs markedly from the practice of most other European countries and the United States.

Under the Danish criminal code, there are three types of punishment: ordinary imprisonment, lenient imprisonment, and fines or community service. Although the main role of the prison and probation service is to "enforce the punishments imposed by the courts," conditions inside Danish prisons are made to correspond to conditions outside as much as possible. In most prisons, inmates cook their own food and shop at the prison grocery store. They enjoy unsupervised visits from relatives, either in single rooms or in their own cells, and they can bring their personal effects to furnish their cells and make them more comfortable.

Danish inmates face the least possible force or restriction while serving their sentences. But inmate units are searched regularly, and there are frequent strip searches to control drugs, since about one-third of Danish inmates are drug addicts. Wardens have a great deal of power to make discretionary decisions within their institutions.

Interestingly, the probation and supervision period for inmates may extend beyond the period of the sentence if necessary. The recidivism rate, defined as new offences within two years after release or the imposition of a suspended sentence, is 45 per cent. Implied in the material on the Danish prison service Web site is the belief in a criminal class: "Compared with the population in general, offenders differ substantially as to sex, age and social background."

Most offenders are young, male, and single; they have no jobs or training and are receiving social security benefits. With the Danish model firmly in his mind, and a totally different country and culture in front of him, Ole Ingstrup directed the Task Force on the Mission and Organizational Development for the Correctional Service of Canada. The Ingstrup task force was set up in the spring of 1985 to find better ways to run the organization by reviewing and rewriting all policy directives. In a speech to the North American Association of Wardens and Superintendents in New York on August 13, 1985,

Ingstrup talked about aging, top-heavy public service organizations that are so bureaucratized that they become dysfunctional – an obvious reference to CSC, although he never formally made mention of the institution for which he worked.

On February 7, 1986, CSC commissioner Rhéal LeBlanc wrote that CSC was "at a crossroads." A new set of political and economic realities meant there would be major changes in the way CSC operated. In March 1988, the results of a $200,000 eighteen-month study of inmates in ten federal institutions in Ontario were published. Funded by the federal solicitor general's office, Edward Zambie, a Queen's University psychologist and professor, interviewed prisoners when they were first incarcerated, four months later, and then a year later. The study began with 133 men, but the numbers dropped to 98 by the third interview.

Zambie and his co-author, Frank Porporino, a senior researcher at CSC headquarters, also published a book called *Coping, Behaviour and Adaptation in Prison Inmates*, which examined what happens to people the first time they go to prison. The authors concluded that prisons were "practically useless" when it came to reforming criminal behaviour. They found that inmates were people who did not respond properly to problems either in society or in prisons. They committed criminal offences because they saw them as solutions to life's ordinary problems. Inmates struggled to survive in prison just as they had struggled to survive on the outside.

Zambie and Porporino compared prison to a "deep freeze," where criminals suspend criminal or anti-social behaviour until they get out. Contrary to the myth that imprisonment has a disastrous effect on inmates, the authors found that even though prisoners experience stress when they are first incarcerated, most adapt within a few months: "The Canadian federal prison system is really pretty good as a prison system, but, at the same time, it's practically useless at reforming prisoners."

The best chance to change criminal behaviour came at the end of the sentence, when intensive counselling could help former inmates apply newly learned behaviours to the outside world, or

at the beginning, when the shock of imprisonment opened a window of opportunity. Zambie and Porporino suggested new prison programs that would go beyond the basic life skills then offered, to include short-term problem solving and long-term planning and organization.

Canada's prisons were full to bursting, but the federal government did not want to start building new penitentiaries to accommodate the rising inmate populations. Despite the tinkering of a handful of liberal thinkers, everyone who worked within the prison system knew that either judges would have to hand out shorter sentences or the National Parole Board would have to release inmates sooner and hope that the public didn't suffer the consequences.

The politicians opted for the latter option, candy-coated with a new philosophy based on the unproven notion that inmates would do better serving part or all of their sentences beyond prison walls. After a year of study, a Commons committee looking into the criminal justice system concluded that prisons should be reserved for those who committed the most serious crimes, because prisons were too expensive to operate and did little to rehabilitate criminals or reduce the crime rate.

The committee's report, published August 30, 1988, recommended greater use of community service, probation, and victim-offender reconciliation. Like the Canadian Bar Association, the committee endorsed electronic monitoring for non-violent offenders. Headed by Conservative MP David Daubney, it made one hundred recommendations, including better programs for natives and women. With rising bills that no one wanted to incur, incarceration was losing favour as the principal means of dealing with the country's criminals.

After a two-year stint as chairman of the National Parole Board, from May 1986 to June 1988, Ole Ingstrup was appointed CSC commissioner on June 13, 1988. He immediately began putting his European policies into practice in Canada. Faced with serious overcrowding (394 federal inmates were double-bunked in Ontario

alone), CSC began to consider the construction of another medium-security prison or the earlier release of non-violent inmates.

As always, CSC's liberal policies were occasionally tempered by spectacular failures in early-release experimentation. Tighter release rules were imposed, for example, after Melvin Stanton, convicted of three rapes and a murder, walked away from a North Toronto halfway house where he was on a forty-eight-hour pass and raped and murdered twenty-five-year-old Tema Conter on January 27, 1988. Another of Stanton's rapes had taken place ten years earlier when he was on day parole.

At a meeting in Ottawa in early June 1988 called by the inter-church Council on Justice and Corrections to discuss sentencing reform, the position taken by many in attendance was that crime is an offence against people, not the law. Sentencing should not be about imposing sanctions to promote respect for the law; rather, it should be concerned with restoring broken community relationships, something it was argued that prison simply didn't do. In fact, participants argued that imprisoning poor and unemployed people who committed crimes merely temporarily warehoused the offenders and further alienated them from society.

The modern liberal theory of criminology and penology is that most people who commit crimes are themselves victims – of poverty, abuse, addiction, or racism – and are therefore not really responsible for their behaviour. One mustn't punish the criminal but reform him. Seven out of ten offenders, for example, have a serious problem with drugs or alcohol, and over half are behind bars because of crimes related to substance abuse. So if enough appropriate programs are offered, offenders will eventually see the error of their ways and become different people. It is a theory that has little time for the neo-conservative view that it is the offender, not society, who must assume responsibility for his actions and that retributive justice is an important part not only of correcting criminal behaviour but of demonstrating to the rest of society that felons pay for their crimes.

Although academics and administrators within CSC wanted to release more offenders earlier, they faced a very suspicious public. In fact, by the late 1980s Canadians were alarmed by the early release of so many dangerous offenders. A spate of spectacular disasters had undermined public confidence in the parole system. The examples seemed absurd. Edmonton serial rapist Larry Takahashi was given escorted temporary absences to play golf only five years after receiving three life sentences for a series of vicious assaults against seven women. James Sweeney, a murderer and sexual sadist, raped and murdered a twenty-one-year-old halfway house worker named Celia Ruygrok in 1985.

The public was also alarmed at high-profile escapes. Daniel Gringas, a murderer, escaped while on a birthday pass to West Edmonton Mall in 1987 by overpowering his unarmed escort. Guards at the main gate of Edmonton Institution had challenged the warden about letting Gringas out on the pass but were ordered to release him. Gringas killed two people and was at large for fifty-seven days. CSC censored the official report of this bloody fiasco. Allan Légère, known as the Monster of Miramichi for a string of rapes and murders in New Brunswick, escaped in 1989 while on his way to hospital. He raped and murdered three women and beat a priest to death.

Powerful institutions like CSC routinely control public access to information to deflect criticism. At the April 1987 Ontario provincial inquest into the murder of Celia Ruygrok, Ontario's chief coroner, Dr. Ross Bennett, criticized the federal government for trying to use intimidation to limit damning evidence. Sweeney had murdered Ruygrok while he was on parole for a similar mutilation-murder in 1975. Before he sent the jury out to consider recommendations, Bennett said, "From day one, I think it was obvious Corrections had blown it and were not going to admit it. I think efforts were made at the outset of this to keep records confidential." Throughout the five-week inquest, lawyers for the NPB and CSC had maintained that a provincial inquiry had no constitutional right to question the workings of federally

appointed agencies. In other words, public institutions argued that they were above accountability.

Public controversy over killings by parolees led to the demand for meaningful guidelines and turned a searchlight on Canada's secretive prison system. Many NPB members were part-time patronage appointees rather than justice professionals. It was an odd situation: guards were supposed to get better training and education to handle the job of supervising prisoners, but the government was using amateurs to decide which dangerous criminals would get parole.

On March 1, 1988, Ingstrup, as chairman of the National Parole Board, had sent a memo to all NPB members that for the first time laid out formal guidelines to be taken into account in parole decisions. Essentially, more paperwork would have to be done before inmates' cases were heard by the parole board. Although the NPB decides whether to release a prisoner, it is CSC that provides the board with the information used to make the decision. CSC develops the Correctional Plan, which is "the basis on which release is predicated. It is the basis upon which discretionary release is either supported or denied . . . by the NPB." Despite CSC's often stated claim that the parole board decides who gets out of prison, CSC is chief puppeteer to the board's marionette.

Although the workload increased for CSC classification officers in the wake of Ingstrup's reforms, there was no new funding. Under the new guidelines, the NPB could not proceed with hearings unless all the reports on inmates were available. The parole board now also had to read police reports of the crimes committed by the inmates. Over the next year the controversy and new guidelines slowed down the parole hearing process, creating a backlog at the NPB and even greater tensions inside the country's prisons.

The same month the new guidelines were issued, John Hill, the director of the Queen's University Correctional Law Project, stepped in to help inmate Ross William Evans, the first inmate in Canada to be denied mandatory release after serving two-thirds of his sentence. The NPB had refused to release him because it considered him too dangerous. At a second hearing, Hill

convinced the board to release Evans to a Toronto halfway house. Evans walked away and immediately raped a thirty-year-old woman at knifepoint.

In a desperate effort to restore confidence in the prison system, Tory solicitor general James Kelleher proposed sweeping reforms to the parole system in July 1988, including a stipulation that all federal prisoners serve half their sentences, rather than one-third, before becoming eligible for parole. Kelleher consulted broadly with interest groups, the public, and provincial attorneys general before abandoning his plans. Graham Stewart of the John Howard Society labelled Kelleher's proposal "obscene" and accused the minister of trying to score political points by exploiting the public's fears about crime. Kelleher later amended his proposal to apply only to violent offenders. But he had no stomach to take on prisoners' rights groups. In early August 1988, he told an international conference on sentencing, parole, and early release, "Canadians are telling me that they are prepared to give non-violent offenders an early opportunity to redeem themselves." Kelleher lost his seat in the November 1988 election and was replaced as solicitor general by Perrin Beatty.

While many people wanted to close halfway houses and get tough with inmates, the new commissioner of CSC pressed ahead with his mission statement, which stressed the need to reintegrate offenders as soon as possible. Although Ingstrup knew how to handle politicians and bureaucrats, there was a power struggle within CSC at the prison level over the old and new philosophies. The move toward a European-style prison system imposed on very different North American realities was a hard sell behind the prison walls. But Ingstrup provided only part of the impetus for this momentous change. The Charter of Rights made it inevitable that prisoners' rights groups would press for greater and greater freedoms for inmates in Canada. And as one former colleague of Ingstrup put it, the commissioner was an "astute" reader of the impact the Charter would have on the operations of the CSC.

The CSC "Mission," as it was called with an almost religious fervour, was approved at a famous meeting in Banff in 1988. It was a huge tome that laid down what the system would do for the inmate in great detail, while remaining silent on what the inmate had to do for society as a result of his having committed crimes. The total absence of such obligations did not go unnoticed by some of the most experienced executives in CSC. As Tom Epp puts it, "There's very little there that talks about what obligations the citizen as offender has. And that's where I part company with [Ingstrup] because we were running places where one would think that . . . in the crucible of corrections, there's a number of things that come into play. One is, of course, what we will do for offenders to heal them, to make them whole, to get them to see the errors of their ways. Pick a word – paternalism, teacher, rehabilitator, assister, facilitator, ass-kicker, whatever – but you've got to pour into that mix something that they bring to the trans-action, which is the will to change, the will to participate. What we found at every turn was that as Ingstrup got more and more established, he was looking at policies, changing policies around visiting, around searching, around other things that conveyed this notion that anything we can do for the offender to return them in a productive way to society we'll do. But we have very little to say about the onus of the offender to play in that game. And that bothered me because – well, I just think it's flawed thinking."

There are five "core values" included in the mission. One: "We respect the dignity of individuals, the rights of all members of society, and the potential for human growth and development." Two: "We recognize that the offender has the potential to live as a law-abiding citizen." Three: "We believe that our strength and our major resource in achieving our objectives is our staff and that human relationships are the cornerstone of our endeavour." Four: "We believe that the sharing of ideas, knowledge, values and experience, nationally and internationally, is essential to the achievement of our Mission." Five: "We believe in managing

the Service with openness and integrity and we are accountable to the Solicitor General."

Ingstrup's mission statement was rolled into the Corrections and Conditional Release Act (CCRA), the law that governs Canada's prison system. Proclaimed in November 1992, it replaced two previous pieces of legislation, the Penitentiary Act and the Parole Act, and made fundamental changes to the way CSC operates. One purpose of the mission is to give direction to CSC employees: "It offers practical guidance for today and inspiration for meeting the challenges of tomorrow." It is also the CSC's constitution, defining the management of the organization as well as the management of offenders in its care. The mission is based on the principle that offenders retain all their rights, except for those expressly removed or restricted as a result of their sentence.

Commissioner Ingstrup liked to have his ministers, parole officers, program officers, and unit managers sign his mission statement, which first came into effect in February 1989. Every solicitor general from Pierre Blais to Lawrence MacAulay added his endorsement to the document. It was a quasi-religious act, a kind of initiation into Ole's World, and the commissioner constantly quoted from the mission statement as a parson in an earlier age might have quoted from the Scriptures.

Under Ingstrup, CSC carefully created a culture in which staff work within a framework of shared values. "We're supposed to act like Moonies," one guard says. "Follow the leader, no matter what's really happening inside." There is no doubt about the group-think imposed from Ottawa. According to the report of the Task Force on Security, chaired by Helgi Eyjolfsson, director of general security for CSC, "Managers and staff must live by the values enunciated in our Mission in carrying out their responsibilities."

In addition to the CCRA, there are regulations, commissioner's directives, institutional standing orders, post orders, and policy manuals – a veritable thicket of regulation ostensibly aimed at preserving public safety while using the least restrictive options on convicted offenders to accomplish that. It is poorly understood

that the CSC does not simply administer a sentence imposed by the courts. It also works to rehabilitate inmates and wields tremendous influence over how long they remain behind bars, even though it is technically up to the parole board to grant early release.

At the same time as Ingstrup's European model was being imposed on North American offenders whose criminal careers didn't rest on bicycle theft, inmates and prisoners' rights groups were mounting a whole range of court challenges over various alleged rights, including the right to vote and the right to have conjugal visits with people other than spouses. It was a highly successful campaign, ending in legal decisions that prohibited or restricted the right of CSC to strip-search for drugs or impose widespread urinalysis testing as a means of fighting drug use. At an inquest into the death of a Collins Bay inmate, Dennis Lepik, from a heroin overdose in 1990, one witness testified that over a ten-year period, she had successfully smuggled drugs into federal institutions eighty-five times, most often by wrapping them in a condom and "hooping" them.

Critics of the rights campaign fumed over the fact that funding and support for these inmate-friendly court challenges came from Ottawa's Court Challenges Program and other taxpayer-funded programs. The Charter of Rights had wide-ranging implications for CSC, which had a lawyer review thirty-five thousand pages of CSC directives and other documents to ensure that they did not conflict with it. Searches, transfers, the monitoring of inmate calls, and a host of other practices were all examined to see if they conflicted with the new legislation.

The most famous user of Canada's taxpayer-funded court challenge system was Clifford Olson, the serial killer who was convicted in 1982 of the brutal murders of eleven children, ages nine to eighteen. He sued the warden of Kingston Pen seventeen times over various perceived injustices, including the fact that he was locked up in segregation twenty-three hours a day for his own protection. Olson argued that this was cruel and unusual punishment, and the Supreme Court agreed to hear his case in 1989. His

victims' families planned a protest over Olson's hearing. The same court had turned down the bid by the families to overturn the $100,000 cash-for-bodies deal between Olson and the RCMP, which led police to the final resting places of the killer's victims.

Although funding existed for prisoners to challenge the system, the criminal justice system was losing funding to catch and incarcerate them. When the Tories slashed government spending in the November 1990 budget, for example, CSC lost $14 million of its $900-million budget, and the RCMP lost $13.9 million of its $1.1-billion budget.

After Ingstrup's first four-year stint as head of CSC from 1988 to 1992, John Edwards became commissioner. (From 1992 to 1995, Ingstrup was principal of the Canadian Centre for Management Development, then a senior adviser to the Privy Council Office. He was reappointed CSC commissioner in 1996 by the Chrétien government.) Mentored by Ingstrup, Edwards was also a reformer who strongly supported alternatives to prison. He believed that rehabilitation was more successful in the community than it was in prison. As to those who had to be imprisoned because they were dangerous, Edwards thought that prisons should teach them how to maintain good relationships with people in an environment that was as close to the outside world as possible – in effect, give prisoners the "socialization" they had never received in the outside world. Canada was becoming an elephant-sized Denmark as the reformers pressed on with their agenda of liberalization.

Despite his agreement with Ole Ingstrup's mission statement, John Edwards realized that the document needed modifications to catch up with the reality in the prisons, including an embarrassing number of "walk-aways" from the low-security institutions in the system. Edwards formed a working group of the CSC executive committee to shorten and revise the mission statement, a decision that was supported by all the members of the working group with the exception of Pierre Allard, a Baptist minister who was one of Ole Ingstrup's closest friends. Despite Allard's dissent, the working group spent a year revising the mission statement with the help of

parole and correctional officials from across the country. When the work was done, the proposed changes were approved by the executive committee. Solicitor General Herb Gray approved the changes with the caveat that they had to be administered "while respecting the rule of law." All that was left to do was make the formal announcement of the new mission statement, which diluted some of the "statist" or big-government elements of the old document and spelled out the onus on offenders to accept their responsibilities in the rehabilitation process.

But it was not to be. In 1996, after being reappointed CSC commissioner, Ole Ingstrup showed up at the penultimate meeting of the executive committee's working group, across from CSC headquarters at 340 Laurier Street. Tom Epp, a member of the committee, remembers the demeanour of the commissioner when he was presented with the proposed changes to his original mission statement, which had been cleverly included in the act of Parliament, the CCRA, that covers the correctional service.

"He comes to this meeting, and we hear about his anger about what's happened there, and what an awful thing it was and how his vision had been sullied. We started briefing him on what we had done, and you can tell right away he's not buying what we are telling him. Some of us are born to speak our mind. So I look around the room and no one was going to say the obvious, so I said, 'Commissioner, this document has been in revision for a year. It reflects everything I told you earlier in terms of consultation and input and the key changes.' I went over all that. I said, 'It's been approved by your executive. We feel strongly that this is a more balanced document than the original one.' . . . He made some vague response which suggested that he wasn't buying it. Then he said something to the effect that he was going to ask Pierre Allard to assist him in reviewing it. And that was the end of it that morning. We sputtered and fiddled around in the afternoon on the thing, but we all sensed it was in his hands."

Two weeks later, Tom Epp made one final stab at defending the revision of the original mission statement. While Ole Ingstrup

looked on, unmoved by Epp's arguments, one of his lieutenants, Brendan Reynolds, went after Epp. "I asked the question, what's to become of the mission revisions? And I repeated my argument. Stupid," Epp recalls. "And of course all of a sudden it was really interesting: I'm arguing with Wayne Gretzky and suddenly I've got Dave Semenko in my face. Brendan Reynolds, the self-appointed policeman, has now taken me on, and the Danish prince was sitting up there, not having to do anything. Suddenly I realized the game in town. So I lost. I'm sitting in the room looking at all my former friends. We had been at this table together for two years. Nobody says a goddamned thing. And I'm thinking, 'Boy, you guys are stupid.'"

Epp, who had long observed that one went to executive meetings with Ole Ingstrup to be "edified, not to participate," applied for a job outside of headquarters and was told he could be a lead investigator within CSC working out of Kingston, whenever it was "administratively convenient" to make the move. He was happy to exchange the realm of the philosopher king for the dark calamities of the prison system. "I'm doing something that's very focused, like train wrecks and rock slides and unhappiness, murders and suicides and escapes, as sort of the permanent chair of national investigations for eastern Canada. It was a relief."

At a meeting of CSC assistant deputy commissioners held in June 1998 at William Head Institution in Victoria, one of the subjects recorded in the notes of the meeting had to do with spreading the commissioner's vision. "The Commissioner wants all staff to read his speeches and those of the Minister. The EA–ACCOP [Executive Assistant–Assistant Commissioner Correctional Operations and Programming] will discuss with Communications the need to get the Commissioner's speeches on the Intranet sooner."

As for his live performances, many of which were taped for posterity, there was not much Ingstrup's colleagues could do but listen to two-hour doctrinal dirges. Tom Epp recalls: "Ole's blindness was just simply believing that because he said it, it was true and

we'd accept it. Adult education at its root doesn't work that way. Adults learn by doing, by believing, by participating. They don't like to be lectured. We would react as any caged group with no way to the exits would act. You have no power, what the hell can you do? Some submit stoically, some snigger behind their hands; human behaviour is multi-faceted. But the one thing in common was that people just accepted it. It was probably like sitting through one of Castro's two-cigar speeches. You are stuck – you just hope your bladder holds out."

The increasingly imperial style of the commissioner was less easily ignored than his speeches. Despite budget cuts to maximum-security facilities like Kingston Penitentiary, the commissioner and his Ontario deputy found themselves on the front pages of the country's newspapers for spending $200,000 on international travel over a three-year period.

Ingstrup's personal travel bill for 1998-1999 was over $71,000. His fifty-one days of foreign travel included two visits to his native Denmark as well as trips to London, New Orleans, Israel, Orlando, Detroit, Bermuda, the Persian Gulf, Lithuania, and France. His expenses included a $1,507 dinner for twenty-two, a relative bargain compared with the feasting on the *Bernier*. The commissioner also spent $4 million on a seven-seat Swiss-built Pelatus aircraft, ostensibly to transport high-risk inmates in the Ontario and Quebec regions to other institutions. That way, these inmates would not suffer the inconvenience of having to wait for one of the RCMP's thirty planes to transport them. (Low-risk prisoners fly on commercial airlines.)

In April 1999, in a "protected" twenty-six-page draft cost-benefit analysis that CSC used to justify the acquisition, bureaucrats claimed that "confidential meetings" could be held on the plane while management travelled in a group. The plane would also enable CSC to fly delegations from other countries into state-of-the-art federal correctional facilities such as Okimaw Ohci, Pê Sâkâstêw,

and Fenbrook. But despite CSC's best attempts to justify buying the aircraft, there was no changing the bottom line: a mere one-third of the single-engine Pelatus's air time would be dedicated to inmate transportation; the other two-thirds was for the travel of senior CSC management. The Canadian public had essentially purchased a private plane for CSC brass.

One sentence jumped out of CSC's attempt to justify the purchase of the Pelatus. "With [an] expected increase in violent offenders profile, continued transportation of inmates on commercial airlines could become a costly and public safety issue." Exactly what the bureaucrats meant is unclear, but if CSC officials knew that there was going to be an increase in violent offenders, they certainly weren't talking about it. From 1979 to 1997, the proportion of offenders who were imprisoned for non-violent offences dropped from 32 per cent to 12 per cent. According to CSC statistics, in 1997, 80 per cent of offenders actually in institutions were incarcerated for violent crimes.

One victims' rights advocate, Steve Sullivan, was so disturbed by news of the intended purchase that he wrote to the solicitor general: "One cannot help but wonder how many more rehabilitative programs that $4 million could pay for, or how many more psychologists or teachers. It is ironic how victims of crime must often beg for public support to attend parole hearings, while their assailants may now have their own plane."

The commissioner also authorized spending $78,000 for a glossy millennium calendar that was given to federal prisoners, parolees, guards, and parole officers as a public education exercise. Ingstrup was so incensed by the negative coverage he was getting in the press for the first time in his career that on January 11, 2000, he sent a long memo to all CSC managers and union executives concerning stories published by the Sun Media chain. In his view, the stories presented "a very negative and distorted view of CSC, and myself as the Commissioner."

The headline on a January 8, 2000 story by Alain Cairns in the *Toronto Sun* was "Prison Boss Ingstrup Out of Control." The

article claimed that CSC had a $70-million deficit, $50 million of it at headquarters in Ottawa. As usual, Ingstrup could not be reached for public comment. But in a letter to CSC managers the commissioner wrote: "I find these articles distressing, not only because they are a personal attack on my leadership, but also because they make allegations which are absolutely false." Regarding reports that CSC was facing a deficit at the end of the 1999-2000 year, "That is simply not true," wrote the commissioner.

According to Ingstrup, there had been no reduction in the fixed allocations that the regions had received at the beginning of the year. But that was not the whole story: "However, as a result of extensive financial review earlier this year," the commissioner wrote, "we became aware that some regions were in danger of coming in over budget, largely due to unexpectedly high overtime payments. We took immediate and decisive actions to rectify this situation. As a result, I can inform you today that every Regional Deputy Commissioner and Sector Head has assured me in writing that they will come in on budget, without compromising the safety and security of Canadians, CSC staff, or offenders." The words were comforting but the reality was not. How does an organization that blames deficits on overtime payments make cutbacks in staffing without affecting security?

As Cairns had reported, there was a deficit, and CSC managers across the system were scrambling to deal with it. In fact, a memo entitled "Recent Budget Restrictions" was sent to KP staff on December 9, 1999: "This week the following measures were put in place in the Ontario Region to assist in off setting the Ontario Region deficit of $6.5 million. The 15 cost-cutting measures put in place included: #8 – 'Institutions are to review minimum staffing procedures' and #10 – A review of all casual and term positions (non CX) is to be conducted at all institutions for potential terminations effective January 1." In 2000, nine correctional officers at KP were laid off. In the midst of budget deficits, Commissioner Ingstrup drew fresh fire from opposition MPs for allegedly preparing to spend millions of taxpayers' dollars over

what they saw as a major exercise in empire building: Ingstrup's proposed International Institute for Correctional Excellence.

On the morning of January 7, 1998, there had been a "brainstorming" session in the fourth-floor boardroom at CSC headquarters to gather ideas for the new institute. The discussion was chaired by the commissioner himself. Nineteen CSC officials, including Assistant Commissioner Joe Price and Senior Deputy Commissioner Lucie McClung, were invited to "please bring your good ideas to the table." Two months later, Ingstrup's brainchild had been christened and kick-started. The International Institute for Correctional Excellence was the first new order of business on the agenda of a second meeting at CSC headquarters. "The Commissioner noted that his Millennium Initiative to establish an International Institute for Correctional Excellence is currently being managed by different sectors within CSC, and that it would be important to bring cohesion to the process and to work as a team to ensure the success of this project."

By March 4, a draft of a discussion paper was ready to be presented at the First International Round Table for Correctional Excellence, a component of a conference called Beyond Prisons, being held in Kingston later that month. The proposed new institute would be based in Ottawa and would function as a non-profit international organization paid for by Canadian taxpayers. Its mission statement grandly declared: "The International Institute for Correctional Excellence will contribute together with partners, agencies, jurisdictions and individuals to the protection of society and global peace by actively improving correctional management and practices around the world."

Beneath all the rhetorical helium, the facts were considerably plainer. The institute would be a vehicle for spreading CSC's current philosophy of corrections around the world at the expense of taxpayers, despite the fact that inmates in Canadian jails had a higher standard of living than the citizens of many Third World countries. A corrections system that didn't have the money to put guards in towers or provide them with hot lunches was willing to

seek major public funding to promote the notion that locking criminals up was an antiquated idea.

A draft proposal for the institute was presented at the Beyond Prisons conference, which was attended by a hundred delegates from forty countries. Kingston had been hard hit by the January 1998 ice storm, and Commissioner Ingstrup opened the conference with a comment that acknowledged the growing public criticism that CSC policies were beginning to generate: "It's a lot safer to talk about the weather than it is to talk about criminal justice policy." But he was undeterred in his correctional evangelism, as he showed in a quote from the anthropologist Margaret Mead: "Never doubt that a small group of thoughtful, committed people can change the world. Indeed it's the only thing that ever has." Ingstrup told the audience that they were there to learn "what is known about the excessive use of incarceration as a response to crime. . . . We are here to move beyond prisons." It was a forum not so much to exchange ideas as to export them.

In a letter of April 1, 1998, to Alex Himelfarb, deputy secretary of the Treasury Board Secretariat, Ingstrup wrote: "Through its establishment, the institute would meet a number of policy objectives of the Government of Canada. It would, among others, increase Canada's international profile as a 'big legacy' project, in keeping with one of the major areas outlined in the Government's Millennium initiative. As well, it would serve as a vehicle to help promote Canadian public sector expertise abroad. It would also be completely consistent with a number of our foreign policy positions, such as those related to good governance, sustainable development and the projection of Canadian values."

Every detail of navigating the funding process was carefully dealt with. CSC retained John McLure, senior vice-president of Hill & Knowlton Canada Limited, a public relations firm with experience in the development and operation of national and international organizations. His task was to prepare the development plan for the international institute before CSC's proposal went up to the minister for final approval. McLure, a former deputy minister himself,

had worked on a number of high-profile international assignments and knew exactly what was needed. In a letter to Ingstrup, McLure said he required four full-time and five part-time members of Ingstrup's staff for the "IICE Task Force," as well as the co-operation of "all members of your organization." The task force would also, of course, require guidance from the commissioner from time to time.

A draft memo was prepared for Ingstrup to send to senior members of Treasury Board. It said that there had been unanimous agreement among the forty countries represented at the Kingston conference "that Canada should play a leadership role in establishing a global partnership." The memo boasted, "This is an overwhelming acknowledgement of Canada's reputation in the field of corrections around the world, and a tribute to all employees of CSC."

Suddenly, however, after months of planning, staffing, lobbying, and spending, the IICE disappeared from the bureaucratic radar screen of CSC in late 1998. Two things had happened. Word had begun to leak out in official Ottawa that the institute would cost Canadians $50 million, enraging critics of the CSC and putting Commissioner Ingstrup on the defensive. Second, Solicitor General Andy Scott was forced to resign after an indiscreet conversation he had held on an airplane was reported to Parliament by an NDP MP from the Maritimes.

A new solicitor general was sworn in. A small-C conservative from Prince Edward Island, Lawrence MacAulay may have been moved less by his commissioner's promise of "world peace" through the IICE than by the more homespun conviction that CSC's real job was to keep dangerous felons behind bars.

In place of the institute, CSC created the International Corrections and Prisons Association (ICPA), a vastly scaled-down version of the IICE that would cost Canadians $528,000 to set up. Jennifer Oades became the executive director of the ICPA. She had been the lead policy analyst on an initiative called Corrections Population Growth, a project designed to reduce Canada's "over-reliance on incarceration." The mission statement of the ICPA echoed the

grandiose aim of its doomed forerunner. It would be an international forum to share ideas about correctional systems and best practices with those forty countries that had once been in favour of the IICE.

When criticized for its empire building, CSC again claimed that "Canada was asked by the international corrections community to take the lead in organizing a forum to help countries to share ideas." No mention was made of the fact that the commissioner and his inner circle had been planning the institute two months before the international corrections community even gathered in Kingston. And there was another problem with the claim that other countries had pressed Canada to create the new institute. In a speech he gave in Vancouver on October 18, 1998, to the Eighteenth Annual Asian and Pacific Conference of Correctional Administrators, Ingstrup himself said that he and a small group of international corrections academics and practitioners had met in Toronto earlier in the year, and "we decided to create an international association."

Less than impressed with Ingstrup's obfuscations about the roots and purpose of his international institute, opposition MPs attacked the commissioner for wasting public funds. The commissioner replied that his critics had been misled about the funding levels for his venture and were confusing the ICPA with an earlier "proposal" for the IICE. Reform (later Canadian Alliance) MP Myron Thompson, who believed the commissioner had simply misled the justice committee about his grandiose plans, called his explanation "pure nonsense." After all, how many international institutes could come out of the same conference?

Declaring his work complete, Ole Ingstrup announced his resignation on August 8, 2000. "There comes a time when you've done what you had to do in the public service," he said. Answering Ottawa's busy rumour mill, abuzz with the story that the career bureaucrat had worn out his welcome with the new solicitor general, Ingstrup pronounced his stewardship of CSC a success: "I have thirty-five years in the public service behind me,

and I'm satisfied with the work we've done. . . . There were no external factors."

The outgoing commissioner couldn't resist giving himself one more pat on the back for the revolution he had brought to Canadian corrections. "We have placed ourselves in the international community as a leader in the area of correctional services. It has been a delight to see how many people are rallying around our philosophy and how many other countries have sent visitors to view our facilities."

While correctional officers at Kingston Penitentiary were fighting to keep their cafeteria open, Ole Ingstrup spent his last two weeks in the job out of the country. He attended two international conferences in South Africa. First came the prison chaplains' conference in Kroonstad, and then it was off to Cape Town for a five-day annual general meeting of the International Corrections and Prisons Association in September 2000. Ole Ingstrup was its founding president.

Although the philosopher king had departed, the torch at CSC was passed to a loyal subject, his former senior deputy commissioner, Lucie McClung. McClung was one of the top-ranking guests on the Booze Cruise and the hands-on worker at headquarters who had transformed the commissioner's vision into reality. One of the former parole officer's first acts was to refuse interviews when her appointment became public. While inmate advocacy groups were delighted with McClung's appointment because it meant that there wouldn't be a "right-wing takeover" of CSC policy, Myron Thompson, his party's corrections critic, quipped, "We're getting the same old thing in a different package."

7

HIGHER AND HIGHER

It is the Canadian prison system's biggest lie. Despite Commissioner's Directive 585, which lays out CSC's zero-tolerance national drug strategy, literally every drug available on the street can be purchased in Canada's most secure prisons. Alcohol is also produced in large quantities, with no meaningful sanctions against its inmate brewmasters when they are caught. Illicit drugs and alcohol are a central driving force in the lives of inmates: they not only supply ways of escaping the deadening routine of doing time but also confer currency, collateral, and power on their dealers. Just as on the street, substance abuse in prison leads to violence and further crime.

Although no one knows the amount of alcohol and drugs consumed by federal inmates, the data on internal drug interdiction suggest it is huge: in 1999 alone, staff at federal prisons seized 2.2 kilograms of cocaine, 164 grams of opiates, 5.4 kilograms of cannabis, and 8,918 litres (1,962 gallons) of brew. One visitor at Kingston Penitentiary was arrested with a quantity of Dilaudid, a highly addictive narcotic painkiller, worth an estimated $51,000 on the street.

The profit on prison drugs is enormous, with markups commonly up to 300 per cent and sometimes even higher, depending on the classic forces of supply and demand. A single hit of heroin can cost $50, and inmates never know with certainty the strength of the drug they are taking. Their only security is the assumption, sometimes unfounded, that dealers are not in the business of killing their customers. Most of the drugs are paid for by transactions that take place on the street, the proceeds going into outside bank accounts belonging to inmates.

"Ninety per cent of it is outside the walls," one intelligence officer says. "We find lists of bank accounts all the time. On the street, one con's visitor will contact another visitor's wife – that type of thing, and they set up the transaction. Usually it's simple. They meet at a McDonald's somewhere, the money is exchanged, or a bank account number is exchanged. . . . A lot of these inmates have a lot of money in bank accounts on the street, waiting to get out – I mean hundreds of thousands of dollars when it comes to the Jamaican and Asian gangs. We find records of drug debts too. A lot of times you find sheets of gambling debts. The cons are getting smart, though; they are now putting all these on disks and encrypting them. There are some smart computer guys, inmate-wise, inside."

Drug use is as staggering as its consequences. From August 1998 to August 1999, 15 per cent of the total inmate population of 230 at one federal institution in Ontario were hospitalized after taking various kinds of intoxicants. There were also thirty-eight violent disturbances, during which forty inmates and six officers were injured. Drugs and alcohol, used separately and in combination, spark almost all serious prison violence.

Shortly after a major retrofit at Kingston Penitentiary in 1996, inmates went on a rampage, destroying thousands of dollars worth of the renovations. Since officers are rarely authorized to use force to stop property destruction, they stood by and watched helplessly until the pill- and alcohol-induced frenzy played itself out. "If you

get the wrong inmates into the brew, mixing it with pills, the repercussions are unbelievable," one of the guards present at the riot says. "Whole ranges have been destroyed. Like the one range, Upper E. They smashed all the windows, it was just after the retrofit. CSC put drywall up on the ranges. They ripped all the drywall out. There was about $80,000 in damages by the time they were done."

Public property isn't the only casualty. In September 2000 a coroner's jury ruled that a Millhaven inmate, Lawrence Stocking, had died of an accidental heroin overdose. As R. Jeff Anderson, a Justice Department lawyer, put it in his closing address to the jury, Stocking "chose to go on a little trip that day and he didn't come back." Stocking, a contract killer who was serving a life sentence for first-degree murder, had been transferred from Joyceville to Millhaven after he threatened another inmate. In November 1998, he injected a high-purity dose of heroin. In the wake of Stocking's apparently accidental death, the jury recommended that CSC "continue to employ strong deterrents" to drug use in prison. It was a strange choice of words. The current maximum fine for drug trafficking while in federal custody is $50, a negligible cost of doing business, given the profit margins involved. Usually the penalty is only a short-term loss of privileges, and often drug violations aren't even written up. "Staff shall ensure that reasonable steps are taken to resolve matters informally, whenever possible," according to CD 585.

Prisoners find clever ways to hide their drugs. Guards at Collins Bay found a hundred grams of heroin in the base of an inmate's fan in June 1998. A syringe was discovered in the removable lining of a small wooden box in his cell. The heroin problem became so great in places like Kingston Pen that the institution was locked down in August 2000 for an "exceptional search" of every cell and work area, following a series of drug-related disturbances. Three inmates in the Kingston area had died of suspected heroin overdoses in just seventeen days: one at KP, a second at minimum-security Frontenac, and a third at Joyceville.

More drugs than usual had been getting in and inmate debts had mounted, destabilizing the institution. Although even an exceptional search does not allow an inspection of body cavities, each cell was checked and 402 inmates were taken to the showers for a strip search. The drug situation was so severe that authorities considered imposing closed visits on the entire prison for a thirty-day period to help dry up the heroin supply. But as one of the intelligence officers involved in the abortive project observed, the plan never got off the ground: "There was a rash of drug incidents in every institution across Canada. Mostly it was heroin. And so what happened was they quashed the closed visits idea because it was going to cause too many problems. They put a dollar figure on how much damage there would be to the institution, cons flipping out, staff overtime, the Emergency Response Team being used, all the investigations that would have to be done. They said this is going to cost us way too much money, so they quashed it."

There is no mystery about how massive amounts of illegal drugs find their way into supposedly secure penal institutions. In March 1999 a bulletin entitled *Say No to Drugs* was posted in the main visiting area of KP. "The level of drug activity at Kingston Penitentiary is very high," the bulletin read, "and our intelligence confirms that the vast majority of drugs are being introduced through visits."

In the case of PFVs (private family visits), the opportunities for drug smuggling are unmatched. In 1998, neither the doors nor the windows of the individual family units at KP where the visits take place had alarms. The fences separating the units could easily be scaled, allowing contraband to be passed back and forth at will. Inmates close to the units could manually pick up any drugs that were tossed over the fence.

Given the rampant drug use, in March 1999 management at KP decided that all inmates would be frisked when they went to visits and strip-searched when they returned. Drug violations would be reported to an inmate's parole officer. An inmate who was intoxicated would be reported to the officer in charge of his unit,

segregated, or placed under "house arrest" – confined to his cell. Visitors bringing in drugs would be severely dealt with.

It wasn't long before the public found out what that meant. Officials at KP learned from electronic surveillance of telephone calls that drugs would be coming into the institution during a visit with inmate Frank Horgen on October 29, 1999. As required, permission was sought from the warden to authorize the search of a visitor. Before such a search can be carried out, Commissioner's Directive 571 (about searches of persons) is read to the visitors, and forms must be filled out. The targets are then informed that correctional authorities have received information (often by anonymous phone calls) that they are carrying contraband and that a strip search needs to be done.

The visitors/smugglers are then told that refusal to submit to a search could result in cancelled or closed visits. They are also informed that a refusal does not necessarily mean that they are assumed to be guilty, and that they are free to voluntarily leave the institution. The suspected "mules," usually female, are then given time to think about their options. Visitors are not permitted to use the washroom prior to the search to prevent the suspected drugs from being flushed down the toilet. Drugs are frequently wrapped in cellophane and then a knotted condom before being hidden in a body cavity. A "cavity search" can be done only with the signed permission of the visitor and the head of the institution, and must be conducted by a doctor in the presence of a witness of the same sex as the subject being searched. Visitors must also give authorities a written consent before a strip search can be conducted. "The washroom in the V&C [Visits and Correspondence] area is used for intrusive searches if a visitor must be searched. The officers that work at V&C have been told, 'We've got it shoved so far up it, you'll never find it,'" one guard says.

"I'll give you an example of something I was involved in," a KP guard says. "We were called on an emergency to a PFV because there was a woman that was bleeding from her vagina. And they

thought it was an assault and whatnot. . . . We went with the woman in an ambulance to the hospital. The end result was she was bleeding from her vagina because she pulled drugs out of it and had ruptured something on the way out. They never searched the inmate, they never found the drugs. There was no charge, nothing. The trailer visit continued after that."

A Kingston woman, Sheryl Galway-Jones, was interviewed when she arrived in KP's visiting area to see Frank Horgen. Initially she denied any wrongdoing, but finally she admitted to having drugs secreted in a body cavity. A package containing seven grams of crack cocaine, sixty-two five-milligram tablets of Dilaudid, and thirty grams of marijuana was seized. In what guards describe as a "highly unusual" move, police were informed and Galway-Jones was charged, something that rarely happens when drugs are found on a non-inmate at a federal institution.

The thirty-four-year-old woman had met Horgen while doing volunteer work with the John Howard Society. Her lawyer, Stephen Zap, told the court that his client was a victim of strong-arm tactics by the prisoners. She had received an anonymous phone call the day before, telling her to pick up a package at the bus station and deliver it to the prison. If she refused, her caller warned, Horgen would be assaulted or killed.

In June 2000, Galway-Jones pleaded guilty to bringing the drugs into KP and apologized for her actions. After assuring the court that it would never happen again, she was sentenced to six months' house arrest, during which she could not leave her home between 6:00 p.m. and 7:00 a.m. During working hours, she was allowed out only for medical reasons or to buy groceries. She would also have to perform seventy-five hours of community service and be placed on probation for nine months. When he sentenced Galway-Jones, Mr. Justice Rommel Masse said, "Now if somebody asks you to pick up a package at the bus station, you know better."

A lot of drugs also make their way into prison on the persons of inmates returning from temporary absences, as in the case of Paul Roger of Archambault Institution in Sainte-Anne-des-Plaines,

Quebec. After his return from an outside visit with family, Roger was placed in a dry cell to see if he had suitcased drugs in his body. The next morning, Roger presented the intelligence officer on duty with two condoms containing a total of sixty-six grams of marijuana. Charges were laid and the inmate was placed in segregation without any further penalty.

When another offender was transferred from the Regional Reception Centre to Archambault Institution, his personal effects were searched and authorities discovered 104 grams of hashish hidden in the soles of his running shoes. His penalty? A short trip to segregation.

One former inmate claims to know of an offender who actually took down the drug orders of other inmates before he went out on his Christmas Day pass. At the time, in 1992, hashish and tranquilizers like Valium and Seconal were the most prevalent drugs on his range, although crack cocaine was also making its debut. Inmates got to know which guards were easy on the "dopers" and then used drugs openly during their shifts. There is no doubt in this inmate's mind that the system knew about and tolerated drug use. "They don't mind a few guys on their range sleeping all afternoon. It makes it less tense. Fewer fights," he says. "Fewer demands from those doped-up inmates and less of a custodial problem." And no rehabilitation.

On November 24, 1999, numerous pills were found in the cell of a Matsqui Institution inmate. During a strip search while he was being processed for administrative segregation, staff found a package in the pocket of the inmate's sweatpants. Three inches long and one inch wide, the package was wrapped in three separate condoms, cellophane, and toilet paper. It had seven flaps of paper containing a white powder that proved to be heroin.

David Proulx arrived at Leclerc Institution in Laval, Quebec, on December 6, 1999, after his parole was suspended. An intelligence officer had received information that Proulx would be bringing drugs into the institution. The inmate denied the allegations but refused to go to an outside hospital for X-rays, so he

was placed in a dry cell. He requested a change of clothing and was observed throwing a package into the laundry bin, which staff retrieved. It contained forty-five grams of hashish.

At 19:30 on December 19, 1999, an officer in Tower 2 at Leclerc noticed three inmates in an unusual area of the exercise yard. The officer contacted the mobile patrol, which recovered a baseball-like object on the ground near the outside fence. It contained eight-five grams of hashish.

Inmate socials are another favourite way to get drugs into a prison. Socials are held several times a year at most federal prisons. Inmates and approved visitors, including children, take part in the party-like events, which include barbecues, games, and entertainment. Normal security is suspended. When, for example, an inmate has an open visit in the V&C area, he is observed at close proximity by correctional officers. Inmates understand they can also be recorded by audio or video, and may be strip-searched after a visit. But at socials, inmates have access to a large area inside and outside the prison building away from the vigilant eyes of custodial staff.

Such a social was held on Saturday, June 24, 2000, at Joyceville Institution. Provincial police were on hand to screen the seventy-two visitors. But even with the assistance of a drug dog borrowed from Canada Customs, it was impossible to search everyone. (According to a CSC document, only "passive" dogs are used; they are trained to point from a distance to indicate the presence of narcotics.) Visitors suspected of carrying drugs were asked to submit to a search. Eleven were denied entry on suspicion of trying to smuggle drugs into the social after they refused the search.

The medium-security prison had 427 inmates that weekend. At 19:50 on Sunday evening, inmate Paul Iwaszczenco, age thirty-one, serving four years for robbery, was found in his cell coughing up blood. Believed to be suffering from a drug overdose, the unconscious inmate was taken to Kingston General Hospital, where his condition was upgraded from critical to guarded. Two hours later, another inmate on the same cellblock was found unconscious

in his cell. John Paul Bolyantu, age thirty-eight, was serving twenty-eight months for possession and trafficking. Bolyantu wasn't as lucky as Iwaszczenco. He died of a suspected drug overdose on his way to hospital.

The Ontario Provincial Police Penitentiary Squad suspected that bad drugs had been smuggled into the prison during the social, and four drug dogs were taken inside to conduct a search. Reports indicated that morphine was the likely cause of the overdoses. A 1998 survey of Joyceville inmates found that 24 per cent used intravenous drugs in prison, with a quarter of those users having taken up the habit while in custody.

But inmates and their visitors aren't the only traffickers in the world of federal institutions. There are several documented cases of prison guards smuggling drugs into their workplaces. In 2001, Warden Monty Bourke of Kingston Penitentiary fired nine guards and took disciplinary action against seven others after a three-year joint probe by the RCMP, the OPP, and the Kingston police uncovered alleged violations of the Standard of Professional Conduct and the Code of Discipline within CSC. Some alleged violations included running drugs, alcohol, and contraband such as pizza and pornography to inmates such as Paul Bernardo. Interestingly, no criminal charges have been laid in the case to date, and CSC has not made the findings of the police investigation public. Confidential information about the probe was made public when a memo left in Warden Bourke's wastebasket was recovered by an inmate cleaner. The firings and suspensions followed the apparent suicide in late December 2000 of two married guards at KP, who were being investigated for running drugs to the inmates, an allegation the couple's friends claim is absurd.

Some of the fired guards were key players in the ouster of their old union, an affiliate of the Public Service Alliance of Canada, in February 2001. The new, militant Union of Canadian Correctional Officers helped four officers start a class action suit against CSC, the solicitor general, and CSC officials for $130 million, claiming that

entrapment tactics were used during the investigation and that inmates received transfers and other rewards for their help in compromising guards. The case has yet to be heard.

The business of drug dealing is just as much a factor behind prison violence and sexual predation as drug use. Drummond Institution in Drummondville, Quebec, experienced a hostage taking because an inmate owed twenty pouches of tobacco to his prison drug dealer. The death of Jody McCauley at Joyceville on January 25, 1998, was a typical drug murder. Just twenty-eight, McCauley was stabbed in the neck and back with a sharpened butter knife by an inmate to whom he owed money. McCauley's wife, Christie, had raised some money from his father to deposit in the accounts of those he owed, but not enough to wipe out his debts. On the day before he was killed, McCauley asked his wife to bring a small quantity of marijuana into Joyceville during a social, explaining that he would then be debt-free. She refused, and the next day her husband was dead.

One enterprising inmate decided to finance his escape from Millhaven's J Unit with some major drug deals directed from prison. Four years into a seventeen-year sentence for drug trafficking, Hugo Delconti used a cellular phone smuggled into prison concealed in computer game parts to arrange the deals through Costa Rica and Miami and to set up the escape. Delconti planned to get an escorted pass to see his ailing father in Toronto. Friends armed with two fully automatic rifles and a .50-calibre machine gun were then to ambush the van transporting Delconti. In the event that Plan A failed, Delconti would turn to Plan B: his heavily armed associates were to make a direct assault on Millhaven itself. The plans were foiled by authorities.

This was not the only example of a business run from inside a Canadian prison. Two inmates, both of them convicted pedophiles, ran a child pornography ring from Warkworth Institution and the Toronto West Detention Centre. Two dozen members of the ring distributed photos and videos of boys aged five to fourteen engaged

in sex acts with adults and other children. The pornography was distributed on the Internet.

In August 1999, several KP inmates made the allegation that they had been raped or used as sex slaves by Michel Huneault, a convicted killer and armed robber. According to one alleged victim, Huneault was also the drug kingpin at KP, which had experienced a substantial increase in supply after his transfer from Joyceville in May 1998. According to inmate informants, Huneault had $1,500 in cash at all times, as well as a stockpile of assorted drugs stored in various cells. One informant told authorities that he had personally "held" and sorted drugs for Huneault. He claimed that the ex-biker had raped many others, sometimes at knifepoint, but because of his "muscle" both inside and outside KP, he was able to command silence and co-operation from his victims.

Forty-four-year-old Huneault had been in prison since 1982. Although he had been eligible for parole since 1992, he had not applied. Huneault had been "red-flagged" as a sexual predator at two previous institutions for numerous offences against fellow inmates, but true to the prison "rat code," which can carry a death penalty for those who break it, no one had come forward.

In addition to his suspected drug dealing, Huneault was also chairman of the inmate committee, a position that allowed him to roam freely through the prison, including the segregation unit. He was known among the guards for appropriating appliances out of the trailers used for family visits and taking them to his range.

Management had also supplied him with a computer, accidentally forgetting to erase sensitive files about KP's guards. When he saw what Huneault had in his possession, one of those guards, Eddie Castle, complained to KP's warden. "He had documents about me. Tons of documents. I went to Monty [Bourke]. Monty said, 'Who? Can you prove it?' I said, 'Here are documents. And this is a document about my car being vandalized in the parking [lot]. Here's a document with your response. And here's a document with the response of your unit manager.' This was from an inmate!"

Huneault bolstered his power inside through his drug business. One alleged victim said that over a seven-month period Huneault had given him home brew and pills and coerced him into sex. Another told authorities that the stocky and muscular Huneault had "controlled" him from June 1998 to June 1999, during which time he was repeatedly raped. This inmate also claimed that Huneault boasted of his connections with Rock Machine biker crews and other criminal gangs on both sides of the prison walls.

One inmate informant was so frightened by possible reprisals from Huneault that he refused to go to the yard. He was even afraid that Huneault would arrange to have his food laced with poison, telling one officer that if he was forced to stay, "KP will have a corpse on their hands." The inmate wanted an immediate transfer out of KP, following in the tracks of several other alleged victims of Huneault. Instead, it was Huneault who got the transfer, all the way to the super-maximum unit in Sainte-Anne-des-Plaines, Quebec. After investigating for several months, the OPP laid sexual assault charges against Huneault. The trial is scheduled for the fall of 2002.

Fear of poisoning was no outbreak of paranoia. In October 1999, Millhaven deputy warden Paul Snyder was briefed by the OPP Penitentiary Squad about the cause of death of inmate Barnett in July 1999. The initial investigation suggested that the inmate had died of a drug overdose. He had stopped breathing for seventeen minutes, and there was a swelling on his brain consistent with a lethal dose of drugs. But forensic tests eliminated the drug overdose theory and confirmed the real cause of Barnett's death: cyanide poisoning.

The cells of the inmates suspected in the death were searched. Warden Lou Kelly sent a memo to staff reminding them to wear gloves and protective clothing. They were not to open, inspect, or smell any unknown substance they found. Instead, it was to be sealed and handed over to the appropriate authorities for identification. Staff were also reminded to wash their hands before eating, drinking, or smoking. They were not to leave open beverages where

inmates had access and not to accept food or drinks from inmates — a tall order since inmates ran the kitchen.

Cyanide takes the form of white granules, flakes, or dust. It can absorb moisture from the air and form a wet solid or solution; when dry, it is odourless. Damp or wet, it smells like bitter almonds. As dust or in solution, the chemical is taken in quickly through the skin or eyes. If swallowed, it is rapidly absorbed. According to the Canadian Centre for Occupational Health and Safety, mild or early cyanide poisoning symptoms include general weakness, heaviness of arms and legs, difficulty breathing, headache, giddiness, nausea, vomiting, and breath that smells of bitter almonds. Severe symptoms include nausea and vomiting, and gasping for breath.

Barnett's breathing was at first rapid and deep. He then began to gasp as fluid filled his lungs. His heartbeat became irregular and his chest tightened. Toward the end, his skin turned bright pink. Convulsions, loss of consciousness, and death followed. Massive exposures can produce sudden collapse and death. An airborne concentration of cyanide dust of just 270 parts per million is fatal in under a minute.

Authorities at KP had intelligence that the heroin showing up in the prison was being cut with cyanide. Warden Monty Bourke issued a notice to inmates about the cyanide risk, inadvertently recording the essential contradiction between common practice in Canadian prisons and CSC's stated drug policy of zero tolerance: "Although management does not condone the use of any type of non-prescription drugs, it is our obligation to inform the offender population of this potential risk, especially those offenders who participate in the drug trade at this Institution." The notice went on to list the symptoms of cyanide poisoning and precautions that should be taken.

Illegal drug use and the violence that comes with it became so rampant at medium-security Joyceville Institution that correctional officers set up a picket at regional headquarters to protest the fact that managers had, in effect, ceded control of the prison to the inmates. Signs read "Management is out of control" and

"Hey Warden, just say no to drugs." The Joyceville officers were reacting to events at the institution over the July 1-2, 2000, weekend and to the fact that management would not take meaningful action against inmates who broke the rules.

It was the latest in a string of incidents at Joyceville: a rampage by inmates in the recreation building that cost $100,000 to repair, an escape attempt by the killer of a police officer, rumours that cyanide had been smuggled into the prison, and the usual security problems caused by drugs, brew, and homemade weapons. John Edmunds, the national vice-president of the Union of Solicitor General Employees, claimed, "We're either dismissed or we're lied to." He also said that there had been numerous incidents where guards were pricked by drug needles or exposed to the blood of inmates infected with hepatitis or HIV.

Eleven days after the events at Joyceville, James Hilton, a thirty-one-year-old inmate at Kingston Penitentiary, died of a suspected drug overdose. Again, a lethal dose of morphine was suspected. Just half an hour after Hilton's body was discovered, two "wired" inmates refused to return to their cells. They began smashing up their cellblock with a broken broom handle and a metal pole. It was suspected that they were under the influence of an intoxicant. Concluding that lives were in jeopardy, authorities authorized the firing of three canisters of tear gas. The rampage continued. The ERT was assembled, but a senior officer finally managed to talk the men into surrendering. Earlier in the evening, another prisoner was attacked and stabbed by two inmates in the yard. The attackers joined the two would-be rioters in segregation.

Despite all the dangers, inmates can be fierce about their sense of drug entitlement. At medium-security Collins Bay Institution, inmates held a three-week work stoppage in April 1995 to protest a drug crackdown. They threatened to bomb the institution unless the ion scanner used to check visitors for drugs was removed from the prison. The written threats also demanded the reinstatement of visiting privileges that had been suspended because of drug violations. Two inmates had recently died of drug overdoses,

and urinalysis tests showed that 40 per cent of those tested used drugs at the institution. A major blood study conducted at Joyceville from 1994 to 1998 showed a 24 per cent increase in intravenous drug use in the prison over the course of the study.

During cell searches for drugs, alcohol, and weapons at KP, staff also found unauthorized televisions and stereos – a clear sign of debt collection by prison drug dealers. But that didn't stop one angry inmate from starting a fire in his cell when items he had muscled from other inmates over drug debts were removed from his possession. Managers hastily met with the inmate committee and agreed to stop removing TVs and stereos, if the prisoners agreed to behave. According to one senior guard with more than twenty years of service, the CSC's real policy toward the illegal use of drugs and alcohol in federal prisons could be summed up in two words: tolerance and appeasement.

"There's a huge degree of tolerance! A lot of inmates are actually caught with narcotics on them, and nothing is done," the guard says. "Or very little is done. Even something like segregation isn't practised and charges have been shredded. Myself personally, I've had a keeper come to me and try to smooth over things because the inmate committee chairman a couple of years ago was caught trying to pass marijuana on to another range. It was all smoothed over because this guy was a committee chairman, and we were asked to kind of look the other way."

Realizing that CSC management will not stand behind them in the war on drugs, many guards, like a veteran keeper at Warkworth, cope with their frustrations by simply giving up on Commissioner's Directive 585.

"They don't want the drugs out of there because they can't deal with withdrawal. As a guard, you have to develop the attitude that you can't stop it. They don't want you to stop it. The management won't let you stop it. So why get all worked up about it? A lot of times you'll walk a range and you'll smell marijuana, and you know, you may not be able to pinpoint where it is, but you know that there is no use even looking for it because all you are going to

do is raise a stink. The keeper on the shift is not going to back you, they are not going to lock the area down and search, they are not going to bring in drug dogs, they are not going to charge anybody if you do find it, so really, why even bother?"

A veteran guard at KP agrees: "You go after them and they blow smoke rings in your face and defy you to find their stash. When they start mixing the dope with brew, that's when the really dangerous situations get going. Yet management won't get tough with these guys."

A December 1999 memo from the acting deputy warden of KP, Mike Ryan, tacitly confirmed the officers' sense that their managers saw illicit drugs as a way of pacifying the inmate population. Ryan wrote that the festive season was quickly approaching and "there is an increase in risk for a number of our offenders to commit self-harm. . . . This risk has also been heightened as a result of the increased impact of the drug interdiction strategies employed at Kingston Penitentiary during the past few weeks. Illegal substances are not as readily available and you may see an increase in tension between inmates and inmates, as well as between inmates and staff. Further, you will undoubtedly see an increase in brewmaking."

In 1995, CSC spent $165,000 to fund the first national survey of attitudes among male federal prisoners in Canada. All participants were guaranteed anonymity, and therefore immunity, for taking part in the survey. Forty per cent of the 4,285 respondents admitted that they had used an illegal drug at least once in their current prison term: marijuana, crack cocaine, or heroin.

When CSC reintroduced random urine tests in the late 1990s, the inmates simply switched to drugs that were less detectable. Since the chemicals in soft drugs like marijuana and hashish stay in the body longer, they began injecting opiates, which are metabolized much more quickly. Accordingly, many inmates using drugs were able to test drug-free, despite their continued substance abuse. But there was a much simpler way of beating the drug tests, and 50 per cent of suspected drug users at KP were quick to use it;

they simply refused the test. Addressing a staff assembly in September 1998, the prison's warden, Monty Bourke, effectively admitted to staff that there was nothing they could do when prisoners said no to urine tests in the late 1990s.

"We must follow CSC policy, this is something we cannot change. Inmates know there is no immediate consequence, but the refusals and the charges will follow the inmate and have long-term consequences. It is important we have a record of all this activity. . . . We are restricted by rules and regulations, but we are communicating with NHQ Legal on new initiatives."

Faced with such lukewarm support, many guards simply let inmates sleep off the effects of booze and drugs rather than waste time on paper charges that went nowhere. But no one is under any illusion about the bottom line of the unofficial indulgence of substance abuse in Canadian prisons. As one member of a crack ERT team puts it, "You don't need the drugs to run the institution and keep it under control. You just have to change the internal procedures, which they are not willing to do. The way they want to run it, then you do need the drugs. Inmates are being taught almost the exact opposite of what we are supposed to be doing here. They call it rehabilitation. Well, do you think the city police are going to tolerate most of this behaviour that is allowed inside when these guys get out?"

With a blatant drug problem right across the prison system, Commissioner Ingstrup's New Age correctional philosophy started to get bad press, and his political masters began to twitch. In May 2000, a subcommittee of the Commons justice committee examining the CCRA suggested that every person entering a penal institution should first be searched, but only in a "non-intrusive way." The committee members, who found the legislation, policies, and institutions "complex and at times confusing," were apparently untroubled by the essential contradiction in their recommendation.

A month earlier Solicitor General Lawrence MacAulay had announced new initiatives to combat the supply of drugs in federal

prisons. Drug dogs would be used and ion scanners would be in every medium- and maximum-security institution by the end of May. MacAulay, an admitted alcoholic who credits Alcoholics Anonymous with getting his affliction under control, even used the word "punishment" to describe part of the process that offenders should be subjected to for their crimes, a word that had been stricken from the lexicon of correctional managers under Ole Ingstrup. But as a Kingston guard who has seen several ministers come and go observes, vigilance works only if there is a will to impose it: "A lot of times if a visitor goes over that limit [of drugs detected by an ion scanner], they are restricted from the prison for so long, usually thirty days, and then the person's back in. They may be placed on closed visits for up to as many as six months, but the point is the person still gets in the front door. The operators are supposed to call the keeper and say, 'Well, we have this level of drug detected,' but a lot of times keepers just go, 'Well, that's OK, let them in.' Everyone knows they'll be getting in later anyway. Why piss off the inmate?"

A February 1999 internal report, *Review of CSC Drug Strategy*, stated that CSC was facing an epidemic of infectious diseases because of intravenous drug use, tattooing, body piercing, and unprotected sex. Although sexual activity is officially forbidden in Canadian prisons because they are considered to be public places, it is a prohibition honoured more in the breach than in the observance.

On August 9, 1998, while working in Tower 1 at KP during visiting hours, an officer noted an inmate and his female visitor engaged in "unacceptable acts." "The female visitor was seen straddling the I/M [inmate], resting her head on his lap and rubbing his groin area. The I/M was observed reaching his hands up her top and down her pants, all in view of other I/M's, and their visitors, including small children." The officer who reported the activity from the tower felt that since this would not be tolerated in the community, it should not be tolerated at KP. She felt it would be devastating for the young children. However the most

troubling aspect of all of this for the writer is what message is Kingston Pen (CSC) sending to the public?"

Despite the official prohibition of sex inside, condoms and safe sex guides are distributed to new inmates. HIV/AIDS infection rates are ten times higher in the prison population than in the general population. Although condoms are available, two-thirds of the sexually active inmates don't use them. Even though these same inmates fear prisoners with AIDS, they regularly have unprotected sex and share drug needles. According to CSC's 2001 performance report, an estimated 19 per cent of all federal offenders and 40 per cent of female offenders have hepatitis C, and 90 per cent of intravenous drug users in prison are infected. Hepatitis C is also spread by tattooing and body piercing. Although both activities are prohibited in federal institutions, it is estimated by authorities that 90 per cent of inmates have a tattoo done in prison as a rite of passage.

Although inmates are told that drug use will not be tolerated in prison, the CSC also provides bleach kits to clean needles. The taxpayer-supplied kits consist of a one-ounce plastic bottle of 4 per cent bleach and a one-ounce plastic bottle for rinse water. Bleach dispensers are set up at various locations around the prison to allow inmates privacy when they need to refill their containers. When a group of officers tried to invoke their right to refuse work under the health and safety provisions of Subsection 128 (1) of the Canada Labour Code, protesting that the bleach could be thrown at them, used as poison, or combined with other ingredients to make a bomb, their grievance was turned down.

Despite the ease of access to drugs, "brew" is still the most widely available intoxicant inside Canadian prisons. It is also the compromise drug when inmates can't get their high of choice. A pouch of tobacco, worth $3.75 at the inmates' canteen, is the currency for the underground prison economy. Ten ounces of brew commands a price of four pouches of tobacco, so it is worth about $15, or the same as one-fifth of a gram of hashish or marijuana. (The maximum pay for a federal inmate is $40 a week.)

A brewmaster makes between ninety and nine hundred ounces in a batch. Depending on available ingredients (yeast, sugar, fruit, ketchup, rice, and bread from the prison kitchen), the process takes anywhere from one to four days. "Dunkers," small homemade immersion heaters with two wires that plug into the wall, are used to keep the mash warm. To prevent guards from sniffing out the brew, inmates use electric fans that circulate burning incense or fabric softeners from their laundry kits. According to a veteran guard, "You'll see most of the inmates, they'll have, like, three or four fans in their cells, and they'll put down Bounce sheets, and the breeze from the fans will clear the room of other smells."

Prisons are never more dangerous than when they are awash in alcohol. "When the cons get into drinking brew, that's the worst thing, from my point of view as a security officer. I'd much rather see them shoot heroin or take crack or smoke marijuana, because the brew brings out the violence," one guard says. "Most of the violent smash-ups and stuff, it's because the inmates were into the brew. They can make it in large quantities. They can make it from everything that's inside the jail right now. All you need is fruit, sugar, and water. They make it sometimes in garbage pail sizes. They can get the whole range drunk because you only need a cup, it's so potent. A lot of times we'll go through the entire institution and it's not uncommon to find fifty gallons."

By prison standards, brew is big business. The brewmaster can pull in $135 to $1,350 per batch. Despite the institutional mayhem they provoke, brewmasters are treated to the same lax sanctions as drug dealers. A thirty-year-old brewmaster identified in KP documents only as "S.D. b May 21/70" had a brew- and drug-related disciplinary file that started in September 1996. One of his guards estimated that for every time S.D. was caught, there were four or five more times when he sold his brew and made major deposits to his outside bank account.

Sanctioned thirty-seven times for making brew, S.D. was sent to segregation only twice. On both occasions, his penalty was served in his own living unit. On February 22, 1999, S.D. was fined $50

after being found with ten gallons of brew in his possession, worth more than ten times the amount of the fine. Three more charges followed, two for brewmaking and one for possession of a hashish pipe. But these charges were withdrawn by prison officials because S.D. was released from the institution on parole. Charges without consequences, or no charges at all, have put officer morale in CSC at rock bottom.

"Just before Christmas, every day we took at least five gallons off different ranges. That's every day – not every week, every day. And nobody was getting charged. We just throw it out. They don't go to the hole, we throw it out, they make it again. We throw it out," one guard said.

Oranges, a favourite ingredient of brewmasters, were temporarily banned at KP because of the extent of the illicit alcohol problem. But the ban didn't hold, and the fruit soon reappeared on inmates' food carts. Guards at Kingston were even issued special flashlights able to pick up the presence of brew in individual cells. During midnight shifts, officers were supposed to point flashlights into the cells of suspected brewmasters, the way police use the same device in routine traffic stops to check for alcohol in a vehicle. Even though guards discovered a lot of brew with their flashlights, an order came down the line to discontinue their use.

According to one guard, "The flashlights had a light that goes on in the presence of alcohol. Again they claimed that we didn't have proper training, or they didn't have time to train us and whatnot, and they removed them. They were $800 flashlights that they bought, three or four of them. We used them maybe for a week or so, and then they were removed."

As readily available as it is, sometimes inmates aren't satisfied with the quality of alcohol available from the prison system's many enterprising brewmasters. Inmate Gabriel Warner at minimum-security Rockwood Institution in Stony Mountain, Manitoba, was found to be missing on December 29, 1999, at 21:30. But authorities needn't have worried; he had merely "left" the premises to buy beer. Escape was the last thing on his mind. In fact, Warner

paid three individuals from the community $20 to drive him back to Rockwood after his beer stop.

Warner was apprehended at 22:00 when he was dropped off at the institution; he was transferred to Stony Mountain prison, in Winnipeg. The RCMP laid an escape charge against the twenty-two-year-old inmate. This comical episode loses some of its humour when Warner's sentence is considered: he was serving twelve years for four counts of robbery, use of a firearm while committing the robbery, disguise with intent, and attempted murder. His sentence had commenced on September 20, 1996, yet after only three years, he had been transferred to a reduced-security institution. Warner was following what is getting to be a time-honoured tradition in the Canadian prison system. In 1999–2000, ninety-six inmates escaped from federal custody, 95 per cent of them from minimum-security institutions. One hundred and fourteen federal inmates had escaped the previous year.

Fining brewmasters is a dubious sanction, to say the least. Not only are the fines negligible, but since brewmaking is such a time-consuming activity, brewmasters often don't work at regular prison jobs. As a result, they don't have money in their institutional bank accounts, which means that when a fine is levied, it often can't be recovered. Nor do they pay for the public property they use to distill their brew. Parts for prison stills are stolen from refrigerators, coolers, water fountains, wall clocks, radios, TV sets, and other appliances within the institution. Taxpayers foot the bill for most of the replacements.

Modernizing institutional security was considered to be a big step toward reducing the drug and alcohol flow to Canada's convicted criminals. Despite $43 million worth of renovations to Kingston Penitentiary between 1989 and 1998 (including poisoning all the sparrows that nested in the ancient prison), the facility was in some ways more inmate-friendly after the overhaul. Inmates found the perfect spot to brew alcohol behind the radiators in the hollow space between the new drywall and the old stone walls. They took off the radiator covers, cut holes in the drywall, and

inserted bags with the brew ingredients inside. Heat from the radiators was useful, since it accelerated the fermentation process.

Prison regulations also work to the inmates' benefit. Before a "special" search of a cell, a correctional officer must first convince the officer in charge that he has reasonable and probable grounds to believe that there is brew or drugs on the premises. In the case of native inmates, the native liaison officer must be present during the cell search to ensure that no sacred objects are disturbed.

The hunt for drugs and brew is often an exercise in bureaucratic window dressing. On March 2, 1999, officers at KP were informed that they would have to do six routine cell searches in half an hour, starting at 9:15 and ending at 9:45. The allotted time was ludicrously inadequate, given the object of their mission: to uncover brew and weapons. It amounted to just five minutes per cell, and even less than that considering travel time between ranges and inmate pat-downs. Weapons and drugs are rarely left in plain view, and it took a lot of time to sift through clothing, bedding, boxes, and papers. In fact, to thoroughly search a cell can take hours, not minutes.

But even a five-minute search is better than what happened on the evening of September 13, 2000, after officers at KP discovered that most of the inmates on Lower B Range were drunk. Several fights broke out and the range was locked down at 20:00 for the night. The next morning, officers wanted to keep the range locked until a search could be completed. But the correctional supervisor informed her officers that that wouldn't be necessary. Instead, the inmate committee was going to remove any contraband and turn it over to the keeper! As one astonished intelligence officer exclaimed, "Since when does the inmate committee search ranges and remove contraband? Management wanted them to do it so the range could be unlocked and the inmates wouldn't be angry. Can you believe this?"

In October 1999, Pierre Rolland, a CX2 at Drummond Institution in Quebec, heard that disciplinary sanctions were going to be standardized throughout Quebec as part of the national drug

strategy of CSC. Commissioner Ingstrup had once more proclaimed that the CSC would not tolerate drug or alcohol use or
trafficking, as well as related activities such as muscling and extortion. Every institution was ordered to develop and implement
drug and alcohol strategies to balance detection, deterrence, and
treatment. The commissioner said that drug and alcohol abuses
must be considered "serious" offences. Under the CCRA, a serious
offence can merit a thirty-day stretch in segregation. (After
September 15, 1999, prison authorities lost the power to impose
such penalties on their own, regardless of what inmates had done.
On that date, the Supreme Court of Canada ruled unanimously
that prisoners facing solitary confinement because of disciplinary
charges were entitled to legal aid.)

Rolland had fifteen years of "on-the-floor" experience with
brew in federal prisons and was an expert on the danger that
it presented to guards and inmates alike. He was completely unimpressed with the proposed $20 fine for possession or trafficking of
illegal alcohol. As Rolland saw it, the reverse onus provision of the
proposal grossly favoured the inmate offender. The officer who
finds the brew must show up at the inmate's hearing, sometimes
on his day off or after his shift. Unlike the inmate, he is without
legal assistance, but he is cross-examined by the taxpayer-supplied
lawyer for the inmate accused. Every working day, the officer also
has to face the aggressive attitude of the inmate he charges.
Dismissing the proposed fine as meaningless, Rolland felt that anything less than segregation added to a monetary penalty would
never deter inmates from brewing, selling, and using alcohol
behind bars.

There was only one thing wrong with his suggestion. Segregation,
the once-dreaded "hole" of Hollywood movies, is not what it used
to be in Canada. Solitary really isn't very solitary any more. The
CCRA spells out that inmates placed in segregation retain the same
rights, privileges, and conditions of detention as other inmates,
except for those that can be enjoyed only in association with other

inmates and can be reasonably granted under security requirements. At KP, for example, up to four inmates can be locked in the cells of other segregated inmates for cell studies, card and computer games, or a bull session, at the discretion of the officer in charge. The only proviso is that visiting inmates return to their own cells for all counts.

At Kingston Penitentiary, Lower H Range became a segregation unit after the warden ordered the doors of the former "hole" welded shut in May 1999 to celebrate the commissioner's New Age approach to corrections. During stays in the new segregation unit, prisoners have their meals delivered to them by food stewards, not guards, and enjoy cable television and stereos. A staff memo from Millhaven dated July 30, 1998, and signed by Deputy Warden Paul Snyder lays out the rules. If an inmate goes to segregation peacefully, he can pack his cigarettes, some of his canteen, and a few clothes in a pillowcase and carry these items with him. If he remains in segregation after a twenty-four-hour review of his situation, then his TV, stereo, and fan will be taken to Admission and Discharge, searched and tagged, then delivered to the inmate. But even if an inmate resists admission to segregation, he is deprived of his cell effects for only twenty-four hours. Should the decision be made to hold the inmate beyond twenty-four hours, "then a Correctional Officer will follow the above procedure on behalf of the inmate." In other words, if the inmate can do without his effects for a day, room service will deliver his personal effects in the person of a guard.

"The prisoners end up running the place, man," one officer on medical leave from KP says. "It's like their own culture, their own society in there."

8

JUNGLE JUSTICE

If, as many of CSC's employees believe, convicts run Canada's prisons, then it is an underworld that comes with a justice system much harsher than the one that put the offenders behind bars in the first place: it is the law of the jungle.

Most of the trouble for inmates comes from their own justice system, not the one imposed on them by society for their crimes. Known child rapists or killers, like Clifford Olson and Paul Bernardo, have to be placed in protective segregation. If they were assigned to the ordinary population, they would be swiftly killed by other inmates, sometimes under the very nose of armed guards who cannot use their weapons without orders.

Phil Whaley, a veteran guard now retired from Kingston Penitentiary, had to watch helplessly from his gun cage while a sex offender was assaulted by a posse of inmates out for a little prison justice. "He [the victim] started walking back through the rec yard, and there was about twelve, fourteen cons, just like a mass movement to go and use the washroom facilities. And about twenty feet away from the cage – the rifle was leaning up against the wall right beside me – they all closed around him and then they

walked away from him. He got stabbed seventeen times and was laying on the ground."

According to CSC statistics, from 1990 to 1999 there were 775 serious, violent incidents in federal prisons, including 32 major assaults on staff, 136 suicides, 474 major assaults on offenders, and 51 murders of inmates. As noted earlier, although sexual activity is prohibited by law in federal penitentiaries, condoms and safe sex guides are distributed to new inmates entering the system, and with good reason. In a 1995 survey, 6 per cent of federal inmates reported that they had been pressured for sex, the same percentage that reported they had had voluntary sex with other inmates. Three per cent of federal inmates claimed that they had been sexually assaulted while inside. The jungle, supposedly a secured environment, can be a very dangerous place.

At 22:25 on Friday, December 26, 1997, KP inmate Victor Nickerson was locked up for the night. The evening shift officer, Chad Parslow, commenced his count of Lower G Range shortly after lock-up. It had been a quiet night. There were thirty-three inmates on the range and Nickerson, a cocky black hustler with connections to the black drug gangs, was accounted for in his cell.

A little over half an hour later, at 23:07, the shift officer, Pedro Sousa-Diaz, did his first count. Again, inmate Nickerson was accounted for in his cell. Sousa-Diaz did a range walk a little after midnight and once every hour after that until the next full inmate count. At 4:58 on December 27, Sousa-Diaz again certified that Nickerson was in his cell, although, as usual, it was difficult to see clearly into the cells because of the privacy blankets inmates use to cover the bars. According to the call-out sheet, Nickerson had the day off, so Sousa-Diaz did not awaken him at 5:15 when he opened the cells of the other inmates who worked in the kitchen.

After the 5:00 count was certified – fifteen inmates on the second floor, and eighteen more on the first floor – Sousa-Diaz drew keys from the Keeper's Hall and opened the kitchen for the food stewards. At 5:45, the officer on kitchen duty admitted

the workers to the kitchen and provided a roll call to the Keeper's Hall. "Jug-up" was scheduled for 7:25. The kitchen and the serving line corridor at KP do not have catwalks or cages for armed staff, although there is a staff office in the area. Tool control in the kitchen consists of a shadow board in a locked "crib." Knives are designed to be used with a cable that locks them into a fixed location. Although its shadow is still on the board, the meat cleaver has been permanently removed from the kitchen at KP. The last time it was seen, guards were using it to test the strength of the metal cables designed to secure other kitchen knives to their workstation.

While Sousa-Diaz was in the kitchen, another officer did the 6:00 walk of the ranges. Once again, inmate Nickerson was accounted for in his cell. Officers were on the range throughout the morning of the 27th. Although only eight cells were supposed to be open at once, all the cells were unlocked when jug-up was called, since most of the inmates on the range worked in the kitchen, and it was a holiday weekend. Some officers, especially the new ones trained to "interact" with the inmates, leave all the cells open rather than having a constant battle over staggered releases. According to the men who worked it, G Block was a difficult post filled with "high-needs" inmates who were constantly "in your face," looking for favours or challenging authority. It was an assignment where vigilance was especially important. But on this particular Saturday morning, in the hollow aftermath of a prison Christmas, the cellblock was quiet.

At 7:00, the diabetics on the range were released for medication. Jug-up went off smoothly at 7:25. At KP the food line winds around a secure corridor in front of the serving line, which is enclosed behind barred windows and glass. Inmates move along the line pointing out what they want, and staff on the other side of the glass place it on their trays. When they reach the end of the line, they receive their food from a pass-through slot designed to prevent inmates from muscling for extra food, or the kitchen workers from showing favouritism to friends. Large dining halls

and recreational areas are hot spots for trouble in prisons, so there is no prisoners' mess at the institution. Except for segregation inmates, who get their food brought to them on lightweight, thermoplastic carts, offenders at KP take all their meals in their cells.

On the day that Victor Nickerson's body was discovered by inmates, Officer Ross Boulter was working the 7:00 to 15:00 shift on Lower G Range. His walks had been uneventful. Inmates Armstrong and Fish were called for V&C at 8:50. Boulter made his rounds at 7:00, 8:30, and 9:30. He had just called for count-up at 10:30, when he was informed by inmates trickling back from the recreation yard that not all of them had arrived back. Awaiting the stragglers, Boulter delayed the count.

At 11:15, there was a sudden commotion on the lower range of G Block. Boulter heard an inmate shout, "Get the nurse!" and he immediately radioed the central control post requesting medical assistance. As an added precaution, he also asked for backup officers. He entered the range from the second-floor control post, while the other officers came through the Lower G sliding barrier. Officer Robert Trainor, the "float" or auxiliary guard who went where he was needed during his shift, was in the staff mess when the call went out for assistance on Lower G.

The officers rushed toward cell G-1-11. When they arrived, Trainor saw inmates coming out of Victor Nickerson's cell, in the centre of the block in the heavily travelled general common area. Officers Boulter and Trainor found Nickerson hanging at the back of his cell. The inmate was facing the front of his cell and had a strip of blue sheeting and a white shoelace around his neck. The sheet and shoelace were attached to the air vent above the sink.

A third officer, Cal Mullins, also entered the cell, which at the time did not have a blanket covering its entrance. (Officers would later talk about the fact that inmates had been playing cards in front of Nickerson's cell earlier that morning.) Mullins noted that there was a sheet bundled up at the foot of the bed, but the rest of the mattress was not cluttered with anything that could be mistaken for a sleeping body. Nor did he see urine or feces beneath

Nickerson's body, an unusual fact given the way he had apparently died. Although there was swelling in the lip and mouth area, his eyes were closed. Mullins noted, "Did not appear to be a traumatic death, too calm." In the grim vernacular of prison, Victor Nickerson had become a "wind chime."

Trainor steadied the lifeless body while Boulter cut the homemade rope with an emergency knife. Like many inmates unhappy with the height of the bunk/desk combination that had been installed during renovations, Nickerson had preferred placing his mattress on the floor when sleeping. The two officers gently laid the inmate's body on the mattress directly in front of the celldoor, then locked up. Mullins went for a stretcher, haunted by the image of the white shoelace knotted tightly around Nickerson's throat.

Next to shivs and the occasional zip gun (a homemade weapon that can fire standard cartridges or brass projectiles using a propellant and a wick detonated by a match), shoelaces are one of the more popular weapons in prison. They have two advantages: virtually no elasticity and a very high breakage point. They are also issued to prisoners on a regular basis, and no one can be charged for carrying a lethal weapon if they happen to be found with shoelaces during a search. (Endlessly creative, inmates at Millhaven and KP have even used dental floss and Ajax cleanser to cut through steel bars with relative ease.)

Guards at KP were well aware of what a shoelace could do. Lloyd Wilson, a convicted murderer, had a shoelace in his pocket when he took seventy-four-year-old Hubert Rockey from his cell in the Regional Treatment Centre at KP and pushed his wheelchair to the showers. Rockey, disabled and only about five-foot-two, was serving ten years for sex crimes. The six-foot-three-inch, 280-pound Wilson wanted to kill Rockey for his disgusting crimes. A few years earlier, Wilson had thrown a cup of bleach in a fellow inmate's face before trying to stab him. Once he got Rockey in the showers, Wilson took the shoelace from his pocket and twice attempted to strangle the old man.

Wilson later told police there was nothing personal in the murder attempt: "Today, when I woke up, I just thought it was a pretty good day to do it." Wilson pleaded guilty to the attempted murder. Asked by the sentencing judge if he had anything to say, Wilson said, "I realize what I did was wrong, but I don't regret it one bit. I was sexually abused when I was eight, so I don't regret it one bit." The judge sentenced the unrepentant inmate to another fifteen-year term to go with the life sentence he was already serving for a 1982 murder in Toronto. (As a result of the brutal attack, his second intended victim is now incontinent, bedridden, and fed through a tube.)

Deputy Warden Janet DeLaat was called at 11:23, along with various unit managers and the regional duty officer, Syl Riel. Victor Nickerson was first examined by a nurse, Gloria Kristic-Smith. She called a doctor, who pronounced the inmate dead at 11:50 and alerted the coroner's office. Officer Beaupré, the acting correctional supervisor, locked the cell with the "crime scene police padlock" until the coroner arrived.

Lockdown was delayed by fifteen minutes as inmates gathered around Nickerson's cell to look at his body. Inmate Hill, who was on the telephone, was given two minutes to finish his conversation before he too was locked in his cell. Inmates Hill and Alexander Gillis harangued the staff, blaming Ross Boulter for missing Nickerson on his walks. Unit Manager Doreen Natalizio arrived at the cell and asked if the other inmates were all right. Shortly after 12:00, a clergyman and the on-call psychologist were summoned. The unit manager talked to inmate Hill, the inmate range representative, then asked officers to do their walks, which are recorded by an electronic device known as a Deister. Once the range was secured, Trainor asked the other officers to leave the range. He and Boulter then stayed by Nickerson's cell to ensure continuity of evidence until the coroner arrived, or at least they did until Boulter was summoned to the Keeper's Hall.

To senior management, Nickerson's death was an open-and-shut case. The post-mortem of the inmate conducted at the Kingston

General Hospital found that he had died from asphyxiation. A January 28, 1998, memo about the CSC fact-finding investigation into the "suicide" of inmate Nickerson signed by Unit Manager Natalizio declared: "The Coroner had stated that this inmate had been dead for approximately 12 hours. The Coroner arrived at this institution at 15:00, December 27, 1997. This would leave [sic] me to believe the inmate died on the 23:00–07:00 shift December 27, 1997. Mr. Sousa-Diaz asked if there was a margin of error for the Coroner on time of death. I stated I was not aware of any margin of error."

Natalizio had arrived at her conclusion by counting back twelve hours from the time the coroner had viewed the body. Warden Monty Bourke later confirmed that assessment in a memo, in which he wrote, "The Coroner has stated that V. Nickerson had been deceased for approximately 12 hours previous to the time he viewed the body." Given the coroner's arrival time, that would place Nickerson's death squarely on Officer Sousa-Diaz's shift.

But Natalizio's account left out some major inconsistencies that were clearly documented by the prison's own records. In his observation report written on the day that Nickerson was discovered, Officer Robert Trainor noted that Dr. Hinton, the coroner, came to Nickerson's cell at 12:50, not 15:00, and asked several questions about what had happened. Natalizio resolved the inconsistency by summarily rejecting the officer's written report. "Observation report submitted by R. Trainor states that Coroner arrived at cell at 12:50. Visitor's log at Northgate indicates in Dr. Hinton's writing, that he arrived at 15:00. Therefore, it is believed that the Coroner did arrive at time stated in the log at the Northgate."

Natalizio was only partially right. What she did not account for was an earlier entry in the official visitors' registry that same day that showed that the coroner had also signed into the prison at 12:45, an arrival time that tallied perfectly with Trainor's discredited observation report. Having resolved the discrepancy by ignoring the curious double entry in the visitors' registry on the very same page, the system was set to lay blame for Nickerson's

death where it usually did — with the guards. Natalizio concluded in her report: "It is apparent from the information collected and the findings that Mr. Boulter and Mr. Sousa-Diaz did not complete their duties as per CSC policies."

Had authorities calculated the time of Nickerson's presumed suicide from the earlier arrival time of the coroner, they might have concluded that he had died on the evening shift on December 26. And if that was so, KP management would have had to advance the unlikely theory that four guards, counting the officer who did the 6:00 walk while Sousa-Diaz was in the kitchen, had missed the inmate's body. In any case, only in the movies is establishing time of death an exact science.

CSC quickly adopted Natalizio's theory, concluding that Sousa-Diaz could not have looked directly into Nickerson's cell during the count at 5:00, since he didn't notice the dead inmate hanging from the air vent. KP's standing order on counting inmates dated January 29, 1997, stated that particular attention must be paid to "sleeping" inmates, and a "breathing living body" must be seen before a count is considered accurate. But as every guard knows, the only way to be sure is to wake up inmates at every count, a less than advisable policy on a kitchen range, where everyone has to get up for work at 5:00. As one veteran guard puts it, "Unless you wanted to start a riot, you would not normally wake them up to ascertain if they were alive and well."

On January 28, 1998, the internal CSC fact-finding investigation concluded that both Sousa-Diaz and Boulter "were negligent in their duties" since "on all rounds the officers should have ensured that there was a clear view of the inmate. This was not done." A disciplinary hearing was conducted on the morning of February 19, 1998. Warden Bourke decided to postpone further sessions until he clarified police information in light of statements by Officer Sousa-Diaz that Nickerson's death might not have been a suicide. At the hearing, the officer had asked if Nickerson was "dead or hanging" for twelve hours. The warden asked if Sousa-Diaz was "suggesting there was tampering." The officer replied, "I've heard

218 • CON GAME

rumours." Asked by the warden if he remembered "making sure
the inmates were alive on that range," Sousa-Diaz replied, "How
can I do that without waking them up?"

Despite the practical realities, Bourke responded with
Commissioner's Directive 565, which states that employees shall
visibly "ensure count of inmate and sign." The warden insisted
that there was no indication that the body had been tampered
with: "The cause was death by strangulation and the cells are
locked." Asked if he had looked in the cell during the count,
Sousa-Diaz said that he had. The warden replied, "I don't believe
you looked in that cell," in effect calling his officer a liar. Sousa-
Diaz pointed out that to remove cell obstructions, he would have
to open every second or third cell during his walks. He asked the
warden if he wanted him to do that on the midnight shift that
night. "Is that a threat?" the warden replied. "It's not meant to be,
but you can take it that way," the defiant officer shot back.

Sousa-Diaz asked why the officer who did the 6:00 walk while
he was on duty in the kitchen that morning was not included in
the investigation. Bourke assured him that "if there was another
officer who was negligent, we will be looking into it." Sousa-Diaz
asked his most pointed question of the bitter session: "Do you
think we're all lazy and liars and don't do our walks?" Bourke
began to quote the operations manual, but Sousa-Diaz interrupted
him: "Common sense doesn't tell you that something wasn't out of
the ordinary if three officers missed this?" Bourke continued to
insist that Sousa-Diaz had the responsibility. He continued,
"Probability tells me you either didn't count the inmate or you
counted a dead inmate."

On February 24, 1998, the warden wrote to Sousa-Diaz and
lowered the boom: "It is clear to me that you were grossly negligent, in regard to Standard One, Responsible Discharge of Duties,
Code of Discipline, the night of inmate Nickerson's suicide." It
was also clear to the warden that Officer Sousa-Diaz was "not
accepting personal accountability in this serious matter." He was
suspended without pay or benefits for ten days and banned from

the institution during that period. Bourke reiterated what he had already told his suspended officer: "There was no evidence that the body had been moved or tampered with."

For his alleged failure to see Nickerson's body hanging in his cell, Ross Boulter was suspended for two days and registered for a two-day suicide prevention course. (In 1995, Boulter had been commended by the warden of the day for preventing the suicide of a KP inmate.) The third officer, who did the 6:00 walk and also failed to see the inmate's body, was never disciplined. A month later, Sousa-Diaz grieved Bourke's decision through his union, the Union of Solicitor General Employees, and Shop Steward Phil Whaley conducted an informal investigation into the affair to prepare his colleague's defence.

Despite the official version, Officer Sousa-Diaz and several other guards did not believe that Nickerson's death was a suicide: "The reason three officers missed the inmate hanging in the back of the cell is not because we did not look in it (I know I looked in and find it difficult to believe I would have missed him), rather it is because he wasn't [hanging] there at the time. Nickerson did not commit suicide, he was murdered, likely smothered, and hung by his murderer the next day," Sousa-Diaz said.

It was a highly speculative theory, but there were several troubling questions about the death that went unanswered in official reports. How likely was it that three officers on thirteen different walks would either decide not to check inmate Nickerson's cell over a twelve-hour period or miss him hanging from the air vent? Even stranger, why had it taken inmates milling about on Lower G Range over four hours from the time they were let out of their cells to find Nickerson's body and alert staff? Under normal circumstances, they notice every detail on their range as a matter of survival. There was also the question of motive. Why would Nickerson kill himself, when he was just months away from day parole and closing in on his release date for full parole in just over a year?

KP's medical support staff certainly did not see Victor Nickerson as a suicide risk. In fact, just a few days before his death, he was

assessed by the institution's psychologist, who reported that there was no basis for a suicide watch. Members of an inmate peer support group who had been trained to assist other inmates with personal problems agreed. Although the group had been formally disbanded, a number of inmates who had continued to assist staff in counselling and had worked with Nickerson said that they "never felt he was at risk of suicide."

But that didn't mean that the inmate was not at risk. Staff at KP knew that Nickerson's life had been in danger for weeks. On November 10, 1997, just six weeks before Nickerson's "suicide," staff were told by Acting CX3 Tony VanVeghel, the correctional supervisor, "There is a chance that convict Nickerson may be killed." Whaley was sufficiently concerned about the information that he made a logbook entry for Upper and Lower G Ranges at 17:40 during his 3:00–23:00 shift that day. According to Whaley, the deputy warden and the IPSO had also told him to keep his eyes open because there might be "a problem" that night.

A few hours into Whaley's shift, inmate Alexander Gillis, a known drug enforcer, demanded entry to Lower G to "talk to" inmate Nickerson. According to his Criminal Profile Report, Gillis, born January 5, 1968, had "an extensive violent criminal history," which started with conviction for assault and sexual assault with a weapon in 1987. This was followed by three more assaults in 1989 and 1992, and numerous breaches of trust. He had no employment history and supported his family through criminal activities and welfare. Gillis had never filed an income tax return.

The sentence he was serving in 1997 had begun January 12, 1993. He had already had an involuntary transfer to KP from Warkworth after assaulting another inmate. The victim needed over twenty staples to close the wound on the back of his scalp. Gillis had not been "pro-active in participation in programs" but had enrolled in two voluntary programs, "Alternatives to Violence," and "Living, Learning and Caring." There were no final reports from the programs, so there was no way of knowing how he did, or even whether he actually attended classes.

As for his procuring convictions, Gillis claimed that the women he controlled wanted to join his "escort agency." He adamantly denied sexually assaulting anyone. An assessment of sexual behaviour for Gillis was completed at Millhaven in March 1993, during which he denied his offences. His victims, he said, "came on to him" because they needed cash and became addicted to prostitution's easy money. Others wanted to sell themselves for what he called a "thrill."

In May 1996, Gillis told his case management officer, Judith Harrower, that after he was released, he planned to marry and buy a car and a house with a white picket fence. He would finance his new life by finding employment helping others in halfway houses or group homes. Gillis admitted to having emotional problems all his life but blamed his parents for not showing more affection and not spending time with him.

It was not a convincing acting debut. Harrower believed that during his interviews, Gillis had been "giving a performance or press conference" for the benefit of a college student who was present. She concluded that Gillis's risk for both general and violent recidivism was high. In keeping with CSC regulations, a copy of her report was presented to the offender.

Front-line officers were well aware of the real Alexander Gillis. On June 16, 1997, while CXI Jason Godin was in the office on Lower G, speaking to an inmate, Gillis demanded that the officer open the window to talk to him. Godin told him he was already occupied and would speak to him in a minute. Gillis started banging on the window with his fist and yelling, "Open the fucking window!"

Godin opened the window and asked Gillis to stop. The inmate responded, "What's your fucking problem? Have you got a problem with me? Come out here if you got a beef with me." Gillis challenged Godin to "come out and meet me at the barrier door." Godin and others were used to the threats and disturbances on Lower G Range but decided that Gillis had gone too far: "It's time something is done before someone gets hurt," Godin wrote.

Godin reported the incident to his correctional supervisor and the belligerent inmate was locked up for the night.

A week later, at 19:45 on June 23, 1997, Officer Godin was told by CX2 Trainor to bring the inmates back from the recreation area ten at a time. Godin informed the inmates and opened the door. When more than ten of them went to the canteen barrier, Godin refused to open the gate. Gillis began shouting abuse: "This is fuckin' bullshit. What is your fuckin' problem, asshole?" Several other inmates picked up the abusive chant. Godin called Trainor and told him about the situation. Not wanting an incident, Trainor said, "Let them go." As the inmates left, Gillis turned to Godin and said, "Payback is a bitch, you fuckin' goof."

That was the Alexander Gillis that Officer Phil Whaley encountered in November. After refusing Gillis permission to see inmate Nickerson, Whaley had a physical confrontation with the six-foot-four 240-pounder. "Even this guy's shit has muscles," Whaley recalled. Nevertheless, he prevented Gillis from entering the range. After Gillis had gone, Nickerson complained to the veteran officer that he was afraid of "grievous bodily harm" even though he "wasn't anybody's rat." The rest of the shift passed without incident, but Whaley noted his encounter with Gillis.

Phil Whaley wasn't the only guard Nickerson turned to during the final days of his life. In the week prior to his death, he had also approached Officer Leo Prosser, a black guard whom he trusted. According to Prosser, Nickerson told him that his life was in danger, and he wanted a meeting with Prosser and a correctional supervisor who could be trusted. Prosser informed CS Rick Waller of the inmate's request. Prosser and Waller went into an office in the C and D wing, then called the security post on Lower G Range. They asked the officer working the post to send Nickerson to the office. It was a touchy procedure. If his fellow inmates suspected he was ratting them out, they would kill him. To protect Nickerson from fellow inmates, Prosser and Waller told the officer on Lower G to present the meeting as a standard parole officer interview.

During the meeting, Nickerson again explained that he feared for his life and was frustrated about delays in transferring out of KP. He referred to a family link between himself and inmate Eugene Peyton, an Upper G inmate who had died a few months earlier of what CSC called a drug overdose. Nickerson said Peyton's death was not an accident but a murder by one of the factions attempting to control the lucrative drug traffic at KP. Specifically, he claimed to know who did the muscling, who carried and distributed the product, and who the customers were. There were even rumours that staff were involved, something that CSC's own Task Force on Security recognized as a distinct possibility: "We would note that with the rise in organized crime, it is probable that attempts to compromise staff will increase."

Although he had remained silent about what he alleged had happened to Eugene Peyton behind bars, Nickerson believed that his cousin's killers were worried about what he might say once he was safely outside the walls of KP and beyond their reach. According to Prosser, "He says, 'Leo, you've got to make sure I'm off this range today. You've got to make sure I'm off this range.' He was afraid. He believed his life was in danger because he knew about the drugs. He knew that his cousin Peyton was murdered. And he knew who did it." But he wouldn't talk about that or other criminal activities he claimed to know about at KP, until he was guaranteed protection and a transfer to C-7, a low-security area attached to the Regional Treatment Centre.

After the meeting, CS Waller passed along what he had learned to one of KP's intelligence officers. There was little choice but to interview the troubled inmate. The IPSO went to the security post on Lower G and walked the inmate from his range through the main dome to a common room, where he conducted his interview. Several officers remember that this was done during one of the major movements, when most inmates were out of their cells and travelling from one area of the institution to another. In other words, the meeting between Nickerson and the IPSO would instantly have become common knowledge. Sousa-Diaz later

wrote to Warden Bourke, "In my opinion, and that of most correctional officers, [the intelligence officer] might as well have drawn a Bull's Eye on inmate Nickerson's forehead with the word 'RAT' under it." Within a week of the meeting with the IPSO, inmates discovered Nickerson hanging at the back of his cell.

There was one other noteworthy detail. On December 28, 1997, the day after Nickerson's presumed suicide, officers at KP received information that an inmate was planning to smuggle a deceased offender's television from Lower G to Upper E Range. The television was seized by correctional staff for verification of ownership. "T.V. set verified as belonging to inmate Nickerson." The would-be smuggler was Alexander Gillis.

On January 14, 1998, the Ontario deputy commissioner of the CSC, Brendan Reynolds, ordered a regional general security (RGS) investigation into the "suicide" of inmate Nickerson, as required under Section 19 of the CCRA. From the beginning, the investigators assumed they were dealing with a suicide: an incident report prepared for the IPSO and regional and national headquarters on December 27, the day of Nickerson's death, labelled it "suicide." A further report prepared by the IPSO into the "suicide" of inmate Nickerson dated January 5, 1998, stated that "no foul play is suspected at this time." The RGS investigation was completed and a draft report was submitted to Deputy Commissioner Reynolds on February 27, 1998.

The investigation found that some staff did not know that other colleagues had reason to be concerned about the safety of inmate Nickerson. Officers working the upper ranges were assigned to their control posts, where they could review the activities of the previous shift. But officers assigned to the lower ranges took up their posts in the main dome, and had no immediate access to logbooks, where concerns like the one registered by Officer Whaley on November 10, 1997, were recorded. At the time of the presumed suicide, there was no "responsibility framework" to ensure important information was passed between shifts. Sousa-Diaz told

a board of inquiry that he did not know Nickerson and had no previous knowledge that he had personal problems. The board concluded that Sousa-Diaz might indeed not have known about Nickerson's precarious situation.

The RGS investigation found that "Institutional Standing Orders and Post Orders [at KP] are not in compliance with legislation and policy relating to Unit Management, Critical Incident Stress management and the Counting of inmates." The bottom line was no different from Warden Monty Bourke's fact-finding investigation at KP: "The correctional staff member conducting the range walks and count at 05:00 on the morning of 27 December 1997 failed to ensure an accounting for a living, breathing body."

To defend himself against what he considered to be a false charge, Pedro Sousa-Diaz applied under access-to-information legislation to see the documents from the RGS investigation, as well as observation reports written by correctional staff regarding the Nickerson affair. He was flatly denied the observation reports. Although he eventually received a copy of the RGS report, crucial areas had been blacked out.

Officer Phil Whaley was meeting the same wall of official silence in his efforts to help officers Sousa-Diaz and Boulter fight the disciplinary sanctions imposed by the warden. Whaley, the chief shop steward and grievance coordinator, had requested the autopsy and various other investigative reports, but neither the police, the coroner, nor the penitentiary service would release the documents. That left Whaley feeling frustrated and concerned, particularly since his anecdotal knowledge of the case had led him to a conclusion very different from the one reached by the CSC: he believed that Victor Nickerson had not died by his own hand.

On June 7, 1998, he wrote a letter directly to the Ontario Provincial Police Penitentiary Squad, citing his moral and legal obligation as a peace officer. Whaley readily admitted that he was not a professional investigator and that what he was offering the police was a patchwork of rumour, surmise, and fact gathered

during his work on the officer's grievance against the CSC. But there was one explosive allegation made in the nine-page letter Whaley gave to the OPP: that a resident on Lower G Range at the time of the presumed suicide, inmate Fish, had told two correctional officers that another inmate "murdered Nickerson in his cell the evening of December 26, 1997 and placed Nickerson in his bed and went in the cell during yard return the next morning and hung him up."

Leo Prosser was one of those two officers: "I knew Fish. He had information, he gave me information. I was escorting him one time from the diss cells . . . to the hospital, [I] just started talking about the [management] bullshit that was going on with me, and he says, 'Yeah Leo, that's bullshit.' He says, 'Just like the Nickerson case.' I said, 'What are you talking about?' He said, 'Nickerson was murdered.' And then he just stopped, and that was it. Just stopped, didn't say anything else. Then I found out that he had mentioned something to another guard too about the Nickerson case. That he knows, he knew, who actually did the murder."

Whaley concluded his letter to the OPP by volunteering to be interviewed between 10:00 and 14:00 on any working day. He was never questioned. When he later ran into one of the investigators and raised the Nickerson case, Whaley says he was rebuffed. "He told me to drop it and keep my nose out of it."

If inmate Fish did, in fact, know anything about the death of Victor Nickerson, he would be keeping it to himself; according to a brief press report, he died "suddenly" at KP of an apparent drug overdose on November 26, 1999.

The same year that Victor Nickerson died in Kingston Penitentiary, the RCMP began a murder investigation – still ongoing as of this writing – into the death of federal inmate James Mills. In 1991, Mills had been found strangled in his cell at Atlantic Institution in Renous, New Brunswick, where he was serving a life sentence for armed robbery and forcible confinement. At the time, CSC determined that the inmate's death was a suicide.

Despite requests under access-to-information legislation, CSC has refused to make a report into its handling of the inmate's "presumed suicide" public.

On January 26, 1999, Alfred Frank Martin was murdered on Upper G Range at Kingston Penitentiary. "Alfie" Martin, thirty-eight, was serving a ten-year term for attempted murder and aggravated assault after being convicted of stabbing two men in a Toronto apartment while high on alcohol and drugs. He also had convictions for sexual assault and robbery. One of his victims was an eighty-one-year-old woman.

At six feet and 180 pounds, Martin's wiry stature was deceiving. He was one of the most feared inmates in the prison, an accomplished scrapper who wouldn't back down from anyone. He was once jumped by ten inmates in the gym but fought the pack off single-handedly. (Adding to the fear he inspired, he also allegedly had AIDS and hepatitis C, and regularly used his medical condition as a weapon.) Many inmates simply believed he was crazy.

Federal inmates Robert "Bobby" Simpson, Donald "Donny" LaKing, and Pierre Carrière were charged with second-degree murder in Martin's death. They pleaded not guilty. The three had a streak of violence easily as broad as their victim's. For Carrière, it was his third murder charge. In 1994 he gunned down an unarmed corner-store owner during a robbery for the contents of the cash register and a carton of cigarettes. He then shot his own accomplice in the head and dismembered his corpse with a chainsaw. With his girlfriend at his side, Carrière scattered the carefully wrapped body parts along country roads. Simpson had been in fourteen different prisons and was four years into a twelve-year sentence for the manslaughter death of a Montreal woman in 1995. LaKing was entering the nineteenth year of a double life sentence for a pair of murders.

In January 1999, trouble on the notoriously difficult range had been brewing for days. Two days before the murder, Martin had

requested medical attention to have his right eyelid cleaned and Steristripped. He claimed to have split the eyelid when he walked into his cell door. Martin was escorted to the KP hospital by a CX2, Eddie Castle. Earle Young, a CX1 on duty that same day on Upper G Range, had warned in his observation report that Martin might be experiencing difficulty with other inmates. He ended his assessment with the words "Close observation recommended."

On the last day of Alfie Martin's life, Officer Young walked Upper G Range several times. After coming on shift at 14:45, he found things strangely quiet. The only complaint he'd received was directed at the volume control on one inmate's stereo; once again, the man was playing his music too loudly. Although no one gave Young a hard time, he could feel the tension rising among the twenty-eight inmates who were loose on the range as he did his walks.

Just after 15:20, Martin got into a shouting match with Officer McGuire, in the dome area of the prison. Christokos, the chairman of the inmate committee and the so-called "mayor" of KP, had just been fired from his canteen job for possession of drugs. The other inmates, including Martin, were now planning a sit-down protest. After a lengthy confrontation with Officer McGuire, Martin voluntarily returned to his range with the promise to behave.

To the younger guards, it was just a case of another con blowing off steam. But to the veterans, who had worked at KP in the 1970s and 1980s and who now constituted just 20 per cent of KP's workforce, it was the distant thunder of a gathering storm. They knew that for Martin, "flipping out" was a way of signalling authorities that he was in trouble with other inmates and wanted to be admitted to segregation until the situation cooled down.

"He had a habit of – when he wanted to go to the hole, like, he didn't say, 'Boss, take me to the hole,' because he was basically a big shot inside institutions," one veteran guard said. "He'd throw a little bit of a disturbance, just to save face. He knew that when he threatened an officer, cussed him out, the regulations said they had

to take him to the hole. That way he got to go to the hole and also look like a tough guy to the rest of the inmates."

Alfie Martin hadn't exactly endeared himself to KP's senior management. He not only did drugs, drank heavily, and harassed both inmates and guards, he also verbally abused KP's warden, Monty Bourke. One guard who worked in the segregation unit overheard Martin abusing the warden on several occasions: "I worked the seg blocks all the time. That would be Lower H and the dissociation cells. And Monty [Bourke] would come down there and this inmate [Martin] would say, 'I want to talk to you, I want to talk to you,' because they held this inmate in there for a very long period of time for no apparent reason. And Monty wouldn't give him the time of day. It was to the point where this inmate would be calling him names: 'You fucking asshole, you fucking goof.'"

Unsuccessful in his attempt to be sent to segregation, Martin returned to his range. At approximately 15:45, Officer Young witnessed a brief sparring match between inmates Martin and Simpson. Yet when Young jumped up and started for the range door, the two men sauntered toward the office arm in arm, patting each other on the back to indicate that the incident wasn't serious. But no amount of third-rate acting could conceal the fact that something heavy was happening on Upper G Range.

According to one observation report, after this incident it was decided that Martin should go to the diss cells. Backup was called in. Acting Unit Manager Sheri Crisp began negotiating with Martin through a barred door, but he now refused to leave the cellblock. During the exchange with Crisp, Martin appeared to be drunk. He was loud, slurred his words, "appeared to be irrational," and kept repeating himself. Gradually, he seemed to regain control and calmed down. After another promise to improve his behaviour, it was finally agreed that he would remain on the range. Once again, things appeared to settle down on the troubled cellblock.

But at about 16:50, there was another altercation involving Martin and inmate LaKing. LaKing dashed up the range steps to the fourth-floor landing with what appeared to be a metal object in his hand. Although captured on videotape, the scene was not clear enough for guards to determine whether it was a knife. A brief but intense altercation ensued. Acting Unit Manager Crisp spoke to Martin again. This time he agreed to go to the diss cells if he had a guarantee that he would be let out the following day. Officer John McCormack overheard Martin telling Crisp he was drunk and had shot heroin. When the acting unit manager left without agreeing to his terms, Martin became angry and stormed off.

Deputy Warden Alex Lubimiv was informed of the situation and requested that Martin meet him in the courtroom area of the prison for further talks. Sensing a trap, Martin refused. Lubimiv convened a staff meeting in the Keeper's Hall.

Officer Whaley spoke to Martin briefly through the office window on the third floor of G Block: "He was extremely agitated and seemed to be trying to incite the other convicts on 3/4 G to smash the range." But Whaley, a veteran officer with more than thirty years of experience, did not see any "real action" on the range. He was detailed by the deputy warden to take a new gas gun from B-1 Control to Officer McGuire on the fourth floor, and to replace the defective gas gun in the Keeper's Hall with one from another office. He then returned the defective gun to the armouries officer.

By 17:00, the riot squad had been scrambled. Since there is no funding to keep this specialized force on site on a twenty-four-hour basis, its members had to be called from other work posts or from home. At 17:55, inmates were loudly demanding their suppers. After conferring with the Keeper's Hall, Officer Young informed them they would be fed only if they agreed to lock up. They refused, and an already tense situation worsened.

The reluctance of guards to intervene with force was understandable. The Martin incident happened during the much

publicized and racially charged coroner's inquest into the asphyxiation death on October 24, 1993, of twenty-three-year-old Robert Gentles, who had also been an inmate on Upper G Range at KP. Gentles had died during a forcible extraction from his cell. He had been serving a thirty-one-month sentence for failure to comply, uttering death threats, possession of stolen goods, and sexual assault. His family filed a $35-million lawsuit against CSC employees, the attorney general of Canada, and the manufacturers of the Mace used to subdue him.

The police investigation into the incident concluded in 1994 with no charges against CSC staff, but a justice of the peace ruled that a private prosecution launched by the Gentles family could proceed. As a result, six KP staff were charged with manslaughter and criminal negligence causing death. On March 10, 1995, charges against four officers were dropped; three months later, charges against the remaining two officers were withdrawn as a result of insufficient evidence. A week after that, Carmeta Gentles learned that the Ontario Court had ruled that she could not proceed with the private prosecution of the staff members allegedly involved in her son's death.

A coroner's inquest into the Gentles affair began in March 1998 and ended in June 1999, after hearing evidence from ninety-eight witnesses. On June 24, 1999, the inquest found that the inmate's death had been accidental. In releasing its findings, the coroner made seventy-four recommendations and requested that CSC respond to each and every one of them within a year. The first recommendation put a chill over the system's discretion to use force to remove a prisoner from his cell or range: "All alternatives [should] be considered before a cell extraction is ordered."

Regional Instruction 605 for cell and living area extractions stipulated that "only specially trained staff shall enter a cell/living area to remove a resistive inmate, except in situations which a Correctional Supervisor or Officer in Charge deem an emergency." It also stated that the CS or officer in charge "shall exhaust all verbal

attempts to gain compliance from the inmate prior to taking further steps." Despite the judicial exoneration, six careers within CSC had been ruined by the Gentles affair, and one of the charged officers had attempted suicide. The ghost of Robert Gentles may not have been walking the halls of Upper G Range on the night that Alfie Martin died, but he was certainly haunting the thoughts of correctional personnel trying to deal with the rampaging inmate.

Shortly after 18:00, Officer Young began his last walk on the range before the murder took place. Inmate LaKing caught up with the officer as he neared the end of the range. Young, who had seen the videotape of the earlier altercation between Martin and LaKing, said, "Jeez, Donny, I hope that wasn't a shiv I saw when you ran up the stairs at Alfie earlier." LaKing looked down at him and said, "Naw, don't worry about it. But I think you'd better get off the range."

It was an ominous statement coming from LaKing. According to a memo dated January 19, 1999, just a week before the Martin murder, LaKing had requested a transfer to Port-Cartier Institution in Quebec. The reason for the transfer request was recorded in this chilling entry in the report of his case conference: "This inmate is in a very agitated state and is threatening the life of another inmate. Can we get him out of the institution or off the range?"

Although Young worried that LaKing might have a weapon, he couldn't frisk him because twenty-seven other inmates, many of them probably armed, were out of their cells and milling around the range. It was the price front-line guards paid for CSC's so-called "dynamic security," meaning human intuition and knowledge of inmates rather than "static security" – bars and locked doors. Young continued his walk, working hard to maintain his composure. Young was fifty feet from the door when one of the Jamaican inmates called out, "Hey, Father Grim!" – Young's nickname on the range – and they bantered for a few seconds.

Suddenly the range door burst open and an officer grabbed Young and warned him to get out. Acting Unit Manager Crisp and other staff had been watching Young through the main barrier

and the surveillance camera and were worried that he was lingering on a range where conditions seemed to be deteriorating rapidly.

Even though Upper G was known as a "hot" range, it was still "minimum-manned" to save money. When Young went in, he did not have a "float" to watch his back and was outnumbered twenty-eight to one. In one of the enduring ironies of the system, the unarmed guard was walking among inmates who were out of their cells and milling about the two-storey range, many of them high on drugs and brew and armed with homemade knives.

The melodrama on Upper G was entering the final act. At 18:05 Alfie Martin threw what appeared to be soap flakes at the third-floor range door and struck a match. When the substance ignited, it produced flames five feet high that touched off the fire alarm, the automatic sprinkler system, and the automatic shutter at the window near the door. A gas gun was put in position by guards in the fourth-floor office.

Martin's death warrant was quietly delivered at 18:09. An inmate approached the range camera and covered it with a blanket. Fourteen minutes later, at 18:23, Alfie Martin staggered toward the range barrier on the third floor, where he collapsed, bleeding profusely. The sprinkler heads put out thirty-five gallons of water a minute, and Martin's blood was washed away as it gushed out. Officers recalled the flow of water under the door. "It was a river of red," one of them said.

KP's logbooks show that the officer on duty immediately took the stretcher off the wall and readied it at the third-floor door. The officers could not open the door for almost four minutes because Martin's "kid," twenty-year-old inmate Clifford Long, was holding the dying prisoner's hand and refused to move back from the door. When they got to Martin, the officers counted six punctures in his chest, "sucking wounds" so deep that they opened and closed like dark mouths as the air escaped from the dying man's diaphragm. Martin was removed by stretcher at 18:26 and later pronounced dead of multiple stab wounds, including a deep gash to his neck.

The arrival of the riot squad quickly restored order on Upper G Range. Inmates who had earlier refused to lock up returned to their cells, but not before throwing a pile of syringes and shivs out the cellblock window. Knowing that the stabbing would prompt a full-scale security search of their cells, they wanted to make sure that the evidence of any offences was gone before the guards appeared.

By 18:55, Warden Bourke had arrived in the institution and personally taken control of the situation. He immediately asked for a meeting with Christokos, the chairman of the inmate committee. Knowing the inmate code of silence, Christokos refused to comply unless he had an inmate witness who could later confirm that he hadn't ratted out anyone involved in Martin's stabbing. Christokos and inmate LeBlanc met with Bourke from 19:28 to 19:41. At 20:15 the range was locked down and the ERT moved in. According to one team member, you could "hear a pin drop" on the range where just two hours before Martin's enraged shouts had resounded.

In typical CSC fashion, the story the outside world got was very different from the grim reality of what had happened on the killing grounds of Upper G Range. The day after the murder, Assistant Warden John Oddie told the press that he had no idea what had sparked the murder. "We had no indications of there being any problems leading up to this."

It wasn't long before authorities found out what had happened during the blackout after the blanket was draped over the range camera on Upper G. Far from trying to hide their involvement in the murder, two of the perpetrators were actually boasting about it in the press. Simpson and LaKing contacted a newspaper and claimed that Martin died because he was allowed to run amok in the cellblock, high on brew and heroin. They openly admitted to the killing but claimed that they had acted only in self-defence.

The Criminal Code allows a defendant to claim self-defence if a person is "under reasonable apprehension of death or grievous bodily harm" or believes he "cannot otherwise preserve himself." In the landmark 1990 *Lavallée* case, the Supreme Court of Canada

allowed a Manitoba woman to claim she had killed her abusive husband in self-defence, even though he had turned to leave the room when the murder happened. In another case, the Supreme Court allowed a prisoner to plead self-defence in the murder of a fellow prisoner after a psychiatrist testified that the inmate truly believed he would be killed.

According to Bobby Simpson, Martin was the "alpha predator" on the range, an aggressive bully who took whatever he wanted by force. But a veteran guard who had come to know Martin well over the years said age and illness had mellowed the inmate. Drugs and booze had also taken their toll. After years of being the leading force of "the old gang," he was no longer the dominant male on the range.

Simpson claimed he had been in the prison library when he first heard that Martin was drunk and terrorizing other inmates. He returned to Upper G and joined friends near a window; Martin then loomed up and began punching him. When Simpson retreated to his cell to inspect the damage, another inmate rushed in to tell him that Martin had a knife and was coming to kill him. Before reaching him, Simpson said, Martin tried to stab Carrière, but LaKing grappled with him and managed to push him down the stairs near the guards' station. (Carrière and LaKing were best friends.) Enraged, Martin returned to the third floor, shouting, smashing windows, and setting a fire in front of the third-floor door at about 18:10. Smoke quickly filled the range, making it difficult for the officers to see inside.

Martin and Simpson came together for a second time. According to the perpetrator, as Martin reached for his knife, Simpson stabbed him repeatedly with his own ten-inch brass shiv: "He put his hand in his pocket to get a knife or something and I then defended myself and as soon as [Martin] moved two feet away from me, I dropped the knife and walked away." Simpson claimed that other than the blood, he did not see the deadly effect of his frenzied attack: "I was getting hugs from other inmates. I was crying. I was scared to death. I was crying my eyes out," the killer said.

Simpson's recollection of the murder may have been a little self-serving, and his memory faulty. In the press, Simpson claimed that Martin lay bleeding profusely in front of the barrier for thirty to forty minutes while his friend yelled for help. Yet the logbooks clearly show that the officer on duty took the stretcher off the wall immediately and readied it at the third-floor door. The delay lasted approximately three to four minutes because officers could not open the door. There is also strong evidence that Martin was unarmed at the time of his death.

While inmates Simpson and LaKing were at Millhaven, awaiting transfer to the special handling unit at Sainte-Anne-des-Plaines, they applied for a federal grant to launch a constitutional challenge to Commissioner's Directive 551. Under that directive, CSC has the authority to transfer an offender accused of assaulting or murdering someone in prison to the SHU at a super-maximum-security institution.

(By CSC definition, an inmate is dangerous "if his behaviour is such that it causes bodily harm or death or seriously jeopardizes the safety of others." If an inmate commits an act causing serious harm or death while in prison, the regional deputy commissioner reviews his case for admission to the SHU for assessment. It is interesting to note that if an inmate commits a serious assault or murder inside, creating a problem for the CSC, he is sent to the SHU. Yet until very recently, the perpetrator of a violent assault or murder in the community often went to a medium-security institution within months of sentencing.)

John Hill, the lawyer representing Simpson and LaKing, convinced the Court Challenges Program to give his clients $5,000 to make the argument that no prisoner should be sent to the SHU without first being convicted of a crime. Hill called the SHU a form of psychological terror or "living death" for inmates and promised to develop a legal argument "which addresses the unique disadvantage and vulnerable position of prisoners." The case has not been heard yet.

Ontario's minister of corrections, Rob Sampson, was livid. He denounced the federal grant to a pair of convicted killers charged with yet another killing as a travesty of justice: "As far as the Ontario government is concerned, it's the victims of crimes, and not the criminals, who are placed in a disadvantaged and vulnerable position."

Simpson and LaKing were quietly returned to Kingston Penitentiary by CSC. Even though they were placed in segregation on Lower H Range, they still had a good pipeline to inmate witnesses who would testify at their trial. In the end, Alfie Martin's "kid" testified for the defence. On June 22, 2001, Mr. Justice Bernard Hurley found the accused not guilty. In announcing his decision, Hurley told the court that the Crown had not convinced him beyond a reasonable doubt that Robert Simpson and Donald LaKing had not acted in self-defence when they killed Alfie Martin, adding that the case against Pierre Carrière, the third man charged in the incident, was contradictory and confusing.

In a stinging indictment of Ole Ingstrup's offender-indulgent prison system, Alfie Martin's accused killer blamed senior managers at KP for allowing drugs, alcohol, and violence at the institution. It was the fault of a system gone haywire in which everyone was at risk. "I'm a product of the system," Simpson said, "and I've adapted quite well. . . . But if you want me to live in a range like that, where madness reigns supreme and the law of the jungle rules, and I have to defend myself, don't punish me for it."

In the wake of Alfie Martin's murder in what the judge ruled was self-defence, Simpson had some unsolicited advice for Ole Ingstrup. If you want to run an effective prison system, he said, you have to have enough force to keep dangerous inmates under control. Or, as he told one newspaper reporter, "When you have people running around doing triple-life sentences and addicted to heroin, you can't have a woman stand behind a barrier and say, 'Please stop that.' You have to have some type of mechanism to control people. That's why they are in prison."

9

WRONGING THE RIGHTS

Every night, she must watch them masturbate. She has no choice.

Women have worked as guards in federal men's prisons since 1983. Helen Smith, one of eighteen female guards at Kingston Penitentiary, came into the service full of high hopes. Trained as a child and youth worker, she believed in the restorative justice model and the rehabilitation of inmates. But after less than three years in the Correctional Service of Canada, the steady bombardment of verbal sexual abuse from inmates and virtual indifference from management to behaviour that would be punished by law on the street have left her with the conviction that the system is failing both inmates and society.

"I understand that I am coming into a different environment and there is some stuff that I am going to have to take. I understand that they don't see a lot of females. I know I'm not bad looking. But I expect there to be sanctions when they go way over the line. They should never have the right to show themselves naked to me, masturbating night after night, putting their penises through the bars while I do my walks. It just keeps going and going and going. If they did that on the street, they would be

charged. Here, nothing happens. All we are doing is reinforcing their bad attitude, making them worse."

Smith, an attractive woman whose smile isn't marred by the braces she wears, found out early in her career that management didn't necessarily have her best interests at heart in a prison system built on the rights of inmates. In fact, there were times when she felt that her safety was being jeopardized by executive decisions that seemed to place an inordinate amount of trust in people who had already violated it, often in horrible ways. Assigned to the shop dome by herself, Smith noticed that there were a number of "yellow tag" inmates with access to her post, including one named Krauss.

The yellow tag, unique to KP, is management's way of identifying dangerous sex offenders who are never to be left alone with females. Krauss was considered a high risk to females after he showed "abusive behaviour toward hospital nursing staff in a sexual manner," while receiving treatment at a psychiatric facility in 1992. Posters around KP detailing his offences specifically said, "Precautions should be taken to ensure that other staff are present in the same room when this man is interacting with female staff." Officer Smith asked the acting keeper why a lone woman had been assigned to an accessible post with designated sex offenders like Krauss at large. She has never forgotten his answer: "He said, 'Well, you are not alone because you have other inmates there.'"

In 1998, Smith was having a problem with Chilton, a violent sex offender with a long record of hate crimes against women that had landed him in KP's protective segregation. A week before his encounter with Smith, Chilton had verbally abused another female guard so viciously that he was sent to the hole. On the day he got out, Chilton asked Smith for a bedroll. It was 17:00 and the officers who issued blankets had gone home. When Smith explained the situation, the inmate exploded at her: "He said, 'You fucking cunt, you better get it for me.'"

Smith knew that Chilton had gotten out of the hole on a "behaviour contract," in which the inmate wins release in return for a verbal promise to behave. If he breaks the contract, as he did

with her, he is supposed to be returned to the hole. Smith called the keeper, who said he didn't know about the situation and it would be resolved the next day. After a fashion, it was. All through her next shift, Chilton kept up his abusive barrage while management dithered.

"He called me everything. 'Fucking cunt, whore, I'm going to cut your head off and masturbate down your throat. You should be on your knees where you belong. You fat whore, you fat bitch. Bend over and take it like you deserve it.' It was an awful day."

At 14:30, the unit manager informed the distraught officer that he had spoken to the inmate, who again promised to behave if they didn't send him to the hole. If, on the other hand, they sent him to the hole for abusing Officer Smith, Chilton warned that they would have to send in the riot squad to deal with him. "So the unit manager said they were going to leave him on the range that I was working," Smith recalled.

After Smith's strenuous protests, the decision was reluctantly reversed and Chilton was told he would be going back to the hole. The inmate then claimed he had swallowed razor blades, a story which forced officers to call a nurse and have him examined. By the time the nurse arrived, Chilton had changed his story, now saying that he had suitcased the razor blades rather than swallowed them. He was examined with the "wand," a metal detector, and nothing was found. Chilton was finally sent to the hole, but not for long. "A few minutes later, I got a call from Tim Hamilton, the keeper, saying he is on his way back."

When Smith reported to the office, Chilton was already slouched in a chair wearing a big grin. The officer immediately called the hole to find out why he had been released after so egregiously breaking his behaviour contract. The deputy warden and the unit manager met her in the internal courthouse in the dissociation cells. She was informed that they had reversed the decision because the whole misunderstanding was only over a bedroll. Smith was astonished when she heard Warden Monty Bourke's solution to the situation: Smith would attend a focus group on women's issues.

"I said, 'You've got to be kidding me! After all this you are asking me that?' The deputy warden went on to say that Chilton was abused as a child. He was one of those choirboys. I said, 'You are not supporting me with one inmate on my case. Now I am going to have the whole range doing it.'"

She was right. That very day, several other inmates made sexual remarks as Smith did her rounds. As for inmate Chilton, he didn't wait long to celebrate his manipulation of the system. Waiting until she passed his cell (which regulations required her to inspect for a living, breathing body), he whispered, "It smells like fish on the range. They used the wand on me, Helen, and it didn't go off. I hear it goes off for braces. You know, I hear girls with braces can't give good head."

Again, Officer Smith reported Chilton's abuse to the deputy warden, who told her that if he did it again, he would be sent to segregation. "At that point I said, 'When does no mean no, and not, "Don't do it again or else, Buster"?'" Chilton remained on the range, and Smith attended a one-day seminar at the staff college.

Despite management rhetoric that staff are CSC's most important resource, the most basic human rights of front-line correctional workers are violated on a daily basis inside Canadian prisons. If these offences happened in any other workplace, they would be the subject of civil and criminal proceedings. Within Canada's secretive prison system, they are passed off as part of the job. While CSC employees are expected to treat inmates with the utmost respect at all times, they themselves are routinely assaulted, abused, and threatened in outrageous ways with few if any consequences for the inmates.

It is a problem CSC is having trouble hiding. When the Working Group on Human Rights, headed by one of Canada's foremost human rights advocates, Maxwell Yalden, reported on the federal Department of Corrections in May 1999, it noted that the essential rights of offenders were more than adequately reflected in the CCRA. But the working group, which had been commissioned by Ole Ingstrup himself, added that "it would be helpful if a revised

CCRA were to make it clear that staff rights have as much priority as those of offenders."

On paper at least, senior officials in CSC could point to Core Value 3 of the mission statement to prove that staff were respected and independent players in the federal prison system. In fact, one of the guiding principles of Core Value 3 expressly stated, "We believe that staff have a lot to contribute and that they must be able to voice their ideas and concerns, within the service without fear."

Officer Eddie Castle found out exactly how hollow those words were when he tried to warn senior management at Kingston Penitentiary about the danger to the public in releasing inmate Mark Donner in 1999. The thirty-five-year-old inmate was just finishing his third prison term, a sentence of four years, one month, and twenty-three days for assault causing bodily harm and uttering death threats. Castle, a visible-minority officer who had joined CSC in September 1991 and was by then a CX2, knew Donner well. He had even written a commendation about him in the Offender Management System after the tough inmate helped to defuse a dangerous situation on Lower B involving a pair of rampaging inmates.

Donner had spent most of his life in prison and had very limited vocational and educational skills. He also suffered from the substance abuse and anger problems common to so many inmates. Throughout his prison career, he had been used by various factions inside as their muscle, but just as often he was the butt of their jokes because he was illiterate. Castle took Donner under his wing and taught him to read well enough to get through a newspaper.

But the experienced officer knew that even though Donner was about to leave the prison on statutory release, his court-determined debt to society two-thirds paid, he was completely unprepared for life on the street. Castle knew that the inmate was headed for another run-in with the law and that somebody was going to get hurt. The source of that insight was impeccable; Mark Donner himself. "He told me, he said, 'I'm going to go out

and kill somebody before I come back. The only thing I know is prison.' So I put it on paper.''

Shortly before Donner's release, Castle made detailed entries in a casework record log, expressing his fear that Donner was bound for failure when he was released into the community and that innocent people could suffer. "Whose family will be the sacrificial lamb/lambs?" he wrote. Despite the officer's worries, Donner walked through the doors of Kingston Penitentiary on his statutory release date, June 18, 1999. But the story was far from over.

"I got a document back from Alex Lubimiv, the deputy warden, that said, 'I'm asking your unit manager to wipe off all this casework record from this inmate's file because it shouldn't be there,' " Castle said.

The record shows that a month after Donner's release, Lubimiv indeed sent a memo to Castle, criticizing the officer for reports he had included in his inmates' casework record. "Over the last few months, your reports have been digressing from observations and facts, that are a positive contribution to the process, to reports containing opinions that are inflammatory, demonstrate a lack of knowledge of the Mission Statement, Commissioner's Directives and basic policy on a number of basic issues. . . . While I applaud that you took the initiative to complete the casework records, the contents of the records were completely inappropriate and unacceptable as a case management document."

Lubimiv ordered Castle to refrain from including personal comments and opinions in official CSC reports. The officer was also ordered to take a report-writing course, "as the quality of your current reports is not acceptable for use at Kingston Penitentiary." He was further directed to ask senior staff to proofread his reports, and not to copy messages beyond the unit manager level. If he continued his inappropriate reporting, "further action would be taken." It was a strange series of directives for a department whose mission statement said officers were free to voice their concerns within the system "without fear."

It wasn't until July 28, 1999, that Deputy Warden Lubimiv declared his real objection to Officer Castle's recording of his opinions, including concerns about public safety, in official CSC documents. In a memo to a union official about the affair, the deputy warden wrote, "The reports submitted are legal documents and as such are subject to freedom of information requests by inmates and the Public, used in legal proceedings and investigations. I believe it is not responsible for management to allow such documents into the record." The deputy warden didn't want the public or anybody else finding out how CSC conducts its business. Given what happened next, there was good reason.

On September 20, 1999, the Toronto police informed CSC that Mark Donner was back in custody and had incurred new charges. The career criminal, just three months out of prison, had attacked a woman with a butcher knife, inflicting multiple stab wounds on his traumatized victim. Just as he had told Officer Castle at the time of his statutory release, Mark Donner had committed a violent crime and was on his way back to prison: "He went out. He stabbed a woman and physically assaulted her in other ways, and he's coming back. He got five more years. But this is one case. One of many cases. So they are telling us on the one hand we've got to do our casework, we've got to observe things, we've got to report it. But the fact is they don't want us to do that."

The frustration of correctional officers who constantly see their rights ignored or denied have made for a workplace with the highest stress levels in the country. In fact, 17 per cent of guards suffer from post-traumatic stress as a result of their duties. (By comparison, 20 per cent of soldiers who returned from Vietnam suffered from post-traumatic stress.) Assaulted and routinely showered with feces and urine when the inmates don't like their dinners, officers are constantly reminded that while they must operate to the letter of the law, inmate excesses "come with the territory" of working in the prison system. Occasionally, the deference to offenders' rights and the failure to authorize force in the

face of extreme provocation exact a terrible toll on staff, including non–officers.

On Tuesday, November 15, 1994, a keeper at KP received a call from one of the inmates on his range, Tyrone Peard, who reported that he wouldn't be available for the 17:00 count. When the officer asked why not, Peard mockingly replied, "Because I'm up here in the administration office raping the woman you provided me with."

Peard was serving eight years for sexual assault with a weapon and forcible confinement. He also had two previous convictions for sexual assault. His victim had been working as a clerk in the office when Peard came in, looking for his case management officer. The woman couldn't find him and Peard left. Fifteen minutes later, he returned and grabbed the clerk, covering her mouth with his hand. The twenty-year-old inmate was angry because he had been turned down for some programs and a transfer he was seeking. The victim later recalled that Peard made references to the Robert Gentles case, saying the guards had got an inmate and now he had one of CSC's people.

Peard repeatedly raped the woman and made death threats against her. Between rapes, he told her he loved her and asked her not to cry. He also told her that his brother didn't like it when people cried. The woman later testified, "He said if his brother had been there he would have slit my throat and carved my head out like a pumpkin." Peard, who vacillated between throwing furniture against the wall and eerie calm, told her he wished his brother were there. Occasionally, he talked about killing himself. Hoping to ward off another attack, the clerk tried to tell him that she could become pregnant and that she was a Christian, but he raped her again.

Warden Ken Payne would later claim that calm, constant dialogue, including hours of negotiations with KP's inmate committee, helped quell the potentially explosive situation. Not everyone agreed. Standing idly by, watching the atrocities in the administration office while the warden talked with inmates, were a group of

highly trained armed men who could have ended the hostage taking in a matter of seconds. The extent to which the inmates controlled how the crisis was dealt with sickened them: "Those were the worst hours I have ever experienced," a crack member of the ERT said. "We had the ability to walk through that partition wall and take that woman out, yet we had to stand there sweating in full gear watching this animal assault her. Why the prisoners had to be part of the decision of what to do, I'll never know."

At his trial in September 1996, Peard claimed that he recalled nothing about the hostage taking and sexual assaults. He said he was severely intoxicated after taking seven hundred milligrams of Valium washed down with brew. The judge wasn't persuaded. A psychiatrist testified that this was "an almost unbelievably high dose" and that Peard would have been in a toxic coma, or at least noticeably intoxicated. He was neither.

Peard's "horrendous background" included abandonment by his biological father and beatings and emotional abuse from his stepfather. His mother was toxemic during the pregnancy and Peard had to be resuscitated when he was born. He had health problems as a result of his low birth weight and drank kerosene when he was three. Peard, who spent his first seven years with his mother, an alcoholic, was then placed with children's services. He told the judge, "All I really know about my mother is her birthdate." He also claimed he had been sexually abused by his stepfather.

Like 70 to 80 per cent of the inmate population, Tyrone Peard was described by a psychiatrist as having an anti-social personality, with narcissistic and borderline personality characteristics. Dr. Bob McCaldon had Peard under his care for five days in June 1994, while he was at the Regional Treatment Centre at KP for assessment, less than five months before the assault. At the time, Peard claimed that he was depressed.

At first the doctor thought Peard was genuinely depressed and prescribed Prozac to alleviate anxiety; but he quickly came to the conclusion that Peard was trying to manipulate him so that he could serve his time at a treatment facility rather than a prison.

None of the psychiatrists who saw Peard believed he actually wanted to change his behaviour.

Following the assault, Peard was sent to Millhaven, and then to the Oak Ridge assessment centre at Penetanguishene, Ontario, for a court-ordered assessment of his mental competency. But he was sent back to Millhaven for bad behaviour. Peard believed he could beat the charges by claiming mental illness or drug- and alcohol-induced temporary insanity. Instead, he was found competent to stand trial. On September 10, 1996, Peard was found guilty of sexually assaulting and terrorizing his female victim during the hostage taking two years before. The next day he was found dead in his cell with a massive dose of the anti-depressant doxepin in his system. At the inquest, Dr. McCaldon said, "Psychiatrists treat illness very well. They don't treat badness very well."

Intravenous drug use by inmates, and the resultant high incidence of infectious diseases, has become one of the hottest labour issues for CSC front-line employees. Guards are demanding access to the health and medical status records of inmates they work with, so that they may take the appropriate precautions in the course of their duties. According to a union survey released in January 2000, concern about infectious diseases is the number one health and safety issue of correctional officers in Canada. Their union believes that the right of CSC employees to have information that directly affects their own safety and lives overrides any inmate's right to privacy, which until now has been deemed sacrosanct by CSC management. At best, there is still only a grudging acknowledgment of the officers' position. The parliamentary subcommittee reviewing the CCRA, for example, recommended that correctional staff have access to health care information "only to the extent strictly necessary to take steps to protect their own health."

The guards' fear of infection is far from theoretical. In 1997, Officer Roy Tremblay was pricked with a needle while relocating an inmate to a new cell. The inmate had full-blown AIDS. The guards had asked CSC for special anti-puncture safety gloves but

were turned down. In October 1999, KP inmate Thomas Doyle returned to his cell after receiving his medication. According to the official report of the incident, when ordered to comply with the regulation pertaining to cell coverings, Doyle told Officer Eddie Castle to "suck his dick." He then threatened to infect the officer with the AIDS virus. Castle noted that the offender's behaviour had become increasingly difficult: "The subject uses his condition as an excuse rather than complying with his responsibilities," he reported.

In July 1998, while Officers Patrick Ducharme and Neil Baker were trying to escort an intoxicated inmate to segregation, both officers were viciously bitten by the convicted murderer. Because of CSC policy respecting inmates' privacy rights, the officers were not allowed to know if inmate Syd White had any infectious diseases. Through clandestine means, it was learned that White had hepatitis C. The two officers began getting medical checkups and blood tests every six months. Although Collins Bay warden Wayne Scissons initially saw no reason to move White to a higher-security level, union officials kept up the pressure. Eventually, White had seventy-five days added to his sentence and was transferred to J Unit at Millhaven, reserved for some of the worst offenders in the system.

But not for long. Just two months after he was transferred, CSC returned White to Collins Bay without notifying either of the guards he had bitten. Outraged staff told management that they would not perform their duties "if White came through the gates." Regional CSC managers insisted on White's return to Collins Bay. The officers were reduced to desperate measures. In the end, they had themselves registered as victims of crime with the National Parole Board, which would at least make it mandatory for the system to notify them of their assailant's movements in future.

Although officers are routinely in contact with inmate blood, it took until April 1999 for CSC to develop a protocol for employees who are exposed to blood-borne pathogens and other body fluids. The protocol applies to employee exposure from an inmate source only when "the inmate consents to release of medical information regarding infectious disease status." The health care administrator

was waiting for national policy direction "when an inmate refuses to consent to release of information." Nurses were to have "informed, written consent" from the inmate before releasing medical information to the specialist treating the exposed employee. The name of the inmate "source" of the disease was not to be forwarded to the hospital.

It took an officer at William Head Institution, outside Victoria, ten agonizing months to find out the blood status of an inmate who had assaulted him. On October 8, 1999, Officer Rick Justice was working in the units before the 19:00 count. One of his colleagues received reliable intelligence that drugs were about to be moved that night in one of the units. The two officers on the unit and three backups went in to search and found one of the suspected inmates taking a shower. When the inmate found out what they were there for, he began cursing at the guards and pinned one officer against the wall.

Two others tried unsuccessfully to calm him down. "I'm fucking going to kill you!" the inmate screamed. He broke one officer's watch and glasses and tried to kick Justice in the face. He then threatened all three men, saying that he knew people on the outside who would "get" their families; he referred to two Quebec guards shot dead recently by members of a biker gang doing a hit for their friends inside. The inmate was so out of control that he broke the first set of handcuffs used to restrain him, bloodying his wrists. Justice, who had spent twelve and a half years in the military, including a tour of peacekeeping duty in the Middle East, knew that one person had to be in control to secure any violent situation. In his struggle to subdue the inmate, Justice suffered an inch-and-a-half-long cut to his thumb.

The inmate was taken to segregation, demanding that photos be taken to prove that he had been manhandled: "I'm going to sue you!" he screamed. But Justice had weightier matters to deal with. In addition to the cut, he had been exposed to the inmate's blood in his face and mouth. He immediately asked for the inmate's blood status. The keeper told him to go to the hospital,

where he also learned he had a torn rotator in his shoulder as the result of the struggle. Although Justice was given a five-day cocktail of drugs, the attending doctor could not get the inmate's blood status under CSC regulations. As a result, the officer had to take the full, twenty-eight-day course of drugs for HIV, hepatitis C, and other infectious diseases he might have contracted.

Ironically, the officers themselves were then subjected to a full disciplinary investigation for illegal search and seizure, excessive force, and abandoning their posts. In the meantime, word came back through the RCMP that the whole thing had been a set-up by another inmate who controlled the institution's drug trade and who was eager to discredit Justice, one of a handful of guards at William Head who took drug interdiction seriously. Through their searches and seizures, Justice and his conscientious fellow officers were hurting business for the dealers and upsetting the inmates. Officers believe that management at William Head didn't approve of their no-nonsense approach to searches because they didn't want their model institution, one of the cushiest medium-security facilities in the system – with its own tennis courts, fly-fishing dock, and chipping greens – to be associated with a major drug problem.

Although the warden eventually decided not to pursue charges, Justice's wife and eight-year-old son were traumatized by the ordeal. After ten months of worry, blood tests, and drugs, it was finally determined that the inmate had a contact reaction to the hepatitis C virus. It may take up to ten years for the disease to show up in the officer. "This guy destroyed my life," says Justice. "Everything I demanded was refused; everything he wanted he got."

Justice had been exposed to terrible things in the military but says it was nothing compared with working for CSC. Even though he is worn out and fed up with the treatment he received, he vows he is not "giving up." He plans to sue CSC for what they have put him and his family through in the name of protecting an inmate's privacy rights. Although he would like to have his legal bills paid for in any settlement, what he really wants is for the courts to say that CSC is wrong and must stop ignoring the rights

of its own employees in the name of respecting the rights of convicted criminals.

Sometimes even legal drugs can literally cause a riot in prison. On January 4, 2000, at 13:00, sixty-five general-population inmates in Unit 1 at the Atlantic Institution in Renous, New Brunswick, refused to return to their cells for the noon lock-up. The inmates were demanding to be provided with Tylenol and cough syrup, even though both were available for sale in the canteen. They also wanted the return of unauthorized effects seized during a cell search prior to Christmas. The ERT was called in.

At 15:30, the inmates on A and B Ranges began smashing windows and furniture, covering range barriers with blankets to block the view of staff from the control post. The Riot Act was read to the inmates at 16:00. In response, they started a fire on one range. It was put out with a high-pressure water hose. When ERT members attempted to break through the barriers, they discovered that the inmates had tied them shut with fire hoses. Guards fired chemical agents, but since the windows were broken and there was a lot of water on the range, they were virtually ineffective.

At 17:00, the windows in the common room on D Range were smashed out and the RCMP was notified of the riot. At 18:30, D and C Ranges were secured. The ERT used 203 gas cartridges to clear the inmates and remove their jerry-built barricades. With the ERT advancing on them in their black uniforms, shields held high, the offenders on C Range agreed to lock up. By 19:20, the six-member ERT teams from Springhill and Dorchester were en route to Atlantic Institution.

But the riot was far from over. At 20:15, the inmates on A and B Ranges tried to breach the walls of the correctional supervisor's office, giving them entrance to the main hallway. The ERT went onto the roof to get a better view of the inmates, who were now throwing cement blocks and copper pipes at the control post. At 21:35, the team used a fire hose to move back the inmates, who were armed with knives and pipes. At 22:55, the outside ERT teams arrived, but the inmates continued their rampage, setting fires and

screaming at authorities from the ranges until 4:00, when they finally agreed to end the disturbance.

Inmates cleared the debris from the barriers, and some returned to their cells to lock themselves in. A and B Ranges were secured and counted. Since the cells were now unusable, inmates were moved to cells in Unit 3 one by one, by regular security staff. When the count was done at 6:15, all inmates were secured and accounted for. The only thing left was for taxpayers to pick up the tab to repair the prison.

On March 1, 2000, the Fraser Regional Correctional Centre in Maple Ridge, British Columbia, became the first of six maximum-security provincial institutions in that province to impose a no-smoking ban to comply with Workers Compensation Board rules about indoor smoking. The inmates were ready to riot and challenged the ban, arguing it was "cruel and unusual punishment" that violated their Charter rights. They went to court and were given a reprieve; unlike people on the outside, they would not have to obey the laws until further judicial rulings were made. On September 1, 2001, British Columbia's ban on indoor smoking in its prisons went into effect. A Fraser Regional Correctional Centre official explained: "The B.C. province runs their correctional system; in the federal system, the inmates do."

William Canning, who was serving a twenty-two-year sentence, was transferred from Springhill Institution in Nova Scotia to La Macaza Institution in Quebec in 1999. Double-bunked with a smoker for seventeen days, he subsequently took the federal government to court, arguing under the Charter that he had been subjected to the "cruel and unusual punishment" of breathing second-hand smoke. Canning insisted that it was outrageous that he had to breathe smoke in prison when all other federal buildings were smoke-free, including the public areas in correctional facilities. The government argued that allowing inmates to smoke in their cells did not violate CSC policy, and pointed out that on two occasions Canning had actually chosen to share a cell with a

smoker rather than a non-smoker. Nevertheless, CSC quietly settled the case before it reached the Supreme Court. Canning was given $2,500 in compensation.

After a four-day nationwide strike by correctional officers in March 1999 was ended by Bill C-76, a joint union-management committee was struck to study the working conditions of federal correctional officers. For nine months, the committee met with hundreds of officers across the country. The executive summary of its report noted that the officers, often portrayed as subnormal sadists in movies and the popular press, were in fact skilled professionals who required a high level of expertise to do their jobs in the life-and-death conditions in which they routinely worked: "The risk involved in the job, the consequences of making an error, and the constant internal and external scrutiny, add to the already difficult conditions. The job has long-lasting impacts on the personal and professional lives of those who do it."

The committee quickly learned that the biggest problem facing correctional officers was the widely perceived lack of support of front-line workers by management, along with the imposition of policies and procedures that looked much better on paper than they did on the ranges of Canadian prisons. As one senior officer put it to the author, "We are the only group of people whose job is to keep the cons inside the walls. Everyone else is working to get them out of jail. For this, we are the prison doormat. We are being disarmed, our safety equipment removed, or not replaced. I dream of the day when the officers will be treated at least as good as the inmates."

Misunderstood by CSC management, the media, and the general public, guards want recognition of the fact that their job is even more dangerous than that of RCMP officers. Not only are they asked to intervene in violent or emergency situations on a routine basis, they also have daily contact with offenders and are at constant risk of contracting infectious diseases. Despite that, correctional

officers are 20 per cent behind RCMP pay scales and not even on the radar screen when it comes to public respect. Many officers feel that their poor image will never change as long as they are forced to wear uniforms that make them look like fast-food workers or golf instructors.

But correctional officers aren't the only group that CSC has overlooked in its zeal to promote inmates' rights above all else in Canada's prison system. Maxwell Yalden's working group on human rights also noted that victims' rights under the CCRA "may be insufficient to reflect their interests." In the past, victims of crime have not been given specific legal protection by international or domestic human rights law. When the CCRA was passed in 1992, Parliament made provisions for victims' participation in the corrections process for the first time in Canadian history. Since then, a bill has been introduced in Parliament to enhance victims' rights.

A victim of crime in Canada is currently entitled to the following information on request: the offender's name, his offence, the place of the offence, the date the offender began serving his sentence, the length of the sentence, and the dates he is eligible for temporary absences, day parole, and full parole. Most of this information is available in the public domain.

Other information may be provided to the victim if requested, depending on how authorities decide to balance the interests of the victim against the privacy rights of the offender: the age of the offender; the name of the penitentiary where he is serving his sentence; the dates of release on temporary absences, work release, or parole, as well as the conditions and location; the date of a detention hearing; whether the offender is still in custody; and whether he has appealed a National Parole Board decision.

In practice, although the victim can request that information, it is often routinely withheld. Even though the National Parole Board has a community liaison officer at each of its regional offices to provide information to victims, as well as victim coordinators from CSC, caseloads are so heavy that victims frequently complain

that they can't reach the right person. When they do, they are often denied the information they are seeking.

Although inmates have a correctional investigator who oversees their complaints, there is no such ombudsman for victims of crime when they feel their rights have been violated. Prisoners, for example, have been known to walk into a hearing, see their victim, and cancel the session without further explanation. The victim may have used vacation time and a non-refundable ticket to attend a parole board hearing, which causes real hardship if the hearing is delayed or cancelled.

The current law denies the victims of crime information on the programs their offender may be taking in prison. Under the CCRA, victims can be present at an offender's parole hearing, but they must submit an "observer application" to allow for a security check. Observers used to be prohibited from participating in the hearing. Until July 2001, all they could do was submit a written statement prior to the review. By law, the offender had access to the statements of the victims of his crimes. Now victims are allowed to make verbal statements at parole hearings, but they are still prohibited from listening to the board's deliberations.

The parliamentary subcommittee on the CCRA recommended that information on offenders' program participation, institutional conduct, and new offences while on conditional release be made available to interested victims. The parliamentarians also recommended that victims be informed when their offenders are transferred, and that audiotapes of parole board hearings be made available to them on request. The Canadian Police Association, the Office for Victims of Crime of the Ministry of the Attorney General of Ontario, and the Canadian Resource Centre for Victims of Crime have all made similar recommendations. In its May 2000 report, the parliamentary subcommittee recommended that victims be allowed to attend and read statements at the beginning of parole board hearings or to present their statements on tape. This was what finally produced the change in policy in 2001.

Offenders continue to exercise their right to see most case record documentation, to be informed of any decisions that affect their release, and to speak at parole hearings. No information is to be passed on to private individuals or organizations without the consent of the offender.

In a scathing minority report of the CCRA subcommittee, MPs of the official opposition said the primary purpose of the justice system should be to protect law-abiding people. All other considerations, including rehabilitation and the identification of social problems, ought to be secondary to that primary purpose.

Section 4 of the CCRA states that "offenders retain the rights and privileges of all members of society" except those removed or restricted as a consequence of their sentence. The opposition believes offenders should temporarily lose some of those rights as Canadian citizens, beyond their basic Charter rights. They should have to earn other rights and privileges, such as sports programs, conjugal visits, and parole, by demonstrating appropriate behaviour.

The minority report also recommended that, contrary to the current system, privileges should be taken away for inappropriate behaviour. Inmates must face consequences for violence behind bars, the opposition MPs said, noting that guards had no way of dealing with prisoners who destroyed property, fought with other prisoners, or attacked correctional staff both physically and verbally. It singled out Donnacona Institution, a maximum-security prison in Quebec, where there were two separate prisons within a single facility in order to keep rival motorcycle gangs apart: "That suggests to us the prisoners, rather than the prison officials, control those facilities."

Prison staff, and even other prisoners who want to serve their time productively, complained to members of the subcommittee about the lack of control over the most dangerous troublemakers. The minority report recommended that a crime committed inside a facility should be treated with the same judicial consequences it would have if it were committed in the community.

The minority report also recommended that statutory release – automatic release after two-thirds of a sentence – be revoked, arguing that if offenders knew from day one that their release was contingent on their behaviour, they would participate in programs, follow the rules, and make more of an effort to rehabilitate themselves.

Commissioner Ole Ingstrup had told the Commons justice committee in November 1999 that abolition of statutory release would be expensive and even dangerous to public safety, and that it would cost about $750 million to build eight more penitentiaries to house as many as 2,700 more offenders, and an extra $125 million annually in operating costs. After first agreeing to recommend the end of statutory release, the Liberal-controlled CCRA review subcommittee changed its mind. In the words of Conservative MP Peter MacKay, "They back away like cats on a linoleum floor."

The unproven assumption behind statutory release is that the most dangerous person to release from prison is a violent offender who has not taken rehabilitation programs, not qualified for parole, nor even moved from a maximum-security institution during his incarceration. That's because if he serves his full sentence, the offender will be released without any supervision or control. When an offender is automatically released after serving two-thirds of his sentence, he is subject to supervision in the community. But the authors of the minority report wanted to achieve the same effect without discounting the sentences handed down by the courts. They wanted an amendment to the Criminal Code that would require all federally sentenced offenders to have at least six months of supervision after serving their sentences.

Even if he had not qualified for parole during his sentence because of bad behaviour, the offender would still have had supervision when his warrant expired. The Progressive Conservative Party agreed with the Canadian Alliance on the issue of statutory release, as stated in the minority report. "The Canadian Alliance strongly believes in providing a second chance to those who earn

it, but earn it they must. We need to show compassion to those who make a mistake and are remorseful about it. We also need to show a new level of firmness for those who continuously break society's rules."

On January 8, 2001, a woman from Abbotsford, British Columbia, was awarded $215,000 by CSC just minutes before her civil case against the service was to begin. CSC's lawyers had played hardball. While managing a health food store at a mall on January 18, 1998, the woman had been raped at knifepoint by a career criminal named James Armbruster, who had sixty-three convictions, including one for the rape of his own grandmother. The aboriginal man had robbed her and threatened to "cut her up like she's never been cut before." Armbruster had been transferred on statutory release to the Sumas Community Correctional Centre halfway house just four days earlier and was free to come and go in Abbotsford. The settlement was viewed as the first time CSC acknowledged some responsibility for a crime committed by someone who should have remained behind bars. No doubt CSC did not want the publicity of a three-week trial.

In fact, CSC and the NPB rely on confidential settlements and sealed court records to keep lawsuits by victims and their families out of the public eye. Since 1989 there have been more than twenty such lawsuits by people who have been raped or assaulted by offenders on parole or by the families of those murdered by parolees. The Catholic church made similar secret settlements with the families of children abused by priests. Only when the costs of the settlements threatened to bankrupt the church, and the settlements became public, did the bishops finally decide to deal with the problem, rather than simply moving the offending priests to new parishes.

In an ironic twist, the NPB is facing a $1.6-million lawsuit by a paroled prisoner who claims he should not have been paroled. On January 2, 2002, the *Globe and Mail* reported that Mark Turner, an armed robber with a criminal record stretching back to the 1970s

(including drug trafficking and weapons offences), claimed the government should have known better than to release him to a halfway house in 1987 after he had served just four years of an eleven-year sentnce. He landed back in prison in 1993 with an eight-year sentence for conspiracy to commit robbery.

While Turner was on parole, correctional officials were aware that two separate complaints had been made against him, but his parole was not revoked. A woman said Turner had threatened her, and a man claimed he was hospitalized after being beaten by him. In fact, one parole official looking at Turner's case in 1988 wrote, "Something is very rotten in Denmark the way this case is going." Turner alleged he was used as a police informant and cracked under the pressure, which led to his new crime. According to CSC, he is no longer in its system.

High-risk, violent offenders are subject to Chapter 17 of Bill C-55, passed by Parliament in April 1997. It requires judges to impose indeterminate sentences on dangerous offenders. As of September 24, 2000, 276 offenders were deemed dangerous under the Criminal Code, most of them in Ontario and British Columbia. Of that number, 268 were incarcerated, seven were under community supervision, and one had been deported. No female inmates were designated as dangerous offenders. In addition, a designation as a "dangerous sexual offender" targets sex offenders who don't meet the "dangerous offender" criteria. They can be supervised for up to ten years following their release. In 2000 there were fifty-two offenders in this category.

The same day that CSC settled the Abbotsford case out of court, there was a bail hearing for Christopher Renard Wareham. After his release from Dorchester Penitentiary on September 29, 2000, police warned the public that a dangerous sexual offender had been released and was heading toward Halifax. He was charged with the vicious rape of a Halifax woman on New Year's Day, his fourth charge in twelve years. Wareham had shown no remorse, and there was no evidence he had received counselling for his sexual aggression.

Criticized on all sides, CSC has circled the wagons around the philosophy of former commissioner Ole Ingstrup. The controversial department claims that there is no hard evidence that locking people up has a deterrent effect or reduces crime. It notes that the United States has one of the highest incarceration rates in the world but it is still not a safe place to be. It argues that Canada's balanced approach gets tough with high-risk, violent offenders but looks for alternatives to prison for low-risk, non-violent offenders.

Restitution allows judges to order offenders to compensate victims. Alternatives to incarceration include community service, electronic monitoring, or conditional sentencing, in which community service or treatment is required instead of a jail term. Mediation allows the victim to express his feelings to the offender, which then helps the perpetrator of a crime to see the consequences of his actions. Together they agree on a resolution, or at least they do in the paper castles of CSC.

10

OVER THE WALL

Even the commissioner had to admit that CSC had something of an embarrassing problem on its hands. In a speech to his senior managers on May 11, 1999, Ole Ingstrup said, "Minimum [security] wardens obviously have something to think about. In that area, some people should be thinking about how better to ensure that those transferred to minimum-security institutions will actually stay there for the remainder of their sentence."

Nor is the overall picture reassuring. As of October 4, 2001, there were 898 federal escapees and parole violators on Canada-wide warrants on the streets, including nearly 40 killers. That's enough to fill two prisons the size of Kingston Penitentiary. Two hundred and forty-one federal criminals were at large in Ontario alone. Interestingly, parole violation is not a separate offence under the Criminal Code. Offenders are picked up under a Canada-wide warrant of apprehension, and CSC and the National Parole Board then decide whether to return them to prison.

Almost all of the escapes are from minimum-security institutions. One of those who "walked away" was a convicted murderer named Brian Martin, who disappeared on August 15, 2000, from

261

Pittsburgh Institution, a minimum-security facility north of Kingston. He was serving a life sentence for the 1988 murder of an accounting clerk who drove a taxi on weekends. Martin had robbed Michael March of $180 to pay a drug debt and then shot him in the chest. After having breakfast with his seventeen-year-old girlfriend, Martin tried to cross the American border in March's stolen cab. When a border guard tried to check the licence plate, Martin crashed through the barrier and led New York State police on a forty-kilometre chase that reached speeds of 160 kilometres an hour.

Originally charged with first-degree murder, Martin made a deal to plead guilty to second-degree murder and drug possession charges. He was to serve sixteen years without parole. He had served less than eleven years when he was sent to Pittsburgh. Martin had been there for just five months when prison authorities concluded that he was not an escape risk. His behaviour had been "positive" in prison and he had "taken all his programs," according to a CSC spokesperson. The convicted killer was recaptured in what police called a "high-risk" takedown on Queen Street in Mississauga, Ontario, on November 28, 2000.

On December 12, 1999, inmate Claude Daigle left La Macaza Institution in Quebec on an escorted pass to visit his girlfriend in Montreal. He was accompanied by a female correctional officer. After the visit, Daigle and the officer stopped at a restaurant in Sainte-Agathe. While his official escort was in the washroom, Daigle left. The forty-one-year-old inmate was serving a second term of twelve years, two months, and thirty days for seventeen counts of robbery and forcible confinement, assault, the use of force in escaping lawful custody, possession of a weapon, and being unlawfully at large. His sentence had commenced March 31, 1995. Daigle was recaptured and convicted of being unlawfully at large in March 2000 and was transferred to Drummond Institution in Quebec.

It wasn't hard to figure out what William Turchin, a forty-six-year-old inmate serving a lengthy sentence for robbery in Quebec, had on his mind when he was brought to Kingston Penitentiary in

March 1987 to testify at the hostage-taking trial of KP inmate Elmer King. After corrections officials ran a metal scanner over his body, the inmate "voluntarily" removed a metal nail-clipper from his anus. When he was scanned a second time, the alarm again went off.

Turchin was placed in a dry cell over the weekend to allow officers to check his stool for contraband he may have inserted into his body. No one was prepared for what they found. On Monday, Turchin passed a plastic bag which guards recovered from the cell drain. The forensic science lab in Toronto verified that the bag contained all the working components of a zip gun, including a firing pin. In addition, the inmate had injected his own feces into his scrotum to cause an infection so he would be sent to the hospital. Armed with a gun and the nail file attached to the clippers to pick the lock on handcuffs, Turchin had planned to escape during his hospital visit.

Timothy Sappier, a Dorchester Penitentiary inmate, escaped the custody of his sheriff's department escort during a court appearance in Woodstock, New Brunswick. At 8:45 on December 20, 1999, while waiting for court to begin, Sappier was placed in a holding area with a sheriff's deputy. After the deputy removed his handcuffs in preparation for the court appearance (it is considered degrading and unfair for an inmate to make a court appearance in handcuffs), Sappier pushed the deputy aside and left the building. The twenty-three-year-old inmate was serving a sentence of two years and six months for three counts of assault, assault with a weapon, forcible confinement, use of a firearm while committing an offence, and obstructing a peace officer. His sentence had commenced on August 9, 1999. In January 2000 Sappier was recaptured and convicted of being unlawfully at large. He was reassigned to Atlantic Institution, a maximum-security prison in Renous, New Brunswick. In September 2001, he was freed on statutory release in the Atlantic region.

Lee Steven Chapelle was sentenced to fourteen years in 1990 for multiple offences, including gun-running. After he was paroled

from minimum-security Beaver Creek Institution in Gravenhurst, Ontario, in May 1999, Chapelle vanished. The six-foot-three, 220-pound parole jumper was busy robbing a residence in Stouffville, north of Toronto, on February 2, 2000, when the alarm went off. Chapelle, who was armed with a .45-calibre handgun, was followed in his stolen car by a Stouffville man, Gordon Thompson, who called 911 on his cellphone. Thompson tailed the suspect until York Regional Police took over the high-speed chase. Thompson was given a citizen's award of merit by the police for his efforts.

Several recent escapes have resulted in murders and sexual assaults. CSC completed a report on the escapes on July 26, 1999. The situation was so embarrassing that the wardens of the institutions involved met and produced a series of recommended changes to policy and practice aimed at tightening security. But senior CSC management, loyal to Commissioner Ingstrup's vision of kinder and gentler prisons, felt that the changes could be made under existing policies.

Twenty-five per cent of the 114 inmates who escaped in 1998-1999 had prior escapes, and 68 per cent of breakouts happened within the first three months in minimum security. Ironically, Ferndale Institution, a minimum-security facility in Mission, British Columbia, has the most murderers of any federal institution in Canada. Inmate Lee Campbell was missing from the 15:00 count at Ferndale on December 20, 1999. He had last been seen two hours earlier. The thirty-seven-year-old inmate was serving a life sentence for second-degree murder with a ten-year minimum before parole eligibility. He had been in Ferndale for only two months when he became the seventy-fourth inmate to escape from a minimum-security institution in that fiscal year. (A total of ninety-six inmates escaped from federal prisons in 1999-2000.) Campbell was recaptured and convicted of being unlawfully at large in January 2001. He was sent to Matsqui Institution, a medium-security penitentiary in Abbotsford, British Columbia.

The rash of escapes was raising eyebrows in high places in every jurisdiction except Ottawa. In June 2000, two senior members of

the Harris government in Ontario, Corrections Minister Rob Sampson and Solicitor General David Tsubouchi, announced their support for a special police unit that would go after fugitives and parole breakers. An average of five hundred criminals, both federal and provincial, are at large in Ontario on any given day. A six-officer unit, established in Toronto as a pilot project in 1997 with federal funding, has recaptured more than three hundred offenders. Nearly 50 per cent of them escaped from federal custody.

On October 19, 2000, the Ontario government decided to take over funding for the unit, which acts like U.S. marshals to hunt down escapees and parole violators. The thirty-five-officer Repeat Offender Program Enforcement (ROPE) unit would be funded by a $4-million provincial grant. Rob Sampson had a message for fugitives unlawfully at large in Ontario: "If you escape, we will find you." Ottawa kicked in $500,000 for ROPE, just three days before the October 22 federal election call, a tribute to the lobbying expertise of Toronto MP Dennis Mills rather than a sign of any new get-tough attitude within CSC. (In fact, Solicitor General MacAulay had informed Mills in writing of his intention to withdraw funding from the program before Ottawa's eleventh-hour contribution.) On October 10, 2001, Ontario's provincial government finalized ROPE's funding.

There is nothing like a spectacular jailbreak to make folk heroes out of felons. Shortly after 7:00 on Friday, May 7, 1999, the garage supervisor at Kingston Penitentiary called to report that there was a line of canvas belting weighted with a grappling hook hanging outside the east wall close to Tower 5. Ten minutes later, all inmates, including kitchen workers, were returned to their cells for an emergency count. The unthinkable was quickly confirmed. At 7:15, staff searching Upper G Range discovered a "dummy" in Cell 18, where the thirty-two-year-old former resident had been serving an aggregate sentence of over forty-seven years for multiple crimes. With thirty-eight convictions on his record, twenty-five of them for robbery and weapons offences, Tyrone William Conn had gone

over the wall of Kingston Pen. It was the first time in over fifty years that someone had escaped from the formidable prison.

With his escape, Conn gained membership in an exclusive club of convicts. The first, brief escape from KP took place in 1836 when Convict Number 50, Alberzy Nakusilio, went over the twelve-foot wooden fence. (The perimeter wall was not completed for another ten years.) He had hidden in the prison yard before the lock-up, hoping prison officials would conclude he had already escaped when they did the count. His plan was to escape during the early morning hours, but he was caught while climbing over the fence. Given seven lashes in front of the other prisoners, he was then thrown into leg irons as an example to anyone else who had leaving on his mind. The first two female prisoners escaped in 1839, but they were recaptured the next day in Kingston after a $100 reward was posted.

The first guard killed at KP was murdered in 1870 by two prisoners working in the prison quarry. They made their escape with the guard's coat, watch, and pistol but were recaptured two weeks later. One of the most famous escapes was pulled off by the gang led by the bank robber Norman "Red" Ryan in September 1923. After setting fire to the stable next to the east wall, the five men put a ladder against the wall and, under the cover of smoke, went over. They stole a car and managed to outrun the warden and his men. Ryan was soon robbing banks again in Toronto and the American midwest. Three months after his daring escape from KP, he was captured in Minneapolis after a furious gun battle with police at a post office.

The Canada of Ryan's time was no less fascinated by its criminals than Hollywood is today. A reporter named Ernest Hemingway was dispatched by the *Toronto Star* to cover the escape. Not only did the swashbuckling Ryan manage to capture the imagination of the press and the public, but he also attracted the attention of Prime Minister R.B. Bennett. Bennett even visited Ryan at KP and declared that the daring bank robber was reformed. Paroled

from a life sentence in July 1935, Ryan was shot dead just ten months later while robbing a bank in Sarnia, Ontario.

On August 17, 1947, three men escaped from cells on Upper H Range by sawing through their bars and covering the cuts with wax and soot. They went up to an attic, clambered out of the building, and climbed over the wall. They left after the final count at 23:00, and it was several hours before they were discovered to be missing. One inmate, Nicholas Minnelli, was recaptured near San Francisco less than a year later; a second was found dead at about the same time; and the third, the notorious bank robber Mickey MacDonald, was never found.

On April 26, 1948, a prison messenger named John Kennedy, who had been born in an apartment in the west gate at KP, was shot dead during a daring escape by two inmates, Austin Craft and Howard Urqhart. Recaptured the same day, Craft was the last man to be hanged in Kingston. No one was ever actually executed at KP, since the British North America Act of 1867 had made the administration of capital punishment a provincial responsibility. Craft met his maker at the county jail behind the courthouse. In the spring of 1999, with the clock ticking toward the new millennium, Kingston's warden and managers understood how their predecessors had felt.

Hoping against hope that Conn wouldn't use a gun during his flight, the system kicked into high gear. By 7:35, orders had come down that no one was to go into the canvas repair shop, and at 7:46, the canteen was searched. Shortly after 8:00, the inmates were told what was going on. One by one, the diabetics in the institution were escorted to the hospital for insulin and then to the kitchen for jug-up.

Warden Monty Bourke called a meeting for all managers in the warden's boardroom so that the crisis management module could be implemented. All of the shops had been searched by 8:51. The search team was told to search each cell. A log was to be kept of the complete operation. By 9:22, the chairman of the inmate

committee was conducting an unescorted tour of the prison, talking to the inmates about the escape. A red and white helicopter circled the institution and surrounding area. Inside, every attempt was made to ensure that activities continued according to routine.

Support staff were brought in to cook brunch for 10:00. Everything else inside was almost normal. Inmate Chung was escorted down to the hospital. Inmate Sayles was taken to A&D for statutory release and to be picked up by immigration officers. Inmates who needed their methadone were tended to, and the nurse who normally did her medication run on Lower B Range was told to make a list of inmates who needed medication so they could be sent down, one at a time, to the medical room. (Regular procedure is to bring the medication trolley to the cells.)

A staff meeting was called for 12:30. After the inmates were given their lunch and the search of the ranges was finished, staff were instructed that range privileges were to be continued. The native social was cancelled, but the AA social was still on for that night. Management even tried to give the inmates an hour of yard time in the afternoon. The officers on the midnight shift were called to make sure that Conn had not left via an officer's car. If the search was completed by 14:00, the plan was to return the institution to the normal weekend routine, with regular yard, regular visits, including private family visits, and regular meals. Under no circumstances were the inmates to have their privileges upset by the actions of one wayward prisoner.

The preliminary investigation revealed that around 13:00 on May 6, Conn told the canteen he was in the canvas repair shop, and told the canvas repair shop he was in the canteen. Worried that Conn would inspire other inmates to try to escape, management ordered that the whereabouts of escape risks in the institution would have to be known at all times. Shop instructors would have to frisk all inmates coming out of the shops to make sure that all tools were accounted for. Surprisingly, there would be no "exceptional search" in the institution that day. According to log notes,

"We can't punish 300 i/ms because 1 i/m escaped. We have to have reasonable grounds." Jug-up was completed by 14:23, and by 14:30 Kingston Penitentiary was open for the weekend routine.

In February 1999 Warden Monty Bourke had issued a security memo to all KP staff. Over the previous twelve months, there had been a number of serious incidents at the prison, and subsequent investigations had pointed to security weaknesses that needed to be addressed. Information about inmates had to be shared in pre-shift briefings and logbooks, as well as between the living units and the segregation units. Staff were to report all information related to inmate and staff safety, or escape attempts, and officer statements had to be completed following an incident. (Although the unit management model had been in place at KP for several years, staff frequently didn't know the inmates on their caseload very well. The workloads were simply too heavy. The CX2 assigned to Conn, for example, hadn't prepared any casework records on the inmate and had never contacted his parole officer.)

The warden stressed that range patrols were integral to good security, "in that suicide attempts, brew, injured inmates, escape attempts can be detected at an early stage and prevented." In an aside that made guards furious, Bourke also noted that routine searches had not found enough contraband or unauthorized items that later showed up after an incident. In addition, there had been too many cases in which irate inmates had left their own ranges and gone to other areas where they threatened staff. The searching of inmates coming out of Visits and Correspondence, the shop dome, and the kitchen had been sporadic, which had facilitated the circulation of contraband through the prison.

At the time of his escape, Conn was classified as a maximum-security inmate, although staff found him easy to deal with and he faced few institutional charges. He had participated in several pro-grams during his early incarceration. In fact, his case management team thought he was a good candidate for transfer to a minimum-security institution and day parole. The model prisoner seemed to have only one problem: an obsession with escaping.

Despite glowing institutional reports, Conn was not a poster boy for restorative justice. From 1984 to the day of his escape, he had spent only 169 days in the community, 133 of them while he was unlawfully at large. He stole primarily to support himself, mainly targeting banks. His style was menacing and direct; he would enter a bank with a loaded weapon and hand the teller a note demanding money.

Conn was first incarcerated in a federal institution in March 1985, when he was sentenced to three years, eight months, and twenty-seven days. He was released on mandatory supervision (now called statutory release) in December 1986, but his release was suspended in January 1987 and he was returned to custody. He was released again in mid-February 1987 but suspended again in early March. In May 1987, he was charged and convicted of new offences, and his aggregate sentence was now six years, nine months, and twenty-three days.

A handcuff key was found in his cell at Collins Bay Institution along with his will in December 1987. During an escorted absence from Collins Bay in June 1989, he escaped and remained at large for sixty-nine days. He was convicted of new armed robbery charges after he was recaptured. His aggregate sentence was now seventeen years, nine months, and twenty-three days.

In August 1991 the institution received information that Conn was planning to escape from Collins Bay during a private family visit. The visit was interrupted. Although Conn was found in the trailer watching TV, he was dressed entirely in black, a fashion statement that is forbidden in prison for obvious reasons. In November 1991, Conn finally made a daring escape over the wall of Collins Bay, which gained him a certain notoriety and respect among fellow prisoners. He always had a flare for the dramatic. On the day of his escape, he scrawled the words "Gone fishing" on his cell calendar.

It was rumoured in the inmate population that when Conn had escaped from Collins Bay, he scaled the wall only to find himself staring into the lights of a patrol truck. The guard

allegedly panicked and sped off, saying nothing about the escape to his superiors. According to Conn, he remained silent about the close encounter for fear that the officer would be disciplined.

Conn had meticulously planned his November 1991 escape. He read winter survival guides and knew how to build an outdoor shelter. He examined maps, memorized the prison layout, and even estimated police response times. The inmate used the prison library to read bank reports so he could pick the best banks to rob. In a single month, he held up four banks, three in Ottawa and one in Toronto. His weapon of choice was a loaded sawed-off shotgun. A true professional, he also carried a police scanner in his gym bag.

Conn supported himself for forty-five days with robberies and one break-and-enter. On his last day of freedom, December 20, 1991, he walked into Central Guarantee Trust in Ottawa wearing a ski mask and brandishing a revolver. He scooped up $12,000. He was identified on the bank videotape, and a tip later that day led police to a high-rise apartment building about a block from the bank. Police and the Emergency Response Team surrounded the apartment. Conn was spotted climbing from one balcony to another. He gained access to the second apartment by firing his revolver into the glass patio doors. Police contacted him by phone in the apartment, and after two hours of negotiation, Conn gave himself up. He told his Ottawa criminal lawyer, Ian McKechnie, "I'm going to surrender, I'm just having a little fun." The diversion was costly. After the new charges from his latest escape, his aggregate sentence rose to more than forty-seven years.

Conn was sent to Millhaven, and in November 1992, he and a group of inmates attempted to escape by cutting through a fence in the exercise yard. It was recommended that he be sent to the special handling unit of Saskatchewan Penitentiary in Prince Albert. But before the transfer came through, Conn made yet another escape attempt in February 1993 from the Ottawa Detention Centre, where he was discovered with a homemade handcuff key. In 1995 he was returned from Saskatchewan to Millhaven, and later he was moved to KP.

Conn's background was typical of many inmates. Born Ernest Bruce Hayes in 1967, Conn was adopted at age two, when his eighteen-year-old mother could no longer care for him. At age eleven, he was returned to the Children's Aid Society by his adoptive parents; he then went through a series of foster homes. Conn began perfecting his street skills, and by the age of seventeen he had committed his first armed robbery. Conn's mother came back into his life after sixteen years, visiting him regularly in jail.

For most of his incarceration, Conn was considered to be "solid" by his fellow inmates, the highest recommendation a convicted felon can get from his peers. Naturally polite and blessed with a good sense of humour, Conn was viewed as a "good inmate" and trusted by staff. At KP, he was assigned jobs that gave him a greater degree of freedom within the prison walls than other inmates. Management didn't think that this posed a serious security risk, since it was widely believed that no one could escape from the maximum-security institution.

Before his escape from KP, Conn was employed full-time in the canvas repair shop. He was active in the Native Brotherhood and also worked part-time in the prison canteen. Working inmates stay in the canteen while counts are done. Although there is a social development officer present, there is no guard in the canteen. Conn volunteered to go through all the ranges one evening a week collecting orders for bread. (Inmates can order a variety of things from the outside.) The following week, he delivered the orders from cell to cell on what was called the "bread drive."

According to close friends, Conn used this freedom to gather information about the general running of the institution that would later assist in his escape. It was not unusual for him to move between the canvas repair shop and the canteen during the day or be off his range in the evening for the bread drive. He gained the confidence of the staff (and of more than one gullible journalist) and paid close attention to the prison layout. As before his other escape attempts, he determined how he would make his getaway, then waited for the best possible moment to put his plan into action.

During his incarceration, Conn kept up contact with the psychology departments of the various institutions where he had done time. On the advice of one psychologist, he began to commit his feelings to paper. Few mysteries were revealed. Everyone who knew Conn on the inside was well aware that he had difficulty accepting his lengthy sentence and constantly fantasized about going over the wall.

What his fellow inmates and most CSC staff did not know was that Conn was an informer. He provided information to both police and prison officials in order to gain the trust of people he thought might inadvertently give him information he needed to escape. In April 1997, he told the IPSO at Millhaven about ammunition that was supposedly stashed at Collins Bay. Authorities believe that what he really wanted was to gain the confidence of the IPSO at Collins Bay, before seeking transfer back to the institution from which he had successfully escaped in 1991.

After Conn and several other Millhaven inmates were discovered to be involved in an elaborate escape plan in September 1997, the affable inmate began providing information to the IPSO about the other inmates, claiming that he had not really intended to escape. According to CSC's internal investigation of the matter, when the other would-be escapers got wind of his betrayal, Conn's life was in danger. Even in segregation, his safety at Millhaven could not be guaranteed, so he was transferred to protective custody at KP in May 1998. His transfer to the maximum-security institution was made even though he was then classified as a medium-security inmate, his many escapes and escape attempts notwithstanding. According to CSC psychological reports, Conn decided he was going to escape from the moment he arrived at KP.

There were some recent precedents. Inmates Stephen Albert Hall and John Corey Mackay had attempted an escape from KP on November 3, 1995. Considered very dangerous, Hall was serving a concurrent life sentence for manslaughter, attempted murder, kidnapping, robbery, and escaping lawful custody. Imprisoned in 1976, Hall already had one successful escape to his credit in 1981.

He was recaptured four months later. Mackay had been in custody since 1992 and was serving a nine-and-a-half-year sentence for aggravated assault. The men were discovered to be missing during a formal count shortly after 20:00. A guard found a dummy in one cell and alerted security. A second dummy was found in the other cell and the prison was locked down. The two inmates were discovered hiding in the yard a short time later.

A confidential CSC report completed in November 1995 concluded that "some security practices had slipped" during renovations to the prison. Despite KP's reputation as one of the most secure prisons in the system, the inmates had managed to make it to a rooftop in the prison yard. They were back behind bars by 21:00 that night. Whether its authors intended it or not, the internal report was a tacit indictment of Ole Ingstrup's kinder, gentler prison system. It found that information about an escape alert concerning the two men had not been passed on to front-line staff, construction ladders were not properly secured, a door from a cellblock was left unlocked, and inmates occasionally had unsupervised access to other inmates' cells. In 1995-1996, there were fifty-eight escapes from all three security levels of federal institutions.

Conn made good use of his job assignment. Offenders employed in the canvas repair shop at KP mend mailbags for Canada Post. The shop employs eight to ten inmates, who work under an instructor. It is a "locked shop" and considered to be more secure than a work station that allows movement through the institution. L-shaped, the main area of the shop is about four thousand square feet and houses the instructor's office, the canvas machines, and supplies. The entry door is in this area. The other wing is about three thousand square feet and has machines for fabrene (plasticized material) mailbags. A narrow hall connects the two wings.

Although nothing was done about it, there were disconcerting signs about what Conn had on his mind long before he scarpered. In October 1998, a .22-calibre bullet was found in the canvas repair shop. At the time, all the inmates working in the shop agreed to be interviewed by the IPSO – everyone, that is, except Conn. In

November 1998, he admitted to making what he described as a "vest" for an inmate who had back problems. It had pouches in it that held metal weights, supposedly to be worn by the inmate while he jogged. Another description of Conn's handiwork was also health-related: a bulletproof vest.

In December 1998, Conn was sanctioned after it was discovered that he and two other inmates had been planning an escape from KP. When he was caught, Conn served up a less than credible story to authorities. Once again, he claimed that he had been involved in the escape attempt only so that he could provide intelligence to security staff. They already had enough of it to send him to segregation. When he was released on February 5, 1999, Conn attempted to smuggle a letter to his brother using an inmate courier who was leaving on statutory release. When authorities intercepted Conn's letter, they knew that the inmate was not overcome with remorse for his previous escape attempts. The letter asked for maps of the downtown Kingston area, specifically around KP.

Once again, Conn was briefly sent to segregation in March. His security classification was raised from medium to maximum, and his case was reviewed for a transfer to the SHU in Quebec. Unbelievably, Conn's job placements were not reviewed, despite his obvious intention to make a further escape attempt. Prior to his successful escape, neither Conn nor his cell was singled out for special searches, and he continued to move freely throughout the institution on various work details.

Assisted by two other inmates, Conn refined his escape plan. He was actually surprised by the amount of freedom given to inmates at KP and found it amazing that no inmates had made a successful escape in over fifty years. If he broke that long-standing record, he had no intention of coming back. Conn informed friends that if he was caught, he would either escape custody, force police to shoot him, or take his own life. Thanks to the prison's thriving drug business, he boasted that he had enough pills to commit suicide.

The night before he went over the wall, Conn and his two friends made a dummy. They used a shoebox for the torso and

paper towel rolls for an arm and a leg, which were then padded with towels and hockey shin guards. Conn dressed the dummy in the T-shirt and track pants that he regularly wore. The entire operation took just five minutes. There was no need to construct a head. For several weeks now, he had been using a headboard on his bed that blocked the view of his head from outside his cell.

After the retrofit of the ranges at KP in the 1990s, a virtually indestructible moulded fibreglass desk-bed combination was purchased for cells, with the bed above the desk. The inmate is up high, making it difficult to see his face if he sleeps with his head toward the bars. At the time of Conn's escape, an inmate could sleep in whatever location in his cell he chose. Some inmates had even moved their mattresses to the desk, or to the floor under the desk, so it was even more difficult to actually see a sleeping inmate. The dummy was placed in the exact position Conn had assumed for several months during inmate counts.

Inmate counts and the hourly range walks normally take an officer about two or three minutes each per range. Commissioner's Directive 565 requires a minimum of four formal counts of inmates in medium- and maximum-security institutions during each twenty-four-hour period. No inmate movement is allowed during these counts. Since a staff member must be satisfied there is "a breathing, living body" before the count is considered accurate, an officer must shine a flashlight in the inmate's face at night.

At KP, cell doors remain open during the evening between counts, so inmates can visit one another. On the day of his escape, Conn had his friends put the dummy in his bunk about twenty minutes before each of the three formal counts that would take place that evening on Upper G Range – at 16:30, 20:00, and 22:30. When the count was completed, they dismantled the dummy and hid it behind the bed to create the impression that Conn had left the range after each count. The attention to detail was exquisite. The inmates knew that the correctional officers made hourly walks on the range, so his confederates entered his cell before each walk and made small changes to the lighting and

the volume of the TV. They even turned his computer screen on and off.

Conn had clearly thought through every detail of his plan, including some very ingenious ones. If an officer attempted to speak to him while the dummy was in place, an apparatus with a speaker and microphone had been designed to take care of the problem. The microphone was in the cell of a friend, and he was to answer any questions from the officer. The likelihood of a conversation was slim; the inmates on Upper G made the officers reluctant to spend time on the range because of their rude and disrespectful behaviour. They covered the front of their "houses" with blankets, a violation of security rules that staff winked at because management had sent a clear message not to agitate the inmates.

Blankets impede visual inspection of a cell. Even when they are left partially drawn at night, it is difficult to see inside the cell. If an officer bends too close to the bars, or pulls the blanket aside for a better view, he creates a security risk for himself. One officer had his fingers badly cut when he attempted to pull aside a blanket into which its owner had sewn razor blades. Conn's elaborate deception was successful. The officer who worked the evening shift was certain that Conn was in his cell because of the changes he had seen in the cell environment as he did his walks.

The cross-shaped "shop dome" building housing KP's work facilities has a large circular hub with a high ceiling and a curved staircase. Shops and offices on two floors adjoin the central area: carpentry, Admission and Discharge, the mattress shop, the upholstery shop, the school, the barber – and the canvas repair shop on the second floor of the north wing.

On the morning of May 6, 1999, Conn left his cell in Upper G and joined the flow of men through the main dome. He passed through the metal detector and reported for work in the canvas repair shop. Once the inmates were in their designated shops or programs, a call went out by radio to indicate that movement was complete. The shop dome officer then went to each shop to ensure that the instructors had all their assigned inmates. The officer took

the key and locked the instructor and his inmates in for the work period. This officer continued to control all movement in and out of the shops. Written attendance records are kept for the school because of the large numbers of students enrolled, but no such tally sheets are kept for the shops.

Shortly after Conn reported for work, his shop instructor received a call from a staff member in the inmate canteen, asking that Conn be sent there for a work detail. The instructor complied. Conn pressed the buzzer to call the shop dome officer. The officer is supposed to verify with the instructor that the call-out is legitimate, frisk the inmate, and notify the daytime yard officer that the inmate will be leaving the shop dome for a specific reason. In fact, even though the post orders clearly state that inmates are to be frisked as they enter and exit the industrial shops, this was not consistently done at KP. Post orders say that any inmate movement, aside from general movement (called "work-up"), is supposed to be authorized and escorted. Only a few inmates are given passes that allow freedom of movement within the institution without an escort. Remarkably, Conn the escape artist was one of those inmates.

Conn spent most of the morning working in the canteen. He returned to the canvas repair shop just before lunch and went with the other inmates to their cells for lunch and the noon count. After lunch, Conn went back to the shop but said he had been called to the canteen. The area he passed through, the south passage, was open to inmates as they were still going back and forth to appointments, groups, and the hospital. A short time later, Conn was observed walking back to the canvas repair shop by the CXI working the shop dome. He entered the shop at about 13:30, apparently without the instructor or anyone else noticing his arrival.

The moment had come to put his escape plan into action. Conn concealed himself in a cage in a semi-restricted area that held the shop's sewing machines. He was one of the few inmates who had access to the area. He remained in the cage until the shop was cleared and closed for the day at 15:15.

The other inmates were released by the shop dome officer, who is supposed to frisk them and ensure that the instructor is satisfied that all inmates and tools are accounted for. Tool control is done using shadow boards or locked storage cribs. The shop keys are then returned to the instructor, who locks his shop for the night. The shop instructor locked the sewing machine cage, which was always open during the workday. He did not notice Conn hiding inside.

May 6 was the shop dome officer's first day at that post. He had received no specific training for the position, and no post order outlining his duties was available when he arrived. At the time, the canvas repair shop instructor frequently stood at the shop door for all major movements in and out, so that he could check that all inmates were accounted for. Movement could take up to twenty-five minutes, and if the instructor was called to assist a worker already in the shop, he could miss the arrival of other inmates. There was no formal roll call, although the instructor indicated who was in the shop on the pay sheets.

Conn spent the evening making final preparations for his escape. Since there was no ceiling on the locked cage, he simply climbed over the door. Having previously hidden a forty-two-foot length of canvas strapping in the shop, he now used shop equipment to attach a hook made from a sixteen-inch piece of steel-threaded rod. Correctional officers had searched the shop the day before and found nothing. Conn knew that a guard dog would be with the yard officer on the early morning shift, so he armed himself with hockey pads and a knife. He also slipped a small fire extinguisher into a canvas backpack, but at the last minute he decided it was not needed and left it behind in the shop.

A maximum-security audit done at KP in 1998 found that the sodium lights on the inside of the perimeter wall and on the sides of various buildings provided good visibility on the inside grounds after sunset. But there were many sightline problems because of the many buildings that had been constructed over the years. "This made running the facility a labour intensive operation," the audit report stated.

Conn planned to leave between 23:00 and 23:30, since the southeast tower – Tower 5 – was unmanned between 23:00 and 7:00 as an economizing measure. In fact, Tower 5, which overlooks the exercise yard where Conn made his escape, had been unmanned during the night for the previous five years. In making their budget cuts, KP managers drew comfort from an internal CSC report that concluded that a perimeter intrusion detection system (PIDS) and perimeter patrol vehicles were considered more than enough security. There was only one problem. KP had neither a PIDS nor a perimeter mobile patrol, which further frustrated its undermanned security force.

"A tower being down at midnights, not being manned in a maximum-security institution, is just plain crazy," an intelligence officer said. "If they would have had that at KP when Conn climbed the wall, the minute his ladder touched that wall, an alarm would have gone off."

The towers at KP have telephones, but no searchlights or loud-speaker systems. Since there are no gun slots in the towers, staff have to go out onto the catwalks through a tower door in order to discharge a firearm. Although there were thirty-two staff on duty at KP in the evening, only sixteen were assigned by management to watch four hundred inmates between 23:00 and 7:00, a ratio of twenty-five inmates for every guard. Conn knew from observation how many times the yard person walked around the institution and precisely when he picked up the escort dog. Only three patrols were done from 23:00 to 7:00.

Conn pulled two large pieces of canvas, normally used to keep wind and rain out, over the loading doors located in the hallway connecting the two wings of the canvas repair shop. The doors were in line with the yard shack used by the officer, and Conn had cut two small eyeholes in the canvas so that he could watch for the yard officer while he cut the padlock and light chain that locked the loading doors. Just the previous year, a security audit had recommended that "all shop entry doors be examined and that the substandard ones be replaced." The audit team also "found that

shop entrances were often unlocked, permitting inmates to leave their areas undetected." From his hiding place, Conn had a clear view of the yard office.

Lisa Lajeunesse, the officer on yard patrol that night, had performed the same duties more than 150 times in the past three years, exactly as she had been instructed to by several staff members who tutored her when she was first assigned to the post. Although she had never seen an official job description, Lajeunesse had read occasional memos about how to lock or unlock certain doors, as well as CSC procedures for making escorts to KP's hospital. She was never told when to conduct her patrols, but instinctively she made the timing as unpredictable as possible. The dog was a comfort on these "dead of night" patrols, but guards at KP had already come perilously close to losing them.

On October 22, 1998, Deputy Warden Alex Lubimiv had sent a memo to the dog handlers pointing out that it had come to his attention that KP's dogs were soiling the inmate recreation area while on patrol. "The dog handlers' protocol clearly outlines the procedures for allowing the animals to void themselves in areas not used by inmates." Lubimiv expected the immediate attention of the dog handlers to rectify the situation. Lubimiv's memo had come after officers had filed reports that some of the black inmates had been "pestering and antagonizing the K.P. dogs." In one officer's opinion, the inmates were testing the dogs to see how they would respond in a confrontation. While inmates were returning from the yard at 15:15 one February day in 1999, inmate Walker began yelling at an officer and his dog Dillinger. When the dog barked at him, Walker claimed that the animal was "racist" and "an Uncle Tom's dog" because he was protecting the white guard.

With her guard dog in hand, Lajeunesse entered the main exercise yard by the west gate. She proceeded to the southeast tower, clocking in at 23:42. She then walked along the east perimeter wall through the weight pit to the corner of the Regional Treatment Centre, then out through the north gate to the exercise yard. Three minutes later she was in the lower floor of the shop dome. After

completing her first patrol with her canine assistant at 00:05, she returned to the yard shack and groomed the dog. She cleaned the office and did some chiropractic stretching. She also did some knitting to ease the craving to have a cigarette, having given up smoking two years earlier.

Lajeunesse, who had worked overtime on her two previous shifts, changed her location within the shack regularly. It was a tactic she used so that someone observing her from the outside would not see her in a single, fixed location. The shack had a raised chair that provided a good view of the yard, including the loading doors of the canvas repair shop. But two lower chairs, which the officer happened to use that night, permitted only limited visibility through the windows. Lajeunesse had her back to the route Conn would use to enter the exercise yard, but even if she had been facing in the right direction, the chair she was seated in was too low to see out of the exterior windows. The officer could not see the loading dock area and remained unaware that Conn was intently watching her.

Shortly before 4:00, Officer Lajeunesse began her second walk, which lasted for twenty minutes. Deister records – electronic data that record patrols – indicate that she was at the southeast tower at 4:17. Neither she nor the dog noticed a ladder or the unlocked loading doors. Everything appeared to be in order, and she returned to the office.

Once the chain was cut, Conn opened the doors and lowered the ladder he had taken from the canvas repair shop. The unsecured ladder had been in the shop for years and was used to adjust the heating vents in the ceiling. (According to regulations, all ladders were supposed to be secured with chains, after Dr. William Gill used one in 1856 to escape from KP.) Conn climbed to the ground, a distance of seventeen feet, and then quickly carried the ladder 330 feet to the inmate exercise yard in the southeast corner of the grounds. To throw the canine patrol off his scent, Conn spread a bag of cayenne pepper on the ground as he went. The gate to the yard was routinely unlocked and he quietly slipped through. Conn

placed the ladder against the outside limestone wall and climbed to the top. Once astride the wall, he used his grappling hook to climb down to freedom, disappearing up a quiet residential street next to the prison, where authorities believe a car was waiting for him.

Three cameras observe activity in the inmate exercise yard, and Conn was well within camera range on his way to the wall. Although there were three video machines at the north gate, staff thought they were inoperative, so they were not turned on. The monitors for the cameras are located in the principal entrance control centre in the north gate, about fifteen feet behind the officer's desk. The same officer also controls telephone traffic, entry to the facility, and the various prison alarm systems. The August 1998 security audit noted the inadequacy of this arrangement. "This post should be reexamined to determine if staffing levels are at an appropriate level." Correctional officials later estimated that it had taken only seconds for Conn to carry the ladder to the wall and make his escape.

Two months before the Conn escape brought the CSC's security provisions into disrepute, there was a less spectacular incident that showed what can happen under Commissioner Ingstrup's "minimum manning" initiatives. An officer who normally assisted at the north gate had been pulled from the post. Afterwards, a doctor had left the institution through the north gate at 19:55, inadvertently leaving the door ajar. Since there was no second officer present, the officer in charge could not leave his post to close the door. He called his supervisor, and finally the yard officer drove around through the sally port and secured the door manually from the outside. The front door to one of Canada's maximum-security prisons had remained open for fifteen long minutes.

After the 5:00 count, Lisa Lajeunesse began her third patrol at 5:20, again noticing nothing unusual, although she did not specifically recall looking at the wall area where the ladder was found. Her patrol was completed by 5:56. She returned the dog to his kennel and then waited for the garbage truck that was scheduled to arrive at 6:00. After searching the truck, Lajeunesse escorted the

driver to the various prison Dumpsters. Once the count of kitchen workers was verified, she escorted the truck through the gate. Returning to the yard shack, she removed the dog's sleeping mat and water dish and mopped the floor of the kennel. By the time she went to the Keeper's Hall to download the Deister data, Conn was sixty-four kilometres away, saying goodbye to his mother.

Shortly after the escape, Conn telephoned a friend inside KP, and later he sent him a postcard. He even called to thank the newspaper columnist who had written about the fact that Tower 5 was unmanned at night because of budget cuts. Not surprisingly, Conn's favourite movie was *The Shawshank Redemption*.

With the crisis management module in full effect, officers searched the institutional grounds and the forty buildings within the prison walls. A ladder was found leaning against the inside of the east wall near Tower 5. The warden ordered his parole officers to go to houses in the immediate area with pamphlets to alert residents of Conn's escape. The pamphlets had a photo of Conn, his weight and height, and the length of his sentence.

It didn't take long for recriminations to start flying. The guards' union, the Public Service Alliance of Canada, issued a news release on May 11, 1999, condemning CSC for failing to provide adequate training for recently hired correctional officers. This had left them frustrated and concerned for their safety. The news release defended the professionalism of correctional officers, saying the union would "defend any and all members disciplined or made scapegoats for a rapidly deteriorating security environment not of their own making." Strict security practices had eroded because management was always attempting to pacify the inmates. Management would spin-doctor the incident so that guards, not management, were the scapegoats for Conn's escape.

The admission by Lisa Lajeunesse that she could not recall looking at the wall area where the ladder was found during her last patrol on the night of the escape was characterized as negligence and an admission of guilt by management. Justice, or the lack of it, was swift for the female guard. She received a letter of discipline

and was fined ten days' pay. But that was nothing compared with the stress, hostility, and frustration she felt after being "betrayed" by her employer. According to unconfirmed inmate sources, Conn left the institution between 3:00 and 3:30 on May 7. The word of the inmates about the timing of the escape was taken above her word that it could not have happened until after the completion of her second patrol at 4:00. She worried that she would be seen as an unobservant, lazy employee who twice walked past a twenty-foot ladder and open loading doors without seeing them.

Lajeunesse's belief that Conn had waited until after her second or even third patrol to make his escape was never made public, despite the fact that her version of events was entirely possible. The drive from Kingston to Belleville takes only forty-five minutes. In her disciplinary hearing, Lajeunesse denied that Conn could have escaped before her second patrol at 3:59. If he had, she insisted, "I would have seen the evidence of his escape and/or the dog who accompanied me on my rounds would have been alerted to something unusual. My walk route during that second walk took me close to the area where the ladder was located and I would have seen it if it had been there."

Lajeunesse made another good point. The patrol dog lies on a mat in the yard office window with an unobstructed view of the loading dock. The dog would have sensed Conn's movement if he had escaped between 3:00 and 3:30. During her last walk, Lajeunesse had taken a slightly different route that obscured her view of the area where Conn went over the wall.

Management fought back with paper. Even though the yard officer was never shown post orders until after the investigation into the Conn escape began, she was punished for not following what turned out to be the letter of her duties. According to post orders she had never seen, her job required that two complete walks and two partial walks be undertaken on her shift. Although she had done three rather than four walks for more than three years, no one in management had ever told her that she was not completing her duties as required. Lajeunesse grieved the letter of

discipline and fine with her union, which believed she was being publicly humiliated by her employer because CSC was embarrassed by the negative publicity generated by the escape.

Warden Monty Bourke admitted that Tyrone Conn's escape was a serious breach of the community's trust but quickly blamed his guards. The two officers who were deceived by the dummy in Conn's cell each received a ten-day suspension without pay. "I think some staff settled into a complacency with the reputation that we were a secure institution."

After the escape the warden called a meeting where he upbraided his staff; some of his guards didn't sit still for the tongue-lashing from a man they believed had undermined security at the institution. "A couple of days after this, Monty Bourke's in there yelling at us. His face was red, his voice was raised, you know, he said, 'We've got a job to do, we are being too lenient. We have to stop these inmates and check where they are going.' So at that point I said, 'Why are you saying all of this to us? You are the one who gave him a pink pass to travel with the bread drive, and you are the one who allowed him to work in the canteen and have access to tools in the shop.'"

The safety of the public, supposedly CSC's primary mandate, had been jeopardized in order to reduce the budget, but Bourke's management team continued to download the blame in daily shift briefings. According to one guard, the recriminations went on for weeks: "Whenever something happens, it's immediately the guys at the bottom of the feeding trough that basically get it, whether it's our fault or not – things are twisted. And, we were basically told, in the shift briefings, in the morning, 'You guys are responsible for this.' That was done for two or three weeks afterwards, every morning: the correctional officers were responsible for this. It was our fault. We all knew it was coming, it's common practice."

Commissioner Ingstrup convened an internal board of inquiry into Tyrone Conn's escape on May 13, 1999. Members of the board are appointed by the commissioner and report their findings to

him, guaranteeing senior management the opportunity of investigating itself. The board was to provide the commissioner with the facts surrounding the escape, including the background of the incident, a profile of Conn, and a chronology of events. The board began its work by reviewing the security audits of KP and Millhaven dated July 30, 1998, and the investigative reports of Conn's previous prison breaks and the attempted escape by two inmates from KP in November 1995. One person who would never be interviewed by the board was the man at the centre of the controversy, Tyrone Conn.

Acting on a tip on May 20, 1999, police traced Conn to the home of a friend from KP in the west end of Toronto. Members of the Toronto police Emergency Task Force surrounded the house, and Conn asked to be allowed to speak to a friend on the phone. Detective Steve McAteer, the ROPE unit leader, called Theresa Burke and told her that Conn wanted to talk to her. Burke, a producer at CBC-TV's *the fifth estate*, had been a friend of the inmate's for five years, ever since Conn contacted her about a piece her program had produced called "The Trouble with Evan," a story that had reminded Conn of his own calamitous life.

As the two talked, Conn was moving around the basement of the house, trying to get better reception on the cellphone. Just as the connection improved, Conn started to say something. Then Burke heard a shot. The phone went dead. Conn had apparently shot himself in the chest with a shotgun, or at least that's what the contact wound suggested. The Special Investigations Unit, an Ontario government agency mandated to investigate all fatal shootings involving the police, delved into the circumstances of the inmate's strange and sudden death. Conn's mother, Marion Chamberlain, retained the prominent Toronto lawyer Clayton Ruby to look after the family's interests during the probe.

Conn's friend Linden MacIntyre, a host of *the fifth estate*, said that Conn was "the most alive person I have ever met inside an institution." MacIntyre described him as "vibrant, curious, full of

observations about everything under the sun." MacIntyre and Burke had interviewed Conn in prison in Prince Albert, Saskatchewan, in 1994, and the two men had written, phoned, and visited regularly ever since. Conn was upset when MacIntyre wrote a newspaper article after the escape in which he stated, "Ty Conn is a friend of mine. Some time late last week, he violated our friendship by breaking out of Kingston Penitentiary. I wish him well."

Conn was irked by the accusation of betrayal and tried to reach MacIntyre, who was vacationing in Cape Breton. Through a third party, they had arranged to talk on May 23. MacIntyre didn't tell the police about the arranged phone call, because he didn't believe Conn would hurt anyone. The journalist says he planned to urge Conn to turn himself in.

MacIntyre was bewildered by his friend's sudden death. He knew Conn was very fond of Burke, and he could not believe that Conn would kill himself without saying goodbye. Two other facts bothered him; Conn was moving about the room at the time of his death, and the shot had been fired in mid-sentence.

On June 26, 2001, the Ontario coroner decided that there was no reason to call an inquest into Ty Conn's death. The coroner and the Special Investigations Unit cleared police of any wrongdoing. Conn's friends and supporters continued to believe police should have been less aggressive during the incident. MacIntyre, who saw Conn as a victim rather than a career criminal, accused the Emergency Task Force of firing a stun grenade and rubber bullets at Conn during the takedown, a charge the police denied. Although a stun grenade, which flashes and sounds like a shotgun blast, was tossed into the front entrance of the bungalow after about an hour of negotiations, Conn was in the basement apartment one floor below. He admonished the officers, "Don't be doing that again." They complied. Detective Constable Douglas Ducharme, a four-and-a-half-year veteran of the ROPE unit who was actually at the apprehension scene, emphatically recalled, "To my knowledge, no rubber bullets were fired."

Members of ROPE who responded to the tip about the inmate's hiding place said, "It surprised us as much as anyone else that Conn killed himself." They simply weren't expecting it. The Emergency Task Force could see into the basement apartment and watch Conn's movements. Even though Conn was armed with a shotgun, there was no hostage, so they planned to wait it out rather than use force. In fact, the replacement team had just arrived when the fatal blast was heard.

The ROPE officers theorize that Conn had been asleep shortly before they arrived. Dressed only in his underwear, Conn was sitting down with his legs crossed. The sawed-off shotgun was between his legs pointing at his chest. ROPE members believe that Conn moved suddenly and accidentally discharged the weapon. "I don't even think he wanted to do it," says Douglas Ducharme. "Nobody chooses to die in their underwear."

MacIntyre, an anti-capital-punishment ideologue who has taken up the cause of other convicted criminals such as the killer Stanley Faulder, had a professional as well as a personal relationship with the fugitive. He was helping Conn to write his autobiography. MacIntyre described him as a tragic figure to Jonathan Gatehouse of the *National Post*: "The tragedy was a complicated situation made out of the failures of his life, the failures of people in his life, and ultimately the failures of the social organizations we use." Interestingly, there was no mention by MacIntyre of Conn's own failures. It was the same view of the criminal as victim that was at the heart of Commissioner Ingstrup's restorative justice model.

Conn's spectacular escape fascinated the public. He joined a long list of criminals turned into popular heroes by an uncritical press and a doting film industry. Canadians have long romanticized homegrown bank robbers like the Boyd Gang and the armed robber Roger Caron, whose best-selling life story *Go Boy!* won a Governor General's Award in 1978, with the support of establishment figures like Desmond Morton and Pierre Berton. Another robber turned writer, Stephen Reid of the Stopwatch Gang, also

has his faithful supporters, despite his nasty habit of robbing banks and shooting at policemen and young women who get in his way.

MacIntyre was asked by Conn's family to give the eulogy at the funeral in Belleville. He quoted from a letter Conn had written him from Kingston Penitentiary two years before: "My escapes are a way of stealing back some of the time I've lost and whenever I get out, I do my best to collect the widest variety of experiences so that I can recall them later when I'm locked up. Pretty pitiful, eh?" Two weeks before his break from KP, Conn had told his mother that he wanted to be cremated and have his ashes scattered at a secret place outdoors. His family asked sympathizers not to send flowers. Instead, they suggested cash donations to the library at Kingston Penitentiary. The Ty Conn memorial fund received $533. KP's librarian used it to purchase books for the law library.

In death, Tyrone Conn became the poster boy for those who believe criminals are victims of society requiring compassion, not punishment. Conn's lawyer Dan Brodsky claimed that while there had been a potential for violence in the past, Conn was not a violent person. Brodsky did not bother explaining why a supposedly non-violent person would obtain a gun within days of escaping custody or use weapons in eight separate armed robberies. The *Globe and Mail*'s Rick Salutin went into laudatory contortions aimed at transforming Conn into a folk hero who was making a contribution to society by breaking the law. Salutin wrote that Conn had merely robbed some banks, keeping the "cry for social justice audible." Salutin even believed that outlaws were necessary, "in places where those in power are especially venal, nasty, and petty-minded, like . . . Mike Harris's Ontario." The terrified bank employees who were told by Conn that they would be killed if they moved during his many armed robberies would have trouble understanding Salutin's analysis. His admirers could say what they liked, but no one could talk away the bottom line: when Ty Conn robbed banks, his guns were loaded.

The board of inquiry into the Conn escape submitted its findings to Ole Ingstrup on October 6, 1999. The commissioner

kept them under wraps for seven months. The highly embarrassing and heavily censored report was not released until May 2000,
and then only after several access-to-information requests from
news agencies and victims' rights groups.

The principal finding of the report was damning: KP's warden,
Monty Bourke, his deputy warden, and the IPSO at Kingston
had all known that Conn posed a high escape risk. Despite that,
they never shared the crucial information with guards, at least
according to the vast majority of officers who were interviewed
for the report. Guard after guard told the inquiry that they had
no information about Conn's escape-ridden past or his plans to
break out of Kingston. The only people who thought that there
had been a formal briefing on the subject were the warden and
his senior staff.

"Nobody knew this guy," one of KP's most senior officers said.
"I never heard of him being charged for any type of infraction or
breaking any rules. Nobody had any idea that this guy even had
previous escape convictions."

Most correctional officers would never have known that Conn
was an escape risk if John Oddie, KP's assistant warden for management services, hadn't told a newspaper after the escape that KP staff
were well aware of the risk that the inmate posed. "That's a lie. A
blatant lie," one KP officer said. In fact, when guards found the
ladder the morning after the escape, they looked at one another
and said, "Check McArthur's cell." McArthur was an inmate who
was watched very closely because he was known as a high escape
risk. "I know what kind of officer I am," one guard said. "I know
that whenever I was out there, whenever McArthur leaves or goes
anywhere, if I hear his name, if I am going to be the receiving
officer or the sending officer, I am very thorough with McArthur
because all the hype is on McArthur. Had there been any hype
on Conn, I know I would have done the same thing. But there
was none."

The board of inquiry also questioned why Conn had ever been
considered a medium-security inmate, given his bizarre escape

history. Much of the information in his progress summary was from old reports, and the data that were on file were simply listed rather than analyzed. The board also noted that a number of his thirty-eight convictions were not included in his summary of offences. This inadequate information was also being used by parole officers without independent verification.

Management got another black eye over its cost-cutting measures, though ultimately the board pulled its punch. The inquiry found that the "decision to eliminate the southeast tower post created a vulnerable area of the prison." Conn had also been able to hide in a shop area that would previously have been checked by an officer and a specially trained dog every evening. The practice was stopped to save money, but reinstated after the Conn escape.

Remarkably, union claims that staff cutbacks directly contributed to Conn's escape were dismissed as "unfounded" in the report, even though most of the inquiry's criticisms dealt directly with dubious cost-cutting that jeopardized security. It is interesting to note that even though the board claimed that staff cutbacks hadn't contributed to Conn's escape, KP hired thirty new front-line staff and increased the number of managers from eight to thirteen in the months after the episode. The southeast tower is now manned at night, when most escapes take place.

In the wake of the embarrassing escape from their maximum-security institution, chastened senior managers at KP quickly ordered a tightening of basic security measures that ran against the grain of everything they had been doing for years. The "living unit count tickets" for inmate tallies taken on the ranges now read: "This document bearing the signature below does certify a count verifying a live and breathing body. Further, I confirm that a stand-up noon count [approximately 11:30] was a stand-up count." The term "stand-up" is written in bold, black letters and underlined. If anything, it underscores management's about-face on an internal security matter.

Before the Conn escape, management had actively discouraged guards from forcing inmates to stand for the count in order not to

antagonize them. Despite post orders — a written directive that there be a stand-up count to ensure that a live, breathing body was in the cell at noon each day while the prisoners had lunch — neither officers nor inmates could remember the count being enforced at KP. There was a notable exception. From high atop the papers he pushed, far from the real world of KP, John Oddie told the press, "To my knowledge, it has been done."

It had not.

Policy on cell coverings was also reversed, or rather enforced. Staff had had an ongoing battle with inmates over cell coverings for twenty years, and the union had taken the fight to management. They appeared to have scored a victory on January 16, 1997, when one of KP's unit managers had issued a memo advising that blankets should not cover the door portion of a cell. But in January 1998, management at the prison had made a deal with inmates, allowing them to cover their cell bars for privacy.

Tyrone Conn changed all that. On May 25, 1999, Deputy Warden Alex Lubimiv sent a memo to his officers dealing with cell coverings and the use of night lights after 23:30. The cell covering policy would be enforced to the letter, and night lights would now be turned on for the 23:00, 23:30, and 5:30 formal counts. Unit managers were to conduct weekly range inspections, and correctional supervisors would be required to walk all ranges with the range officer once per shift "to provide support to officers, ensure consistency, and achieve institutional compliance."

The rules had not been enforced for so long that the deputy warden felt obliged to send a separate memo to prisoners, advising them that they would no longer be able to cover their entire cell fronts with blankets. As of May 31, 1999, night lights would now be switched on inside each cell before each of the three nighttime head counts.

On December 10, 1999, Officer Eddie Castle was doing a routine walk of the ranges at 23:30. Glancing into Cell 6 on the first floor of B Block, he observed a partial dummy dressed in a blue shirt. The inmate had not escaped but was hiding. The dummy was

removed and turned over to IPSO Rick Rogers. A few months later, on the anniversary of Kingston Penitentiary's most spectacular escape in modern times, inmate Jay Sedore attempted, unsuccessfully, to go over the wall. Though dead and gone, Ty Conn had clearly become something of an inspiration.

11

END GAME

It is widely recognized that offenders need help to reintegrate into the community. Some countries are interested in supervised conditional release – a return to the community with various degrees of monitoring and supervision – for reasons that have nothing to do with punishing the guilty or protecting the public. In the United States, for example, community alternatives to imprisonment are seen as an answer to prison overcrowding and the high cost of incarceration. Australia, the United States, and the United Kingdom have rigid home detention protocols with twenty-four-hour monitoring using electronic bracelets. Denmark, Sweden, and Norway have much laxer monitoring policies. In some European countries, it is believed that prison is actually detrimental to the reintegration of the inmate into society.

It is interesting to note that the pendulum has begun to swing back in Europe. European countries such as Denmark, Ole Ingstrup's birthplace, have retreated from "befriending" the offenders. In the U.K. the home secretary made it clear in 1998 that the core function of the probation service was to protect society from offenders, not befriend them. Parole officers were

now to confront, challenge, and change offending behaviour. Punishment was again viewed as integral to the process that would reassert the balance between assistance and control that is necessary for conditional release to work. Norway has recently been looking at ending or limiting statutory release.

In most countries, treatment for conditions that led to the illegal act – addiction therapy or psychiatric counselling – can be required when there is a clear connection between the treatment and the offence, although it is usually subject to the agreement of the offender. Sweden still allows the committal of an offender to mandatory treatment in the community as a preventive measure. Norway allows offenders to voice an opinion regarding the conditions of their release. If they don't want supervision, it is not applied against their wishes.

In 1995 the report of the Sentencing and Corrections Review Group, which included John Edwards, then commissioner of CSC, and Willie Gibbs, the head of the National Parole Board, as well as the deputy ministers of both the Justice and Solicitor General's Departments, examined the rising prison population. Projections were that the prison population could grow by 50 per cent over the next decade. The report stated, "The current strategy of heavy and undifferentiated reliance on incarceration as the primary means of responding to crime is not the most effective response in many cases, and is financially unsustainable." Solicitor General Herb Gray had already told the House of Commons justice committee that the federal government would work with the provinces to devise alternatives to prison for those offenders who were not dangerous to the public.

Conditional sentencing provisions were added to the Criminal Code under Section 742.1 in the fall of 1996. They allowed offenders to serve time in the community under house arrest. Killers, child molesters, and armed robbers have avoided prison under the provisions. In May 1997 a judge in Ottawa gave a community sentence to a woman convicted of manslaughter in the death of her common-law husband, and Mr. Justice M. Paul

Forestell of the Ontario Court General Division gave a non-custodial sentence to a St. Catharines man who drove drunk and killed two people. A similar crime in North Carolina at the time had earned a life sentence. The prosecutor in that case had asked for the death penalty.

On January 31, 2000, the Supreme Court of Canada ruled that violent offences could not be excluded from conditional sentencing, because it did not want to introduce "unwarranted rigidity" into sentencing. A conditional sentence could be used if the judge found the offender was not a danger to society, even though the charge might be a sexual offence against children, manslaughter, drug trafficking, or dangerous driving causing death. In March 2001, Richard Hall, a former minor league hockey coach who had tricked his players into having sex with him, was released from a five-year prison term by the British Columbia Court of Appeal. The court ruled he would serve a two-year conditional sentence instead, since he posed a low risk of reoffending.

According to a study done by Trevor Saunders of Statistics Canada and Julian Roberts of the University of Ottawa, published in October 2000 in the *Canadian Journal of Behavioural Science*, in the first three years the courts handed down more than 40,000 conditional sentences across Canada. Two thousand were for sexual assault and a "significant number" for homicide. Saunders and Roberts found that 69 per cent of the 1,500 people they surveyed believed sentencing was generally too lenient in Canada.

Asked about specific cases where conditional sentences had been handed out, 97 per cent of respondents would have preferred jail for a man who repeatedly sexually assaulted his five-year-old step-daughter. Seventy-five per cent wanted jail for a man convicted of drunk driving causing grievous bodily harm, and 71 per cent wanted jail time for a lawyer who defrauded his clients of $90,000.

The Working Group on Human Rights headed by Maxwell Yalden, which reported in May 1999, stated that "a country's orientation with respect to parole supervision is as much a matter of societal attitudes and appropriate professional training as it is

of resources." Europeans generally appear to accept the principle that supervision and reintegration of offenders should be carried out in the community. Offenders released in Norway, Denmark, and Sweden can ask to be supervised by a volunteer selected from the offender's community. But the British, American, and Australian parole systems rely on methods such as home confinement and make much less use of community resources.

The working group concluded that written policies exist within CSC dealing with virtually all human rights issues from general directions to the least restrictive interventions consistent with risk management, and even to specific instructions as to what type of offender information is to be given to victims. But, the report concludes, "it is less certain that all parties are clear about the practical implications of any particular policy, let alone whether they accept them as fair and reasonable."

Unlike some provincial correctional services, CSC does not use electronic monitoring, although monitoring has recently been reviewed by the Solicitor General's Department. The most senior levels of CSC and the National Parole Board continue to question the effectiveness and the humaneness of electronic bracelets, while operational managers tend to be more open to the idea. For CSC, it comes down to a question of the rights of offenders.

The working group found that when it came to human rights in community corrections, "On the whole Canada's conditional release system followed internationally recognized principles that an offender should be incarcerated only when there is no other reasonable alternative, and that the offender should be eligible for community release at the earliest possible stage in their sentence."

Yet Yalden found that the task assigned to CSC was "intrinsically problematic" and that the department faced a complex task in balancing the rights of offenders living in the community against legitimate public safety concerns. According to the working group, CSC needed to help Canadians understand that public safety is enhanced when community groups are involved in the reintegration of offenders, tacit acknowledgment that the public isn't

buying into the theory. The group found that when CSC performed surprise home visits and employment verification checks on offenders, two main human rights criteria should be followed: the measure must be "reasonable and necessary" and "consistent with the least restrictive correctional measure available."

The working group stated that the underlying theory of community corrections was that "offenders of virtually all criminal risk categories can, through a process of supervision and support, become more responsible and law-abiding citizens." It noted that this was "a relatively recent" development in Canada's correctional philosophy. But the Yalden report also pointed out that this philosophy was "far from unchallenged, even at the level of theory, and remains to be fully worked out in practical terms." Given public distrust of the justice system and the place that CSC occupies within it, the understatement was staggering.

The Yalden report went on to present four principal arguments in favour of community corrections:

1) That it is intrinsically more consistent with the human rights principle of treating all human beings with as much dignity and respect as possible.
2) That it affords offenders the greatest opportunity to begin to make responsible contributions to the general welfare.
3) That community-based treatment yields more positive results than do equivalent services in institutional settings.
4) That it offers a practical and less expensive alternative to the inefficient and potentially damaging process of incarceration.

Canada has subscribed to the Universal Declaration of Human Rights since it was adopted over fifty years ago. The only major international document that deals specifically with community corrections is the United Nations Standard Minimum Rules for

Non-Custodial Measures, known as the Tokyo Rules. They call for retention of all normal rights, without abridgment because of the offender's situation; the right to enjoy the least restrictive treatment possible, consistent with public safety (that is, alternatives to imprisonment should be explored); entitlement to an appropriate balance of custodial control with rehabilitation; the provision of satisfactory accommodation and a financial allowance to allow the offender to "live decently," visit family, look for work, and so on; no arbitrary special conditions of parole; and assurances that family, friends, and employers will not be subjected to unnecessary intrusion or harassment in order to verify the offender's activities in the community.

On July 4, 2000, a front-page headline in the *National Post* trumpeted: "Criminals' Release Quota Revealed." The *Post* story stated that prisoners were being released from institutions in order to meet a quota that CSC stoutly denied existed. But documents obtained by Steve Sullivan of the Canadian Resource Centre for Victims of Crime under access-to-information legislation had revealed that at least since 1997, wardens had in fact been under steady pressure to boost the number of inmates released on parole. CSC wanted 50 per cent of its inmates in prisons and the other 50 per cent in the community. In a June 1998 internal CSC document, Ole Ingstrup himself wrote: "To reach a 50/50 split by the year 2000 will be a professional challenge – but not all that unattainable."

It was very old news. Ole Ingstrup had been pushing his quota system as a "corporate objective" within CSC since his first tour of duty as commissioner. A 1990 memo from W. J. Gladu, the future associate warden of the Regional Treatment Centre in Kingston, to the warden of Kingston Penitentiary explained why. Gladu wrote: "Having reviewed the [corporate] objectives, and being cognizant of the Commissioner's intention not to construct additional correctional facilities, despite the projected increase in inmate population," there was no choice but to "reintegrate a significantly

larger number of offenders . . . in order to reduce the relative use of incarceration as a major correctional intervention."

Ignoring the evidence to the contrary, in April 2000 Ingstrup insisted in front of the House of Commons justice committee that there was no quota. He did lamely acknowledge that there was "some language out there that, taken out of context, could be interpreted as if there was a goal, something that had to be achieved."

The commissioner's waffling grew more difficult when members of the subcommittee on the CCRA produced a July 3, 1998, memo written by Brendan Reynolds, Ingstrup's Ontario deputy commissioner. In it, wardens were clearly directed to meet targeted numbers of inmates inside and outside prison. *The Ontario Region Reintegration Plan – 1998/99* stated, "To equalize the institutional/community populations, the Ontario Region has committed to the release of a further 660 offenders by December 31, 1999."

Liberal MP Tom Wappel was convinced that the commissioner had played fast and loose with the facts to avoid infuriating the public and embarrassing his political masters: "I very specifically asked, having read and having been infuriated by the memo from Mr. Reynolds. . . . Frankly, I honestly believe there was a quota discussed. I believe it was discussed by the commissioner. He got caught. . . . Both the previous and the current solicitor general slapped him down in the House of Commons, saying there was no such thing, and now they're looking for face-saving." Liberal MP Jacques Saada and Alliance MP Jim Gouk agreed that Ingstrup had misled the committee. But Saada, who was parliamentary secretary to the minister at the time, told the committee on June 2, 1999, "I would be afraid if this thing were to pick up some momentum in the media, this questioning, this doubt about the quota, it would spread undue fear in the population."

In 1999, about 59 per cent of the 22,000 federal offenders were in custody, while the remainder were serving their sentences in the community. Critics of the system, including Steve Sullivan,

believed that the quota was an effort to both save money and reflect the personal philosophy of Ole Ingstrup: "He's not a big believer that prisons are necessary. The consequences are that when you make decisions based not on risk, but based on quotas, you release some people who clearly should not be released."

Public reaction was swift and negative to CSC's undeclared quota system aimed at rushing dangerous criminals from maximum- and super-maximum-security prisons to less secure institutions on their way to early parole. An editorial in the *Post* savaged CSC for its dishonesty as much as for its policy: "The CSC's verbal gymnastics and denials are duplicitous and disgraceful. There must be strong suspicion, to put it no more strongly, that the quotas are kept unacknowledged because the CSC knows they would be deeply unpopular with the public. And the reason they would be unpopular is that it is evidently wrong-headed and dangerous to release criminals into society according to a numerical tally that overrides case by case analysis. The CSC has no right to conduct a secret policy."

Under Commissioner Ingstrup, numerical tallies of many kinds flourished. The data produced have an uncanny way of proving that the commissioner's correctional theories are working. CSC relies heavily on computers to advance its quota system. In fact, the Security Reclassification Scale is a new computer program used to assign risk level to federal inmates for the purpose of determining their required level of security. The program has a scoring range of 7.25 to 38.8 points (higher scores, higher risk). The security reclassification "cut-off" values were designed to distribute 24.5 per cent of inmates to minimum security, 63 per cent to medium, and 12.5 per cent to maximum security. Those inmates at or below 15.8 points go to minimum, those above 26 points go to maximum, and inmates falling between those scores draw medium-security incarceration.

The scale assesses twenty security risk factors: serious institutional incidents; minor incidents (conviction as defined by court);

recorded incident reports; pay grade; segregation periods; urinalysis tests; detention referral; correction plan/program progress; correction plan/program motivation; drug and alcohol rating; abuse affecting one or more life areas; serious abuse affecting several life areas; ETAs; UTAs; work releases; age at review; psychological concerns; Custody Rating Scale (CRS); escape history; and CRS incident history.

Sensitive to the criticism that it was using the computer program to manipulate the system, CSC was quick to deny that computers rather than people decided on an inmate's security classification. "The scale was never intended to replace the judgment of staff but only to be utilized as one more actuarial tool, to provide staff with a research based perspective risk."

According to the latest numbers released by Statistics Canada in July 2001, the overall crime rate in Canada went up from 1999 to 2000. While the number of police-reported property crimes dropped after remaining relatively stable for the last few years, the number of violent crimes reported rose from 291,327 in 1999 to 301,875 in 2000. From 1980 to 2000, violent crime rose 60 per cent.

At the same time, the number of federal offenders in custody decreased from 14,512 in 1996-1997 to 12,898 in 1999-2000. Yet CSC's operating costs rose dramatically during the same period. The department spent $1.39 billion during fiscal year 1999-2000, up from $1.15 billion in 1995-1996. It cost $96,748 a year to keep a male inmate in a maximum-security prison, and $115,465 for a female offender. With superficially favourable crime statistics, and a regime that spends 25 per cent of its budget on human services – case management, programs, and community supervision – Ole Ingstrup was ready to take a bow: "We can safely say we have results that are encouraging."

But the report card on the quota system is far from glowing. The number of escapes from minimum-security prisons increased in 2000 by over 35 per cent, a clear indication that offenders who were moved into lower-security institutions were breaking out of

(or walking away from) prison in record numbers. Statutory release inmates begin the process of so-called "cascading" from maximum to minimum security about eighteen months before their release.

Police charges for violent crimes committed by people on parole or statutory release jumped from 199 in 1999-2000 to 250 in 2000-2001, according to CSC's 2001 performance report. Despite this alarming increase, there is also evidence that CSC has a deliberate plan to reduce the number of parole revocations by not enforcing the letter of release conditions for "minor" violations such as drinking or associating with known criminals.

Under the June 1998 revised reintegration plan for the Ontario region, a systematic review of NPB denials and revocations would be completed within 15 days of the decision. The plan directed that the revocation rate for offenders in the community be reduced by 10 per cent over the previous year. The revocation rate for the region in 1997-1998 was 37 per cent. Operation Bypass was implemented in February 1999 to speed up the process of reintegration by cutting red tape. CSC wardens signed an "accountability contract" with CSC. Corporate Objective 2 of CSC is to "substantially increase the number of offenders safely and effectively reintegrated at or soon after eligibility." The number of releases was measured at monthly executive committee meetings.

For fiscal 1998-1999, warden after warden committed themselves to "meeting the regional release goals" established for their institutions. The warden of KP, Monty Bourke, signed a contract in July 1998 agreeing "to contribute to reintegration by facilitating programming and preparation of offenders for reduction in security classification and transfer to medium security institutions where these offenders can more readily prepare for reintegration to the community." Bourke projected that he would transfer fifty offenders to lower security during the 1998 calendar year, an increase of 35.14 per cent over the previous year.

Wayne Scissons, the warden of Collins Bay, wrote in his October 1998 accountability contract, "I believe that incarceration

should be the last resort as a response to criminal acts in society. It is my goal to assist in the significant shift of the population balance of the Ontario region by December 1999."

Steve Sullivan claims that despite the inherent danger to the public, CSC staff are being discouraged from writing negative reports that could prevent inmates from being released by the National Parole Board at the earliest possible point in their sentence. Warden Al Stevenson of Bath Institution even issued a memo saying that each time the parole board turned down early parole for an inmate, he would personally review the file. This was part of Bath's commitment to Commissioner Ingstrup's "reintegration" plan. The personal review by the warden was to ensure that there had been "no neglect in the management of the case and that nothing can be done at a senior level to open doors which might otherwise remain closed." The CSC was now in the business of opening prison doors, not closing them. At Bath, for example, management was actively working in 1998 toward the release of 169 offenders as part of Ingstrup's undeclared quota system.

"To me, it's intimidation," Sullivan said. "What he's really saying is you shouldn't be making negative recommendations. And if you do, you'd better satisfy me." According to Sullivan, CSC is, in effect, telling front-line staff to release more inmates. Several MPs, including Liberal MP Dan McTeague, have been critical of that practice, as well as the policy of rapidly transferring convicted killers to medium-security institutions.

There was a lot to complain about. In February 2000, Anton "Tony" Lorenz was charged with first-degree murder after he brutally killed his girlfriend. In a plea bargain with the Crown, the charge was reduced to second-degree murder and he was sentenced to life with no chance of parole for ten years. Yet Lorenz served only three months at maximum-security Millhaven Institution before being transferred to Bath, where inmates are prepared for work programs and parole.

The Lorenz case is not an isolated example. Clinton Suzack was given a life sentence for the 1993 murder of Sudbury police

constable Joe MacDonald. Constable MacDonald had pulled Suzack and another man over for a routine traffic stop and was shot five times at close range with a semi-automatic handgun. At the time of the slaying, Suzack was on parole and unlawfully at large from a halfway house.

Suzack had served only four years of his twenty-five-year sentence for the MacDonald murder when he was caught planning to escape from medium-security Joyceville Institution on November 24, 1999. The high-profile offender had a long history of violent crimes, including those he had committed as a drug-debt enforcer inside. Sudbury police chief Alex McCauley considered Suzack "one of the most dangerous criminals in Canada." He was also a friend of Ty Conn when they were both inmates at KP.

An anonymous call alerted authorities at Joyceville to the planned breakout. Acting on the tip, guards found that an inner perimeter fence in the recreation yard had been cut. They also found tools, including an oxyacetylene torch, hidden inside a manhole leading to a pipe that emptied outside the prison. Despite the fact that Suzack had had trouble adjusting to prison life and was on report for threatening staff, he was quickly placed in a medium-security institution according to what guards call the commissioner's "get them out" plan, or GTO for short.

After the aborted Joyceville escape attempt, Suzack was involuntarily sent back to maximum security at Kingston Penitentiary on November 26, 1999. On his way out of the institution, he boasted to guards that his lawyer would have him back in Joyceville in two weeks. In fact, the feat was accomplished in just ten days. The convicted killer was returned to Joyceville on December 6. An internal CSC security report concluded that inmates had indeed exploited lax security at Joyceville to get tools and access to unauthorized areas of the institution. Suzack was identified as the organizer of the escape plot, and although he remained a suspect in the breakout attempt, the OPP Penitentiary Squad felt that there was insufficient evidence to charge him. Suzack returned to the regular population at Joyceville and once

again went to work in the metal shop, where he has access to tools like oxyacetylene torches.

Despite these embarrassing episodes, Ole Ingstrup remained largely hidden from public view. As departures go, Commissioner Ingstrup's was well timed. His resignation, in August 2000, came just a week before the publication of a National Parole Board performance report that showed that the number of serious crimes committed by paroled offenders had jumped by 38 per cent over the previous year. Ingstrup had repeatedly boasted about the recidivism rate dropping while he was in charge of CSC, but 228 federal offenders committed murder, attempted murder, major assaults, robberies, and unlawful confinements after their early return to freedom. The NPB annual performance report cited overall reoffence rates of 14.8 per cent for those on statutory release, 12 per cent for those on full parole, and 5.6 per cent for those on day parole. Critics of Ingstrup's policies pointed to the fifty-fifty parole quota as the obvious reason for the jump in serious parole offences.

On September 21, 2000, twelve days after Ingstrup's resignation took effect, the Kingston police released a shocking report revealing that almost half of all inmates released from federal prisons in the area had committed new crimes. The numbers stood in stark contrast to Ingstrup's boast of only 10 to 12 per cent, results that had routinely been used by CSC to justify conditional release programs. The police study tracked 1,378 inmates released from eight prisons in the Kingston area between 1990 and 1998. CSC routinely notifies police forces about offenders released in their area, and Staff Sergeant Brian Cookman simply ran the names through a national police computer database. He found that 47 per cent (642 offenders) had committed new crimes.

In response, British Columbia MP Randy White, justice critic of the Canadian Alliance, said that CSC and the NPB had deceived the public about how many freed inmates commit new crimes, and that their attitude was that "a little deception won't hurt if we don't get caught."

Given what was really going on in Canada's prison system, the words could serve as the true motto of the CSC.

All offenders released by the National Parole Board, which, like the CSC, reports to the solicitor general, get conditional release. The agency costs taxpayers $30.9 million annually. Released inmates may be on unescorted temporary absences, day or full parole, or statutory release, which in the vast majority of cases is automatic after an offender serves two-thirds of his sentence. Offenders are eligible for full parole after serving just one-third of their sentence, unless a judge sets a longer eligibility period at the time of sentencing. In theory, the degree of supervision is determined by the offender's needs and the risk to the public. Setting the level of supervision on the basis of these two factors is like astrophysics: one part fact, nine parts grasping at straws. As for the supervision itself, high-risk offenders are sometimes seen in parole offices for just fifteen minutes a month because of high caseloads and budgetary cutbacks. It is a system designed for disaster.

Michael John Hector committed his first armed robbery at age eighteen. His later criminal offences included property convictions, using a firearm, and several parole violations. Each time he was released from jail, he was back in court within two years.

On September 28, 1987, Hector, then twenty-three, stole almost $18,000 from the Westford William Credit Union in Thunder Bay. He pulled off the robbery with the help of a .22-calibre sawed-off rifle and a disguise. Hector also had a radio scanner to monitor the police. A plan to rob a Brinks truck was aborted, but on October 30, 1987, Hector dressed a young accomplice in the same disguise and counselled him to rob the Thunder Bay Municipal Employees Credit Union while armed with the sawed-off .22. This copycat crime was calculated to create an alibi for Hector, who was by then a suspect in the September armed robbery.

The Municipal Employees Credit Union robbery was to take place between 3:00 and 3:30 p.m. while Hector was at a therapy session. The accomplice panicked during the getaway and turned

himself in to police, leading to Hector's arrest and conviction for the September robbery. When the legal dust settled, Hector was sent to prison for four years. But in the world of minimum sentences and a prisoner's right to a speedy return to the street, four years didn't mean four years. In fact, it meant less than two.

After doing a risk assessment, the NPB granted the armed robber day parole on April 6, 1989. Parole was granted despite a May 5, 1988, assessment by a Stony Mountain prison psychologist, Dr. R. J. Howes, who noted, "Hector has quite recently behaved in a very calculating, frightening, treacherous manner, however reborn he may currently appear." Hector was granted full parole on October 20, 1989.

Parole was suspended on March 15, 1991, after Hector was charged with conspiracy to commit robbery, wearing a disguise with intent, and illegal use of a firearm. Over $12,000 had been stolen from Hull's Food Store in Winnipeg on January 15, 1991. Hector denied being the culprit and was indignant about the charges. On December 12, 1991, he was convicted on all counts and sentenced to ten years in prison as a second-time armed robber. The sentence was reduced to eight years, six months, and seven days on appeal.

On March 12, 1993, Hector once again applied for day parole. The experienced con knew all the buttons to push. He would reside at the Salvation Army halfway house in Thunder Bay, Ontario, seek employment immediately, enrol in a computer program course, and attend a facilitator training class for a program called "Breaking Barriers." He said, "I am also looking forward to playing an active part in my daughters' lives." Why did he deserve consideration for release? He was a new man: "I know that if I'm given a chance on day parole, I feel quite confident not to reoffend. I feel I have taken the right steps to address the main issue as to why I was reinvolved, that issue being morality. I look forward to explaining this at length during my parole hearing."

Studies have shown that as many as 70 to 80 per cent of federal prisoners could be described as having anti-social personality, with

narcissistic and borderline personality characteristics. Research has shown that criminal psychopaths who undergo cognitive and anger management training before release have an 82 per cent recidivism rate, compared with a recidivism rate of 59 per cent for psychopaths who don't take the programs. According to Dr. Robert Hare, the world's best-known expert on psychopaths, "These guys learn the words but not the music."

Michael Hector had the support of his family, but the Thunder Bay police opposed his release into the community. They noted several potentially violent robbery plans of Hector's that had not been carried out. Dr. Howes assessed Hector and copied the National Parole Board in on his findings. In his updated assessment of May 28, 1993, Howes wrote: "There is something grotesque about a man with Mr. Hector's strengths and abilities who has so frequently chosen the wayward path. He is an intelligent, articulate, energetic young man who even possesses a sometimes poetic nature, and yet he has never translated these qualities into much in the way of meaningful and responsible accomplishment."

Hector complained to Howes that his family had never rewarded success but punished failure. His father had berated him for being a failure when he was still too young to have achieved success, "and this was obviously a stinging rebuke which has affected him ever since," wrote the doctor. As a result, Hector had followed every shortcut to "success" he could devise. According to the psychologist, Hector's two major downfalls were his combination of materialism and impatience, along with a poorly developed value system.

In the two years since he had returned to prison, Hector had completed the "Breaking Barriers" course, was an active member of a weekly psychology group, and had taken a computer correspondence course. He had also quit smoking, something few inmates have the self-discipline to accomplish. Dr. Howes felt that this small personal victory might be a harbinger of greater discipline to come in a young man who hadn't shown much during his criminal career.

Despite the fact that Hector had also received a one-year sentence on May 4, 1993, for the theft of four cars in the Winnipeg

area between September 15, 1990, and February 13, 1991, Howes was not concerned. (Hector was given a one-year sentence consecutive to his eight-years-plus sentence for the Winnipeg armed robbery.) Contrary to Manitoba police information, Dr. Howes believed that Hector had been more of an observer than a participant in the stolen car ring: "He had frequently made inadequate choices of associates and he had an unhealthy attraction to the more notorious, reckless types." In the psychologist's opinion, Hector dearly wanted to prove his worth to his daughters: "I believe he is genuine when he asserts that he never wants to have to lie to them again." Weighing all the variables, it was Howes's "subjective clinical impression that Mr. Hector represents a manageable risk and thus I offer my support for a decision to release him on day parole at this time."

Ironically, his case management team felt that Hector was not ready for day parole. They felt he had not displayed true remorse for his crimes and noted his potential for violence. His case manager was also concerned that adequate supervision was not available in Thunder Bay: "It is imperative that Michael have intense supervision while on day parole, in order to ensure that he is not falling into previous patterns which led him to crime. In this writer's opinion, it is felt that Michael Hector lacks the sincerity and integrity in his commitment to leading a crime free life, and remains a high risk to public safety. The CMT prefer a very structured and gradual release plan for this individual, lest he re-offend in a manner more violent than in the past." No substance abuse was noted in his criminal profile.

Day parole was denied on July 14, 1993, but Hector was transferred from Stony Mountain to the minimum-security Rockwood Institution. He was granted day parole in October 1994 and released in November.

It was noted in Hector's pre-release report that there was "a relatively consistent pattern of increasingly serious offences." When the community assessment for Hector was requested in June 1994, the Thunder Bay police opposed the release of Hector

in their area. The firearms he had used during his offences were loaded, and he had pointed them at his robbery victims. The police believed there was a risk of Hector reoffending and he would be a prime suspect in future robberies.

The 1994 NPB pre-release decision sheet showed that Hector's main problems were his materialism, impatience, negative peer pressure, criminal values, and poor coping skills: "Makes good plans but does not sustain efforts over time." His SIR (Statistical Information on Recidivism) Scale score was −8. Sixty per cent of inmates assigned to that category reoffend.

Hector was assessed by Hugo Foss, a psychologist at Rockwood Institution, in May 1994; Foss found the inmate a "highly criminalized man." Foss noted that while his motivation for crime was economic, Hector mentioned "that he found crime exciting." The psychologist also observed that Hector believed "a crime was not really a crime unless you were caught."

Hector's CSC progress summary was completed on June 10, 1994, by Karen Atkinson. She noted that Hector rationalized his robberies by assuring himself that no one would be hurt in the process: "This appears to indicate to the writer that Hector does not view the psychological harm he caused his victims as significant." When he was arrested, Hector had been carrying several weapons, including a sawed-off shotgun: "He relates the weapons were to be used only for a show of force, however when reviewed against the offender's documented trait of minimizing, the writer feels that Hector may have the potential for violence."

Far from experiencing remorse, Atkinson felt that Hector had glorified his crimes. In an office interview in February 1994, Hector said that he felt he was more intelligent than the average person in prison. He was not "in here for nickel and dime stuff," he said. "I used disguises, police scanners, blueprints et cetera and really know how to plan a heist."

Remarkably, both the psychologist and Hector's case manager recommended day parole, provided there was psychiatric counselling in the community; in fact it was one of his parole conditions.

In the June 1994 community assessment done before release on day parole, CSC noted, "It is strongly suggested that a special condition be recommended: To participate in counselling as arranged by supervisor." But after an initial referral to Dr. Robert Sheppard, head of forensic services, a follow-up assessment was done on April 5, 1995, by Dr. Eugene Hewchuck, a psychiatrist at Lakehead Psychiatric Hospital. After a brief interview, Hewchuck was of the opinion that "it is doubtful Mr. Hector will require ongoing therapy on a regular basis." Therapy would be available locally in the event of a crisis situation.

Hector's parole hearing was reportedly "release focused." The questions were sometimes leading, and the parole board appeared to accept the offender's answers at face value even though he minimized his record, his escalating weapons offences, and his previous parole violations. Hector knew what they wanted to hear. Despite the fact that Hector had always used guns during robberies, the NPB did not consider Hector violent because he had not actually fired them. Hector was released on full parole on April 28, 1995.

Hector's short-term goals included saving money for a lavish engagement and wedding in late 1996. His long-term goals were to be a published writer and to semi-retire as a writer and settle in Australia by the age of forty-five – lofty goals for a man who entered prison with a grade 8 education. It was noted that Hector had the support of his common-law wife and his stepfather, brother, and sister, and that he had "a very stable and positive outlook on life."

(Hector's stepfather, Richard St. Amand, had married Lynne Hector when Michael was three. Michael's brother, Jim, and his mother changed their names, but Michael kept his biological father's name. St. Amand treated the boys as if they were his own sons and was very supportive of Michael.)

The John Howard Society, the prisoners' advocacy group funded by the taxpayer, employed the parole officer who supervised Hector. Although the NPB grants release, supervision in the community is

the responsibility of CSC. Hector's parole supervisor was not provided with key information about his client, including a psychological report that would have described Hector's crime cycle. Nor was he provided with Hector's criminal record, current community assessment, arrest reports, or court and Crown information. In Hector's correctional plan dated January 16, 1996, Ambihapathy Chinniah, the executive director of the John Howard Society in Thunder Bay and the person overseeing Hector's parole under a contract with CSC, noted that Hector was currently being supervised for being part of a stolen car ring in Winnipeg. Chinniah seemed unaware of the more serious armed robbery charges.

Hector's parole supervision consisted of weekly or biweekly meetings at his parole office and the issuing of travel permits for work outside the area. The parole supervisor never visited Hector's home or workplace, nor did he make contact with his family. Although it was known that Hector's financial situation was one of his "criminogenic" factors, financial information was self-reported, and the parole supervisor did not want to pry into Hector's personal life by investigating his finances. Clearly, Chinniah knew something about the Tokyo Rules.

By the end of July 1996, Hector's parole officer thought he was doing so well that he recommended reporting just once a month, noting that Hector was very pleasant to work with. In fact, he accepted everything Hector told him without independent verification. If he had checked, Chinniah would have found out that Hector had no source of income after October 1996, other than what he'd made working as a bouncer at the St. Louis Bar on two occasions. Contract Contracting, a window installation operation Hector had started in April 1996, had gone out of business. Hector's release plan had stated he would be working at his step-father's window manufacturing company.

On December 23, 1996, Hector picked up a .38-calibre Enfield six-shot revolver and a box of fifty Smith and Wesson 145-grain, .38-calibre bullets from a contact at the St. Louis Bar. He then

asked his brother for money to finance a robbery. Hector had not paid his rent for months and had been passing bad cheques, twenty-seven all told, for a cash value of $5,918.46, written on his defunct company for living expenses. He had already been evicted from one residence, owing $3,000 in back rent. Hector changed addresses but not his habits. He was issued another eviction notice for $1,300 in back rent.

In December 1996, Hector failed to report to the police, a condition of his parole. When he finally showed up on January 20, 1997, he claimed that he had "forgot all about the appointment." He also told police that he had lost his parole reporting form. He would continue to report to his parole officer on a monthly basis. His Correctional Plan, dated January 20, 1997, documented a new long-term plan. He was now going to be a publisher as well as a writer, and build a house in Newfoundland in his new girlfriend's hometown. His other ambition was to "continue to be free of crime and be a contributing member of the community." Ambi Chinniah liked what he was hearing. "Michael keeps me informed of all his problems and has been very frank about his future plans."

Despite their chummy relationship, there were a few things the ex-convict did not share with his supervisor – like the fact that eleven days before Chinniah wrote his glowing appraisal, Michael Hector had murdered two men in cold blood.

On January 9, 1997, two friends of Hector, Robert McCollum and Kevin Solomon, were murdered in McCollum's home in Thunder Bay. The victims were involved in a heating installation business, but police allege they supplemented their income by selling illicit handguns and narcotics. The twenty-nine-year-old men were also alleged to be associated with the Hells Angels. The supposed motive for the crime was that McCollum had refused to sell Hector an ounce of cocaine for $2,000 when the asking price was $2,200. According to police, Hector stole the cocaine after killing the two men.

Both McCollum and Solomon were shot in the face and died instantly. McCollum was shot while bending over to snort a line

of cocaine from a blue hand mirror on his kitchen counter. The bullet passed through his chin into his chest. Hector then shot him below the right eye with the .38-calibre Enfield revolver. Solomon was murdered while taking a shower, apparently eliminated because he was a potential witness to the murder that followed the failed drug transaction. He was shot once below the right eye. Before leaving the house, Hector turned off the shower.

On February 3, 1997, Michael Hector robbed Blair Aitkens, aged twenty, of $944, before executing him with the same gun he had used to kill McCollum and Solomon. Aitkens was a pump attendant at the Can-Op gas station near Bay Street in Thunder Bay. He was a hardworking young man with no criminal record and no drug involvement, and was well liked in the community. He had planned to attend community college in the fall of 1997, but he would never have his photo taken again at the family camp he loved so much at Northern Lights Lake, or ride his father's new all-terrain vehicle. After the robbery, Aitkens was taken to a distant part of the garage and shot in the back of the head and then in the ear to make sure he was dead.

Blair Aitkens was found ten minutes later by a customer, lying in a pool of blood. He was rushed to hospital and put on life support. The next day, Jim St. Amand ran into his brother, Michael Hector, at the Victoriaville Mall. The subject of the robbery came up, and Jim told his brother that he had heard on the radio that Aitkens was in critical condition in hospital. Hector replied that he could not be alive and accused his brother of lying. He said, "Once in the back of the head, once in the ear: that kid is not alive." Aitkens died later that day.

Jim St. Amand went to the police and provided a sworn statement to investigators. He also told police that Michael Hector had offered to kill their stepfather for Jim, if it would ease business problems he had with the elder St. Amand. Hector was arrested on February 4, 1997, and charged with illegal possession of an unregistered restricted weapon. The court had banned him from carrying weapons. CSC regional and national headquarters were

notified by telephone and his parole was revoked the next day. The Thunder Bay police told CSC that he would probably be charged with double homicide in the next few days and was also being investigated for the murder of Aitkens. Police wanted him off the street immediately.

Hector pleaded guilty to three counts of first-degree murder before Mr. Justice A.W. Maloney on May 5, 1997. He received a life sentence of twenty-five years without eligibility for parole, concurrent on each charge. At the time of the murders, he had been on parole while serving an eight-and-a-half-year term for armed robbery committed with an unregistered restricted weapon. That armed robbery was committed while he was on parole from a previous armed robbery offence. Members of the community and the relatives of the victims were outraged that the murders were committed by someone on parole for a violent crime.

On February 28, 1997, Commissioner Ingstrup and the chairman of the NPB, Willie Gibbs, appointed Doug McGregor, special assistant to CSC's deputy commissioner for the Pacific region, and Simonne Ferguson, the NPB's regional director for Ontario, as chairs of the board of inquiry into the release and supervision of Michael Hector. Again, CSC and the NPB would investigate themselves. The results of the inquiry are not available to the public. In any case, under Section 154 of the CCRA, no criminal or civil proceedings can be brought against members of the parole board for anything said or done in good faith in the exercise of their duties.

In September 1997 Carolyn Solomon learned through a newspaper report that her son's murderer would be appealing his conviction. When she wrote to the National Parole Board asking why she had not been notified, since she had formally asked to be informed of all changes in Hector's status, she was told "notifying her of Appeal dates was not one of the pieces of information" that either CSC or the NPB shared.

In a CSC document dated April 23, 1998, less than a year after his conviction, Hector requested a transfer from Edmonton Institution, where he was serving his sentence, to Stony Mountain

prison in Winnipeg. Despite the triple first-degree murders committed while he was on parole for a violent offence, Hector was now classified as a medium-security model inmate: "Clearly Hector does not present a problem in an institutional setting." The request was granted by the warden and Hector was transferred on May 11, 1998.

Leo Toneguzzi, the Thunder Bay chief of police, was informed about the transfer by Gordon Aitkens, the father of Blair Aitkens. In a letter to CSC, he stated his strong personal feelings about the transfer: "To put it mildly, I am thoroughly outraged by what I consider a reckless disregard for both the safety of the public and the mental anguish already suffered by the families of the victims. . . . Michael Hector is an extremely dangerous individual who has stated he will escape from prison and kill police officers should he escape. His past record indicates that he is capable of perpetrating any crime."

Hector ended up serving his sentence at Atlantic Institution in New Brunswick. He was appealing his conviction on the basis that his guilty plea was made under duress. His lawyer, Chris Watkins of Thunder Bay, said the appeal was about the "preservation of the integrity of the justice system," not about guilt or innocence. Hector has since married while in prison and qualifies for conjugal visits.

PART THREE

Post-Game

12

NEW DIRECTIONS

The spectacular failures and empty assurances of the Correctional Service of Canada have raised serious doubts about the direction of public policy in the area of crime and punishment. Legislators are looking for better ways to deal with offenders and protect the public, a quest that has rekindled interest in old ideas and led to bold experiments with new ones. Whether they succeed or fail, these new directions are a sign that the status quo is no longer acceptable. Nowhere is the spirit of reform stronger than in the most powerful jurisdiction in the country, a province whose pioneering social policies are frequently followed not only by the other provinces but also by the federal government.

On November 20, 2000, the Ontario government introduced sweeping reforms to the province's prison system, including earned remission of sentence, random drug testing, a grooming code, and contracts with prisoners laying out the terms of their work and rehabilitation programs. In announcing a $500-million "investment" to transform the correctional system in Ontario, Corrections Minister Rob Sampson promised that new jails would ultimately serve the taxpayer by lowering costs and increasing efficiency.

"When I first got this job, I decided to kick the tires for myself," Sampson told the author. "They fell off. When I asked departmental officials what the recidivism rate was, no one could tell me. We didn't even keep those statistics – which, by the way, is the only way to measure the effectiveness of what we're doing. I later received estimates that recidivism was between 70 and 80 per cent in the provincial system. We were running a revolving door in a system that did very little correcting of negative behaviour. At least I then knew why no one was keeping formal statistics."

The feisty minister with the neat moustache promised that there would be no "soft time" or "Club Feds" in Ontario's jails. As he put it, "Criminals will not be rewarded with golf courses, riding stables, or fly fishing. There will be no cocktail dresses and certainly no household pets. Ontario's new jails will keep criminals locked in – and keep drugs and contraband locked out." Sampson confirmed that Ontario prisoners will soon be getting regulation haircuts, losing jewellery and street clothes, and even paying the costs of their own upkeep if they have the means. "It's part of our 1999 electoral promise of 'pay for stay' prisons. Those who are able will pay for their stays in Ontario jails."

The Corrections Accountability Act, some of which directly challenges existing federal law, also lays down the governance rules for privately run prisons and creates local community monitoring boards to ensure public scrutiny of the province's correctional facilities. "By the time we are done," Sampson told me, "I want to have a tough, humane, no-frills prison system that will be able to measure results and which no one will want to call home."

Sampson's bill established accountability for both inmates and correctional facilities. The most dramatic change was a series of provincial regulations that require Ontario's 7,500 inmates, unlike their federal counterparts, to earn the "privilege" of an early release from prison.

As noted earlier, under the current federal statute, widely denounced by victims' rights groups as the "discount law," inmates are automatically released after serving two-thirds of their sentence

even if they have not followed their Correctional Plan. An offender is detained until the end of his sentence ("warrant of expiry") only in exceptional circumstances. In 1999-2000, for example, 4,781 federal inmates were automatically released on statutory release; only 224 were kept past the two-thirds mark after a detention review – the same process that has kept Karla Homolka behind bars.

Under Ontario's new regulations, inmates can still be credited with one-third off their sentences. But their performance will be measured each month, and credits will be awarded or subtracted depending on behaviour. Good behaviour and active participation in programs will both be defined by regulation. In Ontario, statutory release will be revoked if inmates use drugs, refuse to participate in work or rehabilitation programs, or use violence against staff.

An estimated 80 per cent of offenders in provincial jails have some degree of drug or alcohol dependency. In introducing Ontario's reforms, Sampson said, "Unlike the federal government, we will have a zero-tolerance drug policy that means what it says. If you use drugs in our jails and get caught, you will be serving your full sentence." Although the Correctional Service of Canada has an official zero-tolerance policy toward drugs, Ottawa provides inmates with bleach kits for their needles and is currently contemplating a needle exchange program in federal penitentiaries in an attempt to control infectious diseases, which are rampant across the system.

Even if an Ontario inmate accumulates credits for good behaviour under the new system, he can still lose them for breaking the rules. The Ontario regulations fill a void in the federal law, which does not specifically define what constitutes good behaviour. "Our lawyers have looked at it," a senior aide to Sampson said, "and we think these new regulations will survive any challenge."

In December 2000, the Ontario legislature passed the Corrections Accountability Act. At the same time as the Harris government introduced accountability provisions for inmates, it also tabled

governance rules for two new super-jails in Ontario, the Central North Correctional Centre in Penetanguishene and the Central East Correctional Centre in Lindsay. To provide a comparison, the government decided to have Penetanguishene run by the private sector and Lindsay run publicly.

The Harris government also introduced legislation to create local monitoring boards, which will act as independent observers of the care, supervision, and programs being provided to inmates. Board members will have "full and free" access to inspect and tour their local facilities whenever they choose, twenty-four hours a day, seven days a week. Members will be volunteers, appointed by the minister, and appointees will receive training to perform their duties in a safe and secure fashion.

Private operators will be required to comply with standards of operation and performance set by the ministry, to provide the ministry with unrestricted access to offender records and the facilities, and to honour information and privacy legislation, including giving inmates access to the provincial ombudsman. The Ontario government will retain overall authority and accountability for the service provided by its private partners, including "step-in" rights to immediately take over delivery of correctional services if it deems public safety is at risk.

All operators, whether public or private, will be expected to meet the same stringent standards of performance. "When it comes to the publicly-run-versus-privately-run debate, I don't think that either one or the other deserves a monopoly," Sampson told me. "I think that competition will make both types of facility run better. But one thing I do know. Our role models for reform are not in Canada. What the feds are doing is simply wrong."

In the reform of its prison system, Ontario has drawn heavily on the experience of the prison system in the United Kingdom, where the first privately operated prison opened in April 1992. Private prisons were part of a policy initiated by the Conservative government of John Major to make additional prison accommodation

available quickly, and at the same time improve cost-effectiveness. Ontario set out not to copy but rather to adapt the U.K. model. "We don't want to import the mistakes of other jurisdictions," Sampson said. "We want to learn from their mistakes to come up with a made-in-Ontario corrections policy that will be fair, effective, efficient, and, most of all, measurable and accountable."

Ontario faced the same problem of overcrowding that burdened the U.K. prisons. Quinte Detention Centre in Napanee, for example, was designed to hold ninety-six inmates. But on any given weekend, three times that number are behind bars. Nor have staffing levels increased to handle the new caseloads. Increased violence, drug use, and weapons have made conditions inside intolerable. Use of sick time by overstressed prison staff has also jumped. Jails are so overcrowded that officials have occasionally been forced to turn away police when they arrive with new admissions.

The Ontario government is also building a treatment complex in Brockville for inmates with mental health problems. In the early 1990s, many "harmless" patients in psychiatric facilities were turned out onto the street when the government decided that they could return to the community without putting the public at risk. Without the resources to support themselves, many of them ended up trading a psychiatric facility for a jail cell.

From 1992 to 1994 four prisons were built in the U.K., funded by the public sector but run privately. Three more institutions contracted under the Tories opened within twelve months of Tony Blair's Labour government taking office. After looking at the bottom line, Labour decided to proceed with its predecessor's plan to provide four additional Private Finance Initiative (PFI) prisons. Savings have since averaged about 12 per cent per prisoner.

Tim Wilson headed the contracts and competitions program in Her Majesty's Prison Service for three years and oversaw the use of private finance for prison construction. Wilson then took charge of a task force on private finance for the British Treasury. The PFI is a public-sector procurement program for services from private

contractors when a new or renovated capital asset is required. To date, more than 250 PFI contracts have been signed, worth about £16 billion. The services cover a wide range of sectors, including roads and hospitals as well as prisons. Overall, services purchased by public authorities under the PFI are estimated to have yielded about 17 per cent in savings from initial contracts. According to one study evaluated by two professors from the London School of Economics, the PFI appears to offer "excellent value for the money."

In an interview in May 2000, Wilson said that it cost £24,000 a year, or "more than the cost of a place at a top-flight English public school such as Eton," to keep a person behind bars in the U.K. (There are about 65,000 prisoners there.) Britain now runs ten of its 130 prisons privately. Wilson said, "Research undertaken by the Home Office points to the quality of the service in the privately managed prisons and value for money being obtained by these contracts." The "jewel in the crown" is Altcourse in Liverpool, which is the equivalent of a Canadian provincial prison. The research was supported by the independent report of the chief inspector of prisons, Sir David Ramsbotham, in November 1999. He wrote:

> HMP Altcourse is, by some way, the best local prison we have inspected during my time as HM Chief Inspector of Prisons. . . . My team and I frequently had to pinch ourselves and remember that the prison had only been open for slightly less than two years. I am not alone in my views about the excellence of what is being done at Altcourse. During the period of our inspection the Chief Constable of Liverpool visited the prison, telling the Director, that for the first time in his career, he found himself leaving a prison feeling optimistic. I agree wholeheartedly with him. What we found, and what we report upon, proves that all the outcomes that we look for in terms of treatment of and conditions for prisoners in local prison are possible, given the right degree of direction and attitude.

The chief inspector noted that everyone working in the prison, from the director (warden) down to every custodial officer or typist in administration, realized the importance of their role in "treating prisoners with humanity and helping them to live law-abiding lives in prison and on release." Almost 92 percent of the inmates reported they got on well with staff, who treated them with respect, often referring to them as "Mr." or using a first name. Newly received prisoners were offered a cup of tea in the admissions area.

Ramsbotham found that, because Altcourse is a commercial operation, "management response to appeals from the Director for help, or support, is instant, not subject to labyrinthine, public sector, bureaucratic procedures, and it tells." He noted that experienced managers gave clear direction, so staff at the wing level did not feel unsupported or isolated. According to a recent survey, 81 per cent of the inmates said they felt safe at Altcourse. Both prisoners and staff felt safe because, in contrast to Canadian federal prisons, "control" was a priority.

Privately managed jails in the U.K. are subject to very clear contractual performance measures, including the times at which meals should be served, the incidence of assaults, the incidence of contraband being found, the hours of "positive regime" activity for prisoners, even the amount of time it takes visitors to actually get to the prisoners they have come to see.

Wilson was careful to point out that it was never intended that privately managed jails should constitute any more than a proportion of the prisons in the U.K. "This should not be seen in isolation from reforms in directly managed prisons. What it does is provide a benchmark in terms of quality, in terms of cost, that are used by prison service managers within the U.K. in order to reform the management of existing prisons that remain directly managed by the public service." The privately managed jails are part of a program of reform and modernization throughout the public prison service.

Canada's incarceration rate dropped from 136 per 100,000 people in 1994 to 118 per 100,000 in 2000. Although CSC repeatedly says

that Canada's incarceration rate is high relative to those of other Western countries, the incarceration rate in England and Wales was actually slightly higher than ours in 2000, at 124 per 100,000. The U.K. rate had been just 89 per 100,000 in 1993, indicating that the country's soft-on-crime experiment was a failure. The incarceration rates in the United States, New Zealand, Scotland, Australia, Germany, Italy, and even Denmark and Norway have also increased in the last five years. While the numbers in France and Austria have remained static, Canada's incarceration rate has dropped substantially.

Some of Ontario's more controversial prison reforms have been inspired by experiments south of the border. Elements of so-called "shock incarceration" or boot camp have been used in New York State since September 1987. Under the shock incarceration program, inmates are given shorter sentences – say, six months behind bars followed by six months of probation – instead of several years in a conventional prison. In return for the reduced jail time, they are subjected to very strict discipline. These boot camp facilities, originally developed for young adult offenders, screen all candidates who volunteer for the program. Offenders must be non-violent, under thirty-five, and eligible for parole within three years. Military-style discipline features obedience to orders, highly structured days, hard work, and drills. The program provides a total learning environment and is intended to foster self-direction and individual responsibility. The goal is a law-abiding citizen.

The day begins at 5:30 a.m. with a standing count and fifty sit-ups, followed by a five-mile run at 6:00. Offenders are kept busy until the 9:30 p.m. standing count and lights out. There is no free time. Nor are there parcels from home, radios, newspapers, TVs, or magazines. Thirty-seven per cent of the volunteers fail to complete the first phase and are sent to a higher-security institution.

Inmates spend 40 per cent of their time on treatment and education. Thirty-three per cent of time is spent on hard labour: community projects such as cutting firebreaks to contain forest

fires or maintaining public conservation areas in cash-strapped municipalities. Inmates have also helped out in public emergencies such as tornadoes.

Platoons learn to live together as a unit, resolve problems, and develop critical thinking skills, with the objective of teaching inmates to connect their own well-being with the well-being of others. Drug treatment is based on a twelve-step program. About 75 per cent of the women and 50 per cent of the men in the New York program are parents, so authorities believe that a successful intervention can have profound benefits for the next generation. Inmates are evaluated daily and given instant feedback, positive or negative, on their progress. Strict limits on behaviour are a new experience for many of the inmates. Serious violations of the rules lead to dismissal from the program, which is presented as a privilege and an opportunity, not a right.

Although incarceration costs are actually higher per day than for medium-security prisons in the U.S., shorter sentences mean a savings to New York State of $2 million for every hundred shock "graduates." The program saves money by both reducing expenditure for care and custody and avoiding capital costs for new prison construction. When the recidivism rates of the groups were compared, graduates did as well as or better than parolees who did not participate in the program.

At the height of the experiment in strict discipline in the late 1990s, the United States had about fifty boot camps holding approximately 4,500 young offenders. Along with the successes, there have been cases of severe abuse, which in two instances led to death. A fourteen-year-old girl convicted of shoplifting died of heat exhaustion during a forced march at boot camp. Facing searing public criticism over these dramatic failures, many states have begun closing or scaling back on their boot camps, despite the fact that several graduates have gone on to complete college degrees. Missing from the coverage of tragedies at the strict discipline boot camps is the fact that there have always been problems

in conventional youth detention centres, plagued by overcrowding and lack of meaningful programs.

In July 1997, the Ontario government opened Camp Turnaround, a privately run "strict discipline" or boot camp facility for young offenders north of Barrie. The facility got off to an inauspicious start on the eve of the official opening, when two young offenders escaped in a van they had hot-wired. Despite an internal report that concluded that the facility did a good job of delivering rehabilitation programs, a disappointing 40 per cent of the offenders were charged with new offences within a year of being released. Although it had mixed results with Camp Turnaround, the province plans to build two new adult strict discipline facilities to continue with the experiment.

On May 23, 2001, Ontario's minister of education, Janet Ecker, announced that the province would open strict discipline schools for teenagers expelled for violent or disruptive acts in the classroom. The $16-million program, run by seven non-profit groups, began in the fall of 2001. "It provides a good opportunity to deal with someone before they end up graduating into a life of crime," Ecker explained. The strictly regimented schools include regular courses as well as courses in anger management and problem solving.

As many as thirty of Ontario's forty-seven jails and detention centres are slated to close within a few years. Obsolete, crumbling, and expensive to maintain, almost a third of the jails were built in the last century. The new super-jails, designed by Murphy Hilgers Architects of Toronto, are ultra-modern prisons, with smooth, hard surfaces. Central East Correctional Centre in Lindsay and Central North Correctional Centre in Penetanguishene will each accommodate 1,200 prisoners. Octagonal "pods" are linked by spokes radiating from a central administrative building. The pods are open and bright and have excellent sightlines for inmate supervision from the central control station. There is less opportunity for trouble, since there are no dangerous nooks and crannies in the blind spots of the security cameras.

Each self-contained pod has its own program area and outdoor yard designed to hold 192 inmates. The pod in turn is divided into six thirty-two-bed ranges. Inmates on each range eat at tables in their common rooms (which will also be used for recreation), limiting inmate movement through the institution, always a dangerous activity in any prison. The common areas have natural daylight, and each cell has a window. Advanced electronic security provides protection for inmates, staff, and the community.

Not everyone is a fan of the new design. Moffat Kinoshita Architects, the designers of the federal Fenbrook Institution, failed to win the bid for the new Ontario prisons. Gene Kinoshita was critical of the new plan, which he felt displayed a very different philosophy than the federal system. "It's not really built for rehabilitation, but incarceration. It's all to do with price, not quality."

Capacity at the Maplehurst Correctional Complex in Milton, west of Toronto, will be doubled using the same pod design. The $89-million expansion will eventually accommodate 1,500 inmates, making Maplehurst the largest jail in Canada. A 350-bed women's wing is scheduled for completion in 2002.

At the official opening of the expanded prison on March 15, 2001, the minister of correctional services also announced "a new era in correctional services in Ontario." Rob Sampson declared, "We are not just building new jails. We are building a new system of corrections that truly holds offenders accountable for their actions."

The system is not without its problems: food preparation within Ontario prisons is in the process of being privatized. Kitchens at Maplehurst were to produce twenty thousand cook-and-chill meals a day to be sent to other institutions, a concept based on airline food preparation. But instead of costing $5 million, the new kitchen facility cost $9.5 million and could supply food to only six jails, not ten as planned. Two classes of inmates will be employed in the cook-and-chill facility: inmates on work duty, who will not be paid, and inmates whose kitchen service will come with not only a paycheque but also a certificate as food service officers that will

help them find outside employment when their sentence is finished.

Renovations and security upgrades have also taken place in the Hamilton-Wentworth, Toronto West, and Toronto East detention centres, and more are planned for Elgin-Middlesex and Quinte. Expansions and renovations are also taking place in Ottawa and Brockville, and are planned for North Bay, Thunder Bay, and Sault Ste. Marie.

Ontario's two new super-jails were scheduled to open in June 2001, but neither met the deadline. The Lindsay facility remains behind schedule as of this writing, but Penetanguishene accepted its first eighteen prisoners on November 10, 2001.

On May 5, 2001, Minister Sampson announced the signing of a five-year contract with Management and Training Corporation (MTC), a private company based in Utah that won the bid to manage the new jail in Penetanguishene. Approximately five hundred provincial corrections workers have accepted severance packages, and fewer than fifty have agreed to move to the new jail.

MTC manages thirteen correctional centres in the U.S.: seven in Texas, two in Ohio, and one each in California, Arizona, New Mexico, and Utah. Joel Campbell, a spokesperson for MTC, said the company focuses on security as a first priority but also on the rehabilitation of inmates through education and life skills programs. MTC has been in the business of operating private correctional facilities since 1987, but its roots go back to the mid-1960s, when it began operating federal job training programs for youth who were at risk. Today it runs twenty-four Job Corps centres in the U.S. that help troubled youth and welfare recipients learn job skills. MTC claims a corporate culture that rewards innovation and excellence.

It costs more than $50,000 per year to incarcerate an adult inmate in the Ontario provincial system. The average Ontario inmate serves eighty-five days behind bars. Although there has been a 6 per cent decline in the prisoner population in Ontario over the past five years, costs have jumped 19 per cent over the same period. In 2001, Ontario had the highest provincial inmate

cost in Canada, $140 per day, almost twice that of Alberta. (By comparison, in 1999-2000, it cost taxpayers $185.44 per day to keep a man in the federal system and $316.34 per day for a woman. Between the federal, provincial, and territorial systems, Canada spent $2.4 billion operating adult jails in 1999-2000, up from $2.2 billion the previous year – even though the number of offenders in custody is dropping.)

MTC is being paid $34 million a year to run the $87-million Penetanguishene jail – roughly $79 per prisoner per day. The province of Ontario will continue to own the facility, and Corrections Ministry officials will monitor it twenty-four hours a day. Critics of private operators in the U.S. allege that they "warehouse" offenders, and point to the worst example: Youngstown, Ohio. Few critiques mention that nervous bureaucrats in the public system eager to see the private experiment fail sent the worst of the worst to Youngstown, and it wasn't long before disaster struck. Shortly after the private facility opened, six prisoners escaped and twenty were stabbed, six of them fatally.

The Lindsay super-jail will be publicly run. The Ontario government will compare the results of the two new institutions when both are up and running. In the meantime, Rob Sampson points out that before the reform of the provincial jail system, Ontario was getting the worst of two worlds. "Ontario's paying non-warehousing costs and getting warehousing results. . . . There is very little correcting of criminal behaviour going on in corrections." The minister insists that Ontario will not merely ape the American-style system, warts and all, but will create its own model based on local experience and rigorous performance measurements.

Ontario has been looking at other innovative ways to save money and improve security. The provinces are responsible for the custody of adults on remand during the court process, as well as for those serving sentences up to two years less a day. Inmates travel to and from court thousands of times a year. Ontario has proposed that brief, procedural court appearances (some last only a minute) would be safer and more cost-effective if inmates appeared before

a judge using video conferencing. Their lawyer would be in court with the judge, and client and lawyer would be guaranteed private access by phone.

Ontario also plans to use the Global Positioning System (GPS) to keep track of low-risk inmates serving their provincial sentences in the community. GPS works better than electronic monitoring bracelets, which require a telephone to operate. The old-style monitoring bracelets only show "P&A" – presence and absence – working on radio frequency signals linked up between an offender's telephone and the monitoring device he is wearing. Under the GPS or satellite system, authorities can follow the real-time, actual movements of inmates. Ontario will also randomly screen those on parole for drug and alcohol abuse by using sophisticated new tests such as retina scanning and saliva tests, backed up by more reliable urine and hair tests if the initial results are positive.

.According to Rob Sampson, there is one thing Ontario won't be doing in the process of reforming the antiquated provincial jail system: taking any cues from Ottawa.

"The feds have nothing to teach us but how not to handle convicted criminals. Under Ole Ingstrup, Ottawa created a coddled, spoiled, and unrepentant prisoner population and a bureaucracy that is totally unaccountable. When Ingstrup retired, I wrote a letter to the solicitor general of Canada expressing the hope that there might be a new start for federal corrections. I never got a reply. I don't know why, but maybe it was because there is no defence for what they are doing."

13

THE KINGDOM OF SMOKE
AND MIRRORS

In a wide-ranging interview with the author in February 2001, Solicitor General Lawrence MacAulay opined on what the art of governance really came down to: "What you have to do in any system is satisfy the public."

By that measure, the department he oversees, the Correctional Service of Canada, is an abject failure. A major Angus Reid poll done in 1997 revealed that just 6 per cent of Canadians were "very confident" about how effectively convicted criminals are dealt with after they are sentenced by the courts. By comparison, the pollster found that "most Canadians [58 per cent] display little or no faith in the prison system." Only 3 per cent were "very confident" about parole decisions, and 72 per cent said they had little or no faith in the parole system either.

In July 1999, Angus Reid found that the number of respondents who wanted a sentence "to impose a punishment that reflects the seriousness of the crime" equalled the number of people who wanted it to protect the public as a first priority. Only one in six respondents believed that the primary goal of the prison system should be rehabilitation. An astounding 69 per cent of those surveyed felt that sentences were not severe enough. It is difficult

to disagree. On average, federal inmates serve only about 40 per cent of their sentences behind bars, hardly what juries have in mind when they find an offender guilty and look to CSC to administer the sentence.

Earlier polling data had sent the same message to Ottawa: CSC and the public were worlds apart in their notions of post-sentencing justice. In April 1996, Angus Reid reported to the solicitor general that Canadians saw protection of the public, rehabilitation, and punishment as interconnected components of a good penal system. Canadians believed that roughly half of all inmates would eventually reoffend – a number much closer to the truth than the carefully massaged statistics promoted by CSC. Nor did the public have much use for CSC's practice of deeming certain violent offenders "low risk" to reoffend and often placing them in minimum-security prisons. Unlike CSC, respondents in the research study believed risk should be determined by an inmate's offence. They also wanted hard data on recidivism rates.

Not even the man responsible for Corrections Canada has the information they wanted. When asked if he accepted CSC's recidivism statistics, MacAulay's reply revealed how much a minister is the captive of his bureaucrats: "Well, I pretty much accept what's given to me. . . . Like, it would be kind of silly of me to respond to something – like, I don't have an intelligence force of my own."

Minister MacAulay wasn't the only one who was confused. Recidivism – the rate at which offenders who have been through the system commit new crimes – is the only real measure of success for current CSC rehabilitation policies. When Ole Ingstrup retired in August 2000, he told the press, "I am very proud of the fact we have gotten recidivism down to the lowest ever in our history." He boasted that reoffence rates had fallen to 10 to 12 per cent on average, a reiteration of his comments made before the Commons justice committee on May 11, 1999. Ingstrup told parliamentarians, "Our delight in some ways is that the numbers show us there is virtually no difference in the recidivism among people on full parole and people on statutory release. We're talking about

11 per cent for full parole and 12 per cent for those who are on statutory release."

Although CSC did, in fact, have statistics reflecting the numbers quoted by the outgoing commissioner, they were not for recidivism. The percentages quoted by Ingstrup, and repeated by the press, were actually for what the Canadian Centre for Justice Statistics, which publishes CSC stats, calls performance measures. These "success rates" only reflect the number of people who serve their sentence while on parole in the community without committing a new offence during a single year. Ontario, by comparison, defines recidivism "as a return to provincial correctional supervision on a new conviction, either during or following the completion of a community disposition, or following the completion of a custodial sentence."

According to the November 2001 edition of the annual *Corrections and Conditional Release Statistical Overview*, published by the solicitor general, 74.2 per cent of inmates completed full parole successfully in 2000-2001 without a breach of conditions (depending on the case, that could mean failure to report to a parole officer or associating with a known criminal) or a new offence serious enough to send them back to federal prison; 25.8 per cent did not. And 9.8 per cent of inmates on parole committed new offences. In the same one-year period, 59.0 per cent of inmates completed their statutory release successfully, but 41.0 per cent did not. And 14.3 per cent were caught committing new offences.

There are reasons to doubt CSC's commitment to coming up with solid statistics on recidivism. Many obvious reoffenders become new offenders through a number of loopholes contrived by CSC. For example, CSC does not count crimes that are committed by former inmates after their sentences expire. For accountability and statistical purposes, such a crime should be considered recidivism. Under the current system, an offender can commit a murder or rape the day after his writ of expiry and it would not affect CSC "success rates." If a paroled inmate commits a crime that receives a provincial sentence, it is not counted as an offence at all.

In 2000–2001, 7,715 offenders were admitted to the federal corrections system. Of these, only 3,150 offenders were serving time for a first federal offence. The rest were in for repeat offences or parole violations. The numbers imply a failure rate of 60 per cent for CSC's rehabilitation program.

According to Statistics Canada, offenders serving life sentences have a higher risk to reoffend than the general prison population. Eighty-four per cent of lifers are considered at high risk to reoffend, compared with 53 per cent of the other inmates. Yet a footnote in the section of the 2001 *Corrections and Conditional Release Statistical Overview* dealing with success rates reads, "These data do not include offenders serving life or indeterminate sentences as these offenders, by definition, remain under supervision for life." In other words, CSC does not include the offences committed by the offenders who inhabit our nightmares – those who commit first- or second-degree murder or other crimes so vicious they warrant a life sentence.

True recidivism rates must be based on tracking former inmates even after they have completed parole, just as the Kingston police did in their study. Three officials in CSC's own research branch confirmed that recidivism and "success rates" are totally different concepts that should never be used interchangeably, as Commissioner Ingstrup routinely did. CSC has an excellent statistics department, based on an automated system that was established in 1992; yet as one senior CSC researcher admitted in April 2001, "there has been very little research on recidivism." A study is currently under way.

So what is the true recidivism rate for federal prisoners after release? One CSC researcher estimated that 60 per cent of inmates go through the federal system and never return, but the other 40 per cent keep "recycling through the penal system" – a ratio that has existed unchanged for many years. Unofficially, various CSC sources estimate that 35 to 50 per cent of federal offenders will reoffend, figures consistent with the 47 per cent figure published by the Kingston police in their recidivism study, much to the consternation of CSC.

Not all the information about the real recidivism rate is an estimate. A study done by Brian A. Grant, published by CSC's research branch in May 1997, followed all offenders released between 1989 and 1994 for two years. It concluded: "Of the offenders released at their statutory release date, about 35 per cent were sentenced for a new offence. Of the offenders who were detained, less than 20 per cent were convicted of a new offence within the two-year period after their release. This rate was lower than for offenders released on full parole."

Commissioner Ingstrup did not call a press conference to announce the findings of Grant's study. Not only did it blatantly contradict the official spin on recidivism routinely confused with "success rates," it showed that offenders detained beyond their statutory release date actually committed fewer new offences than those who were released at the two-thirds mark of their sentence. For that matter, they committed fewer offences than those who were released on full parole for following their Correctional Plan. In other words, longer incarceration actually reduced the recidivism rate. Statutory release and CSC's vaunted programs didn't seem to be working – at least according to the results of one of the few studies that actually examined the recidivism question.

Brian Riches provides a case in point. In the early morning of November 30, 1998, Jeffrey Hearn was awakened by his girlfriend's screams after she had gone downstairs to answer the door. Hearn rushed down the stairs to the kitchen, where he was struck in the forehead above the right eye with a claw hammer. He was hit more than thirty times, both of his legs were broken, and it took over a hundred staples to close the gaping wounds to his head. His assailant was Brian Riches, a career criminal who hadn't even bothered to apply for day or full parole when he was freed after serving four years of a six-year sentence for armed robbery, aggravated assault, and forcible confinement. Riches was on statutory release when he attacked and maimed Jeffrey Hearn. The National Parole Board never saw the offender before his release from William Head Institution.

Since recidivism rates for offenders released on their "stat dates" were actually higher than for those detained, the practice of statutory release was clearly endangering the public. In fact, according to CSC's own performance report for the period ending March 31, 2001, the number of federal offenders charged with armed holdups, sexual assaults, and other major crimes while free on parole or statutory release had jumped by a staggering 51 per cent over the previous two years. These findings were in direct contradiction to what Ingstrup told the Beyond Prisons conference in March 1998, that "lengthy incarceration has no more deterrent or rehabilitative effect than shorter incarceration."

On April 27, 2001, Dr. Joel Ginsburg, a psychologist with CSC, made a presentation about the Correctional Service of Canada to forty students in the justice and law class of West Carleton High School, just outside Ottawa. During his hour-long presentation, he used charts from headquarters to give an overview of the department's operation. One pie chart projected by Ginsburg dealt with recidivism. It showed that 57 per cent of federal offenders don't come back to prison, while 43 per cent reoffend. The author, who was also there as a guest speaker, pointed out that the recidivism rates quoted by Ginsburg were much higher than the figures routinely used by CSC brass. After the event concluded, Ginsburg sought the author out in the school parking lot and emphasized that he wasn't a member of CSC's communications branch and that his information shouldn't be quoted.

A very different recidivism rate also surfaced in a May 1996 study prepared for the solicitor general by CSC's research branch. The report compared the recidivism rate of child molesters with that of non-sexual offenders, using RCMP records of 191 child molesters and comparing them with 137 non-sexual criminals. Both groups were followed over fifteen to thirty years. There were some startling numbers. Seventy-seven per cent of pedophiles who selected extra-familial boys as their victims reoffended. The average recidivism rate for all the sex offenders studied was 42 per cent. "Although the long-term recidivism rates for the child

molesters were substantial, the recidivism rates for non-sexual criminals were even higher, 61 per cent versus 83.2 per cent, respectively, for any reconviction."

Despite a dissatisfied public and a history of statistical deceit, successive CSC commissioners have boasted that "no one runs prisons better than Canada," pointing out that delegations come from all over the world to marvel at what CSC has achieved. What the commissioners haven't said is that CSC spends millions of dollars promoting itself through various international organizations, conferences, and tours to carefully foster that impression. In fact, the emperor has no clothes.

There are really two prison systems in Canada. One operates in an ideal world where humans behave according to the social theories of the day. It is a version that exists in policy papers, misleading statistics, and guided tours. The real one is behind locked doors or, all too frequently, on the streets. Clifford Howdle, a sex offender, was released on day parole after serving four years of a seven-year sentence for sexual assault and kidnapping. He used his freedom to go on a violent thirty-six-hour rampage that resulted in eighteen charges, including three rapes. In a statement of facts submitted at his trial in May 2001, the parolee said, "I know what I did was wrong. I don't know why I did it."

In his final report to Parliament after ten years as Canada's auditor general, Denis Desautels said that government needed to ensure that senior public servants and ministers answer to Parliament for their use of public resources. In practice, departments don't tell their political masters when errors are made or targets are missed. As a result, parliamentarians receive little or no information on how well government programs are actually working. Desautels believed that the unaccountable administration of the nation's business meant that costly errors and poor choices would continue to be made with few or no consequences for public servants.

Career public servants make policy but often have little operational experience, a clear recipe for disaster. When the fisheries collapsed on both coasts, federal fisheries bureaucrats scrambled to

blame everything but their own mismanagement for the eco-catastrophe. Mel Cappe, who went on to become clerk of the Privy Council, was unable to account for $1 billion of taxpayers' money when he was deputy minister of Human Resources Development Canada. When Cappe testified before the human resources committee of the House of Commons, he observed, "Like you, I wish we were perfect." He explained that the whole thing had happened because his department had become "too client-oriented and not enough taxpayer-oriented." Ingstrup could have offered the same defence on behalf of the CSC.

In its zeal to look after female federal inmates after the P4W scandal, CSC spent over $71 million building and then renovating five new prisons to replace it. Today, they house about 372 women at a construction cost of nearly $200,000 per inmate. But there was not enough money in the CSC budget to man a security tower at night at a maximum-security prison in Kingston, where, according to the warden, 98 per cent of the population is serving time for personal injury offences.

Nor was it difficult to find money for other pet CSC projects. In November 1999, the department decided that convicted murderer Synthia Kavanagh would get a sex-change operation and transfer to serve his/her life sentence at a women's prison. CSC would cover part of the expense of the $14,000 operation. Eleven more prisoners made requests for gender reassignment surgery following the decision. (Only one other prisoner had actually had the operation, a procedure he/she later wished to reverse.)

In 1982, Amina Chaudhary strangled eight-year-old Rajesh Gupta, her lover's nephew, after the man returned to India and married someone else. Under Ole Ingstrup's rehabilitative model, the convicted child killer then had three children while in P4W. The father was another convicted killer brought over from a nearby prison for conjugal visits in one of two houses provided for private family encounters at P4W.

In October 1999, Amina Chaudhary used her children as part of her application for judicial review under Section 745, the

so-called "faint hope" provision of the Criminal Code, which allows convicted murderers to end their twenty-five-year sentences early if the jury hearing their case unanimously agrees. Her file was filled with praise from CSC for being such a loving and devoted parent. Chaudhary's application was rejected, but her jury said she could apply again in October 2004.

Despite the child murderer's court sentence and rejection by the jury of her faint-hope application, CSC granted Amina Chaudhary forty-two hours a week of escorted temporary absences from prison, eight of them for "personal development." It was virtually day parole by another name.

On July 13, 2000, the *Calgary Herald* interviewed Darnell Bass, a former soldier convicted of a failed commando-style robbery of a Brinks guard at a bank in North Hill Mall in November 1998. A prisoner at medium-security Bowden Institution north of Calgary, Bass lived in the farm annex, which he apparently enjoyed: "I have a higher standard of living here than I did in the army." His former home was the Canadian Forces base at Petawawa, west of Ottawa. In fact, many inmates refuse to participate in programs that would shorten their imprisonment. At Kingston Penitentiary, for example, some inmates scheduled for deportation upon release will deliberately lengthen their stay, since a Canadian prison is preferable to living conditions in their own countries.

On December 21, 2001, RCMP Constable Dennis Strongquill, a father of six, was killed in a shootout with two men wanted for parole violations. One suspect, Robert Sand of Westlock, Alberta, had been paroled seven weeks earlier. He had served just three years of a seven-year sentence for robbery. Sand had walked away from an Edmonton halfway house two weeks before the slaying. His brother Danny Sand, who was killed in the shootout, was on statutory release and had failed to show up for a meeting with his parole officer that day. Both men were under the supervision of the Correctional Service of Canada at the time of Strongquill's murder. Robert Sand and a female companion, Laurie Bell, were charged with first-degree murder. CSC and the National Parole Board have

launched a joint investigation, as they do in all "serious" cases. Once again, the responsible agencies will investigate themselves.

Although CSC never fails to mention protection of the public on every public occasion, its guiding principle is very different: to use detention as little as possible and as briefly as possible when dealing with convicted criminals. Senior managers at CSC have cited two powerful forces standing in the way of these objectives: "the current hysteria in support of zero risk" and the fact that the media have a vested interest in spreading anxiety about public safety – namely, to sell papers and advertising. CSC views reporters who interview the victims of crime as being "in cahoots" with the police community, which generally believes that offenders are put back on the street too soon.

The bunker mentality in CSC comes complete with an emergency plan when policies fail and things go terribly wrong. CSC's first step is to contain public relations damage with press spin. Failing that, bureaucrats close ranks to protect themselves and the organization at all costs. When desperate, CSC offers up the heads of a few front-line staff – usually correctional officers – to appease a furious public.

CSC employees interviewed for this book have witnessed suicides, beatings, and murders in prison; they have been threatened by criminal gangs, poisoned, assaulted, and held hostage. Despite the nightmare they call their workplace, almost all said that most of the damage done to them was inflicted by CSC managers advancing their careers by slavishly implementing the latest ideological whim from national headquarters, no matter what the reality inside the prison walls.

It is fashionable in federal government social policy circles to make excuses for criminal behaviour. Society, not the individual, is somehow to blame for an offender's criminal acts. Touched by a bureaucratic magic wand, perpetrators are transformed from criminals into victims who are then entitled to non-judgmental support from everyone, including their victims.

In May 2000, Kim Hancox, the widow of Detective Bill Hancox, an undercover Toronto police officer killed by Rose Cece and Mary Barbara Ann Taylor in 1998, gave the author her first public interview since her husband's murder. CSC had placed the lesbian killers together in Joliette Institution, known within the prison system as "the love shack." Taylor had more than thirty-five previous offences, and she and Cece had been convicted of a violent assault committed while in custody together at the Toronto West Detention Centre. Yet CSC felt the two women should be allowed to "support" each other behind bars. When Solicitor General MacAulay, travelling in the U.S., learned that the two women were sharing a bedroom, he personally intervened. A source in his office said, "Let's just say the phone lines burned up between Washington and the commissioner's office." Toronto-area MPs also let MacAulay know how disgusted they were by the policy.

MacAulay was furious that the justice system was inflicting new miseries on Kim Hancox. When Bill Hancox was killed, the young couple had a two-year-old daughter. A son was born twenty-six days after his father's murder. Now Kim Hancox had to deal with the fact that her husband's killers had been reunited behind bars. MacAulay summoned Ole Ingstrup into his office on May 15, 2000, and told him to review the file. The women were summarily separated. In the House of Commons MacAulay said, "This is a very serious situation. That's why I instructed Corrections Services Canada to make sure that the likes of this situation does not happen again."

Solicitor General MacAulay and the new commissioner, Lucie McClung, have responded to public pressure and brought in other reforms, such as the two-year maximum-security rule for murderers. (Interestingly, CSC's correctional investigator, Ron Stewart, reported that it was illegal to automatically send killers to maximum-security institutions unless Ottawa passes new legislation.) McClung is also re-examining security procedures at minimum-security institutions and doing a cost assessment of the CSC jet ordered by her predecessor.

But when the CSC published its latest performance report in November 2001, it included the statement that while CSC had undergone a change of commissioners, it had not changed its philosophy or direction. McClung, who was widely rumoured to be a favourite of Prime Minister Jean Chrétien during her tenure in the Privy Council Office, is seen as a career civil servant who has ambitions well beyond her current position. Less ideological than Ole Ingstrup, she is also a better media manager. One of the first groups she reached out to was the Canadian Resource Centre for Victims of Crime. "There could be two motives," the centre's executive director, Steve Sullivan, said. "She cares about victims, or she doesn't want us going after her like we did Ole Ingstrup."

McClung also offered an olive branch to correctional officers who had grown bitterly unhappy under Commissioner Ingstrup's tenure. Although McClung initially dealt directly with the Union of Canadian Correctional Officers, the union now finds it is business as usual with the national headquarters of CSC. "They committee us to death," said Jason Godin, president of the Ontario region, in November 2001. "At first she said she wanted to deal with our issues and we were hopeful. But six months later, CSC is dragging its ass and not addressing the problems."

The new commissioner did not respond to a request for an interview for this book.

The conflict between collective rights and individual rights is always a delicate balancing act in a democracy. The focus of CSC since the mid-1980s has been on individual entitlements for the offender rather than on his responsibility for his crime. Ironically, inmates have become the greatest human rights advocates (when their self-interest is at stake), and prisons the focus for much of the human rights case law in Canada. As noted earlier, the money for these Charter challenges, many of which end up making it more difficult for front-line prison staff to do their jobs, is provided by the federal government.

Section 4 of the CCRA states "that offenders retain the rights and privileges of all members of society" except those removed or

restricted as a consequence of their sentences. Section 8 of the Charter protects people against unreasonable search or seizure. Perversely, this section has been used to restrict searches for weapons or drugs in Canada's prisons. These searches must now be conducted under such stringent restrictions as to be virtually useless as security measures.

The rights of victims who expect justice and of the front-line prison staff who deal with the most dangerous people in Canada on a daily basis have been largely ignored by CSC, except in the rich broths of departmental rhetoric served up on every public occasion. If those rights collide with the rights of prisoners, as they often do, inmates can summon their lawyers or see a specialist, and the taxpayer gets the bill. A correctional officer has to pay for the same services and proceeds without any encouragement from management. Veteran officers agree that the old militaristic model of running prisons had to change. But now they believe the pendulum has swung too far in the opposite direction and badly needs a correction. As one of them put it, "It went from [being] a prison to a kindergarten."

In the wake of the September 11, 2001, terrorist attacks in the U.S., the Canadian government rushed through Bill C-36, anti-terrorist legislation that would override certain well-established legal practices and Charter rights. The measure, which the prime minister initially wanted to make permanent (the government later supported a five-year sunset clause), was implemented for the sake of public safety. Justice Minister Anne McLellan told the Commons justice committee that surveillance, compulsory testimony, and preventive arrest – incarcerating people because of what they *might* be about to do – were necessary. "Punishing terrorist attacks after they occur is too late," the minister said. Yet the same government continues to discount major portions of court-imposed sentences and stands on its head to give inmates all the Charter rights shared by law-abiding citizens, even though they have individually terrorized Canadians and continue to pose a real threat to public safety.

The duty owed to the country's criminals is well articulated by Canada's solicitor general. Lawrence MacAulay believes the state has an obligation to rehabilitate offenders, as do most Canadians. MacAulay is dedicated to treating addicted offenders with programs such as AA: "In my humble opinion a lot of the people, though they committed an illegal act to get into the federal institution, that isn't the problem. The problem is their addiction."

In 1999, a senior CSC committee recommended that Ottawa introduce a needle exchange program in all federal prisons to control the spread of infectious diseases. As we have seen, prison authorities already supply drug-using inmates with bleach kits to sterilize their needles.

Asked if he stood behind the CSC's much-stated zero-tolerance policy on drugs, MacAulay said: "Sure, I'm dedicated to it, and nobody would love to get to zero more than I would. Do I expect to get there? I'd highly question it. What you have to do, it's a double aim as far as I'm concerned. The addiction problem within our institutions: you've got addicted people inside, you've got organized criminals who are used to handling the stuff, and you got the stuff inside. What you have to do in my opinion is put everything in place, like the ion scanners, the dogs, which will be at every medium and maximum and should be, but also being on programs within the system. . . . If you happen to be an offender who's addicted and wish to deal with it — and I've talked to a number, quite a number of prisoners in this country and other countries too that have gone through programs, particularly like the AA programs — I think you have to take it from both ends. Keeping it out and the programs within. And if you do both, you can accomplish more."

When asked if these programs were working or could be rated, the minister replied, "I'm not sure I understand what you're asking me."

Asked why the architect of Canada's modern prison system, former commissioner Ingstrup, left CSC when he did, MacAulay

paused for fifteen seconds before replying: "I would never want to indicate anything but the straight truth to you. Ole decided to resign and he did decide to resign. You could indicate probably that he was concerned over things that was coming at him over – what was that word? – quotas, and that kind of stuff. I don't believe that that was the reason the man resigned. If he would have resigned for that, he would have resigned awful quick in the Correctional Service of Canada. He was there for two stints, about eight years, am I correct? And, uh, that's not an easy job, and I can understand where he would like to go somewhere and make more money."

Ole Ingstrup remains head of the International Corrections and Prisons Association, the body he founded, which received $200,000 in funding from CSC in 2001. CSC works with the ICPA in co-operation with the Department of Foreign Affairs and International Trade to develop and promote the concept of "security sector reform." Lyn Ray, national president of the Union of Solicitor General Employees, which represented federal correctional officers until it was voted out by members in 2001 for failing to address their grievances, is now regional vice-chair of the ICPA. CSC also uses the ICPA as an "independent" body of international experts "to validate the effectiveness and integrity of its programs."

In his opening remarks to the justice committee on May 9, 2001, MacAulay said, "All the major indicators continue to show that Canada is among the safest countries in the world. The crime rate has declined for the past ten years, the violent crime rate is down, and the homicide rate continues to fall. In the past fifteen years we've cut the recidivism rate by more than half."

Less than a week later, the media obtained an internal CSC report under the Access to Information Act. A public opinion poll conducted by Environics Research Group for CSC in July 2000 found that despite the minister's sunny rhetoric, the correctional service continues to fail the test of satisfying the public. "There is a prevalent belief that prison conditions are too good in Canada. There is a perception that prisoners lead a better life than some who are not

in prison, especially the homeless." While the numbers were slightly better than those of the Angus Reid poll, once again the respondents expressed little faith in the prison system. While 57 per cent had a high level of confidence in the Ontario Provincial Police, only 15 per cent expressed a high level of confidence in CSC. Faith in the National Parole Board was even lower, just 10 per cent. In the eyes of most Canadians, CSC was neither "satisfying the public" nor doing "a good job."

Occasionally, public opinion moved CSC to drop some of its zanier ideas. The departmental Task Force on Security had recommended that CSC "should strive to eliminate the use of weapons in our service." It had also suggested that razor wire be removed from the perimeters of all institutions because "it gives an inappropriate concentration camp appearance to CSC facilities." After widespread ridicule, both recommendations were dropped. Razor wire was finally installed on the perimeter walls of KP in the summer of 2001. Guards had been asking for it since 1985, long before Ty Conn's spectacular escape.

As firmly entrenched as the restorative justice model is in the federal penal system, Canada's treatment of criminals has become a parody of rehabilitation and redemption. No policy of the federal government is more out of favour with Canadians, who largely believe that offenders are rewarded for their crimes rather than punished. CSC continues to reinforce that impression. In 2001, the correctional investigator reported that it was time to provide inmates with a pay raise and stress counselling.

When asked about the recent 51 per cent increase in charges for violent offences by inmates on statutory release or parole over the last two years, a CSC spokesperson, Michèle Pilon-Santilli, dismissed the numbers. She said that the statistics on charges might not be significant because the number of actual convictions against offenders on parole or statutory release dropped between 1994 and 2001. It was classic CSC bob and weave; skewered on one issue, the increase in charges, you blur the debate by referencing another, the number of convictions over a convenient time frame.

The November 2001 edition of the *Corrections and Conditional Release Statistical Overview*, despite being printed and packed in boxes for shipping, had still not been released by mid-December. It turned out that the report had been embargoed until its release was personally authorized by the commissioner herself. Multiple sources inside and outside the department confirmed that CSC brass wanted to "verify" certain statistics in the report before making the document public. Nevertheless, CSC's statistics department did confirm that Canada's incarceration rate had dropped to 118 per 100,000 in 2000. Despite that fact, CSC was still using the 1997 figure of 129 per 100,000 in the November 2001 document. It used the stale information to support the erroneous claim that "Canada's incarceration rate is still higher than that in other western industrialized nations, except for the United States." In fact, New Zealand, England, and Wales all have higher incarceration rates than Canada.

The CSC makes the claim that it has encouraged fact-based coverage of the department, such as CBC Television's "The Big Picture: Inside Canada's Prisons," which drew the largest viewing audience of any Canadian program in 2001. The CSC-friendly documentary parroted the incorrect incarceration rate of 129 per 100,000. Since CSC presumably has access to its own statistics, it has yet to be explained why the department is putting out false information that leaves the impression that Canada imprisons more of its citizens than it actually does.

And so the con game goes on with a slick and undeclared deal from the bottom of the deck: Canada's politicians have decided that the cost of running a prison system that keeps pace with the crime rate is too high. In New South Wales, Australia, a parliamentary committee at least laid its cards on the table. Set up to deal with an increase in the prison population, the committee recommended that the government abolish all jail terms under six months and expand home detention, community service orders, and other alternative sentences. The numbers tell the story: in New South Wales, it costs A$64,486 a year to keep an inmate in prison, while community rehabilitation programs cost just A$3,000.

In Canada, the same cold calculation not to invest in a correctional system that protects the public, punishes, and, where possible, rehabilitates the offender has been made behind closed doors. Federal politicians have opted for a penal model that minimizes jail time, maximizes alternative sentencing in the community, and resists all accountability. It is a strategy that comes directly from the Prime Minister's Office and the Privy Council Office, by way of the Treasury Board, and it now permeates every sector of the justice system. Sentences are shorter, parole conditions more lax, and the widespread use of conditional sentencing has frequently done away with jail time for even the most serious violent offences. It is one of the ironies of the penal system that a provincial inmate charged with a lesser offence does harder time than his federal counterpart who may have committed a violent crime.

Although the decision to opt for less incarceration and not to build new prisons is routinely linked to the prohibitive costs of jailing offenders, the cost of federal corrections has dramatically increased even though the number of criminals under lock and key has gone down. In 1996-1997, it cost $1.15 billion to incarcerate 14,512 inmates; by 2000-2001, taxpayers were spending $1.4 billion to keep 12,794 offenders behind bars and another 7,575 supervised in the community. Since 1990, the cost of running CSC has increased by more than 50 per cent. As CSC's own statistics are proving, the legacy of a prison system built on speedy release and imagined cost savings will be more innocent victims of preventable crimes. The unstated cost of this con game is anathema to any democracy: a correctional system that is scorned by the public and whose only supporters are the very administrators who so fiercely promote and so furtively run it.

ACKNOWLEDGMENTS

Despite the single name that appears on the dust jacket, many hands go into a book project like this one. I would like to thank my wife, Lynda Harris, who once again has shown that she can work any two people under the table, including the author. Without her diligence, organization, critical intelligence, and spunk there would be no book. David Kilgour, my editor, proved to be a cool collaborator throughout a project that unfolded during a personally trying time for both of us. It was a pleasure to work with such a creative, constructive, and unflappable man. For many years, Doug Gibson, the president and publisher of McClelland & Stewart, has been a solid and supportive mentor. He has worked the minor miracle of getting five manuscripts out of an author who is dedicated to the proposition that the research is never over and the book never quite finished. His compassion during this project will not be forgotten.

Dennis Mills, the MP for Toronto Danforth and a true friend of the arts, poured the author many a glass of good wine over deep discussions of Canada's penitentiary system. This great-hearted public servant was instrumental in gaining me access to federal correctional authorities from Canada's solicitor general, Lawrence MacAulay, to Mike Provan, the finest prison warden in Canada. He was also a true friend when the chips were down. Rob Sampson, Ontario's minister of corrections, was generous with his time, as was his indefatigable chief of staff, Deborah Reid. Steve Sullivan, the workaholic executive director of the Canadian Resource Centre for Victims of Crime, contributed his expertise,

files, and time. The victims of crime in Canada have no more stalwart champion than this man.

The author is very grateful to the members of Ontario's ROPE unit, who shared their insights into the problem of repeat offenders and parole violators. On the federal side, a host of former senior officials in the Correctional Service of Canada were generous in their assistance, none more helpful than Tom Epp. This forthright and talented public servant shared his encyclopedic knowledge of the complex world of corrections. My deepest appreciation also goes to the hundreds of correctional officers who participated in this project despite official prohibitions against speaking about their experiences inside Canada's penitentiaries. Without their courage, generosity, and public-spirited passion for reform, it would have been a much more difficult undertaking. A few of these men and women have since retired from the service or begun new careers, and I would like to publicly acknowledge their help. Phillip Whaley, a thirty-year veteran of Kingston Penitentiary, was a walking history book of corrections, a man whose career has chronicled the many pendulum swings of penal theory that have at various times captured our system. Apart from having the best collection of paperback westerns and the suckiest dogs I have ever seen, this long-serving and decorated prison guard showed me great personal kindness while teaching me what he knew. Jason Godin, whose correctional career is just beginning, shared his knowledge and his hospitality on many occasions, and was even gracious enough to let me win the odd game of pool on one of those long, smoky nights when we did our work. Marc Langlois, a CSC marksman who can shoot the centre out of a loonie at 200 yards and is a true leader of men and women, was indispensable in helping me to understand corrections in Quebec.

To those of you not named, you will never be forgotten.

INDEX

aboriginal inmates: 1988 Commons report, 166; community custody, 90-93; demographics, 82-84; efforts to reduce numbers of, 87-90, 93-95; female, 83, 85-86, 96, 98; Fenbrook, 65, 75; male, 82; Okimaw Ohci Healing Lodge, 85-86, 106; percentage of prison population, 82; Pê Sâkâstêw, 86; recidivism, 24, 87; Saskatchewan, 82; search regulations, 207; view of prison staff, 84

aboriginal people: as prison staff, 84, 85, 87, 91; offering inmate programs, 83-85; social histories, 82-83; view of justice, 83, 86-87

Aboriginal Women's Caucus, 97

accelerated parole review (APR), 2, 23-24

Access to Information Act, 59

Adams, John, 159

age of inmates, 4

Aitkens, Blair, 316-18

Aitkens, Gordon, 318

Alberta incarceration costs, 333

Alberta Provincial Court, 122

Albert, James, 94

alcohol: abuse rates among aboriginal people, 83; annual amount seized, 185; at Joyceville, 198; at KP, 196, 200, 204-5, 206-7; at Millhaven,

21, 33; at P4W, 99; commercial, 11, 205; drug of choice in Atlantic region prisons, 152; fines and other deterrents, 204-5, 206, 208-9; inmate profits, 204; inmates' history of abuse, 4; official zero-tolerance policy, 16, 185; Ontario inmates, 323; search regulations, 207; smuggled in by staff, 193; sparking violence, 186, 204; wide availability, 203-5

Alden (KP inmate), 49

Alexis First Nation, Alberta, 91

Allard, Pierre, 174-75

Altcourse Prison, Liverpool, England, 326-27

Anderson, R. Jeff, 187

Appleton, Robert, 72

APR (accelerated parole review) 2, 23-24

Arbour, Louise, 1, 5, 102-4

Archambault Institution, Sainte-Anne-des-Plaines, Quebec, 190-91

Archambault, Joseph, 150-51, 152

Armbruster, James, 258

armed robbery, by parolees, 5, 309, 316, 339

Armstrong (KP inmate), 213

Ascoby, Renée, 86

Atkinson, Karen, 312

CON GAME

Justice Denied: The Law versus Donald Marshall
Unholy Orders: Tragedy at Mount Cashel
Rare Ambition: The Crosbies of Newfoundland
The Prodigal Husband: The Tragedy of Helmuth and Hanna Buxbaum
The Judas Kiss: The Undercover Life of Patrick Kelly
Lament for an Ocean: The Collapse of the Atlantic Cod Fishery